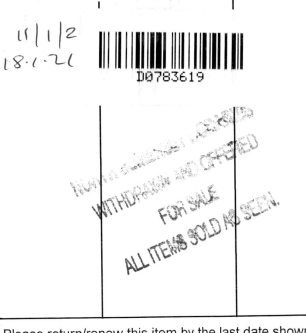

THE KNOWLEDGE

For my parents, Rachel and Michael Lordan

THE KNOWLEDGE

ROBERT LORDAN

Quercus

CONTENTS

INTRODUCTION

'London is far more difficult to see properly than any other place. London is a riddle . . .'

G. K. Chesterton, 'An Essay on Two Cities', 1908

It could have been so different.

As destructive as it was, the Great Fire of 1666 blessed London with an opportunity, a blank canvas. And in the months following the blaze several suggestions for redesigning the city were drawn up by luminaries such as Robert Hooke, John Evelyn and Sir Christopher Wren. All were based upon a sensible grid pattern.

Londoners at the time, however, were creatures of habit. They knew where their homes and businesses once stood and any radical attempt to raise a new city from the ashes would no doubt affect their claims. So instead, they simply rebuilt along the original lines – a slapdash precedent that has seen London mushroom in a messy, haphazard manner ever since.

While other major cities benefit from thoughtful layouts, London is defined by a bewildering jumble of streets that have been cobbled together over time with no apparent respect for logic. There's a strange beauty to this: viewed from a distance, an 'A–Z' map of London resembles a Jackson Pollock.

There's the twisting, turning roads in the historic Square Mile, paths so ancient they were once trod by Romans and Vikings. Move westward and you're hit with 'villages' such as Mayfair and Earl's Court where the densely packed layouts are so confusing it'll make you wonder what on earth the planners were thinking (until you realise there weren't any).

Trickier still are the spaghetti-like tangles of Maida Vale, Hampstead Garden Suburb and Wimbledon Parkside where the roads become so disorientating you half-expect the Minotaur to pop out. Further afield there are peculiarities such as the Haringay Ladder and the Mace Street bowtie.

This is all perplexing enough but there's more: an array of infuriating one-way systems, blocked roads and signs forbidding you from turning this way and that, all of which conspire to lock you in a fiendish game of cat-and-mouse with the authorities.

Despite this chaos, London's cabbies are famous for being able to navigate the streets with ease. Hop into a black taxi, state your destination – whether it be an area, street or place of interest – and the driver will convey you there with confidence.

This skill does not come easily.

It's acquired by undertaking a rigorous course of study known as 'The Knowledge of London', which must be passed in order to obtain the coveted green badge, the licence that allows you to ply for hire anywhere in the city.

There are numerous reasons why someone may wish to apply to become a London taxi driver, although the overriding factor for many is that it's a self-employed role; you are your own boss and can determine your own work pattern as you wish. There is also your pride in earning the right to drive a black taxi, an icon that has long been symbolic of the capital. London cabbies regard their profession as a lifelong career.

Even today, though, there are many Londoners who've never heard of The Knowledge and, for those who have, few have a precise idea as to what it truly entails. This is by no means the public's fault. Apart from the odd documentary and, most famously, the late Jack Rosenthal's much-loved 1979 TV film *The Knowledge*, insights into the process are rare.

Even its origins are an enigma.

The general consensus is that The Knowledge evolved in the wake of the Great Exhibition; the pioneering Victorian expo that took place between May and October 1851. During that period, approximately six million people descended upon the capital to marvel at the mighty Crystal Palace that had been erected in Hyde Park. Such numbers were unprecedented and confronted London's cabbies with their first real test, which they failed miserably, the volume of complaints suggesting the trade was nowhere near fit for purpose.

Gripes against cabmen were nothing new. Letters to the press lambasting their sluggishness, chaotic pricing structure and general unwholesomeness had been a common theme since the first horse-drawn carriages were licensed by Oliver Cromwell in the 1650s.

A letter to the *Sunday Times*, for example, dated 5 March 1837, branded cabmen as 'Ruffians . . . fellows unfit for civilised society and complete nuisances upon the world at large.' Another correspondent, writing a few years after the Great Exhibition, described catching a cab to a party: 'It was raining; the front window was broken; the bottom of the cab was filled with wet straw and by the time we had arrived at our destination my wife was wet through, and her dress completely destroyed.'

Realising something had to be done, the government gradually began to devolve increasing powers for regulating cabs to the Metropolitan Police, culminating in 1869 when the Home Secretary delegated licensing to the Commissioner of Police. In that same year, the Public Carriage Office (PCO) – a neat little brick block for consolidating this new responsibility – opened slap bang in the middle of Great Scotland Yard, visibly demonstrating that the Met were now in charge.

Although no official documentation relating to the implementation of an examination process is known to exist, it was shortly after the opening of the PCO's Scotland Yard office that references to the impressive knowledge of London's cabbies began to appear.

This extract is from February 1872:

> *The knowledge of a London cabman and of local topography is really marvellous. How does he acquire it? Does he study Stanford's or Wyld's maps, or wander about the streets in his years of juvenescence acquiring his geography? However it may be, certain it is he knows it to perfection, much better than the most learned of his fares.*

The new regulations appeared to be working. In 1874, a report from *The Times* stated that 'Within the last few years they [cabs] have decidedly improved in quality, as well as the general character and conduct of their drivers.' The same article also mentions that each potential licensee is 'subjected to an examination about his knowledge of town localities'.

By the eve of the First World War, The Knowledge was beginning to resemble its modern-day counterpart and at least one Knowledge school – run by the British Motor Cab Company – was prepping candidates for the test. In April 1914, a report in the *Manchester Guardian* provided a comprehensive account of the process as it was then:

> *Every applicant for a licence to drive a hackney carriage or taxi-cab within the area under the jurisdiction of Scotland Yard has, after proving his good character and passing a medical examination, to undergo a very severe test as to his knowledge of the streets and public buildings within that area.*

> *He is given a book with about twenty-five lists of questions, similar to those that are eventually put to the applicants. These lists consist of eighteen point-to-point journeys, say from the Royal Exchange to the Elephant and Castle at Newington or the Constitutional Club to Walham Green, and the applicant has to describe the exact route he would follow, street by street.*
>
> *Then follow questions as to the exact position of six squares, six hospitals, six hotels, six buildings, and six clubs. Woe betide the unfortunate driver who takes a retired colonel to the Junior Naval and Military Club instead of the Army and Navy Club.*
>
> *Lately, too, a further examination on the Embassies in London has been added, for it is said that King Alfonso, who was very fond of jumping into taxi-cabs, had found it impossible to discover a driver who knew the Spanish Embassy.*

Today's cabbies and Knowledge students would find this description rather quaint.

In the ensuing decades, the process has become infinitely tougher. The epicentre of The Knowledge is Charing Cross, around which a six-mile radius must be studied and memorised in great detail; from Alexandra Palace in the north to Crystal Palace in the south, Acton in the west, and City Airport in the east.

All told, it's approximately 25,000 streets. Students are also expected to learn the many thousands of 'points' on these roads. These are officially classified as:

> *All the streets; housing estates; parks and open spaces; government offices and departments; financial and commercial centres; diplomatic premises; town halls; registry offices; hospitals; places of worship; sports stadiums and leisure centres; airline offices; stations; hotels; clubs; theatres; cinemas; museums; art galleries; schools; colleges and universities; police stations and headquarters buildings; civil, criminal and coroner's courts; prisons; and places of interests to tourists.*
>
> *In fact, anywhere a taxi passenger might ask to be taken.*

That's from the Blue Book, a dinky A5-sized pamphlet which all Knowledge students receive at the beginning of their quest. The Blue Book contains a list of 320 routes, known as 'runs'. These are the framework for learning The Knowledge. Each run goes from one point to another; the most famous is the first one, Manor House station to Gibson Square.

Students are expected to link the two points via the straightest route possible and commit it to memory. This can only be done physically; you have to get out there and see the roads in person, noting every road, point and restriction.

As well as this, an area covering a quarter-mile radius must be studied in depth at both the start and end point; again this involves clocking every point of interest, street name and restriction. This is known as the 'dumbbell method':

Combined with the routes, these 640 little radii merge and click together like a vast jigsaw, eventually covering the entire Knowledge area.

After completing the first eighty runs, students must attend a written examination involving thirty questions based upon five random runs. The pass mark is 60 per cent. After that, the remainder of the Blue Book must be completed before progressing to an ongoing series of oral exams known as 'appearances', split into three stages with candidates being seen every 56, 28 or 21 days depending on their ability.

It is perhaps not surprising therefore that the average time it takes to pass The Knowledge currently stands at four to five years.

My own awareness of The Knowledge stems from when I was a child.

We were on one of our frequent trips into central London – always an exciting world away from the Metroland suburbs where I grew up – and happened to be walking along Piccadilly when a black cab pulled up beside the kerb, its engine ticking over in the gruff, rickety way that older models used to do. As a suited gentleman hopped out and paid the cabbie through the window, my father informed me that 'taxi drivers have to know everything . . .'

The comment must have stuck with me, but like many cabbies, I spent years in other jobs before undertaking The Knowledge. I had been training to be a secondary school teacher, but had quickly become disillusioned and after leaving that profession, I found myself working in the basement section of a department store.

My father, who'd made the comment about taxi drivers having to 'know everything' years before, once again provided me with the lightbulb moment.

'Reckon you could drive for a living?'

I said yes; I enjoy driving.

'Then maybe you should consider becoming a London cabbie.'

After a spot of research, it wasn't long before I was signed up for The Knowledge and found myself sitting behind a desk in the former Public Carriage Office on Penton Street, Islington, for my 'acceptance interview', a group talk in which an examiner would introduce us to the process and offer advice.

Many cabbies recall the Penton Street building (now the HQ for London's bike hire scheme; the Knowledge office having moved to Southwark) with dread. Although it was a relatively modern 1960s block, the interior was a world away from the colourful optimism of that era. With its dark wooden doors, polished linoleum and generally oppressive aura, it was more akin to a boarding school. Even the air-freshener of choice was sickly and overpowering, which didn't do strained nerves any favours.

The room in which I awaited the talk housed a miniature museum dedicated to the taxi trade. There were several glass cabinets containing mechanical taxi meters, old 'for hire' lights and, on the wall, black and white photographs of old-time cabmen, complete with Edwardian moustaches and bowler hats.

Also in the room were fifteen other newbies. All of us were silent, stewing in an awkward mix of fear and contemplation.

Although Knowledge examiners have a fearsome reputation, the gentleman who gave our talk was quite amiable. But he did make it clear that this introduction was informal; once past this point, things would become serious and regimented.

'From now on,' he told us, 'every time you're up here for an appearance you've got to look the part. We only accept suits. Jackets must be buttoned up. Shoes must be polished. Your hair must be tidy. If you've got a problem with that, you can say so now, ladies and gents, but you'll have to walk afterwards.'

Nobody said a word.

Satisfied, the examiner then imparted some sobering advice.

'Most of you won't pass,' he warned. 'The drop-out rate is around 70 per cent. That's the way it is, folks. Some decide it's not for them; a lot of people can't handle the amounts of information they have to deal with for this. Once you begin The Knowledge, your life is taken over.'

Following this ominous declaration, we were issued with the Blue Book. It was exciting; to me it felt like I was in on a little secret, the key to mastering London.

Most students opt to study The Knowledge on a moped; they are easily recognisable due to the map-board clipped to their handlebars. I, however, decided to use a little car, a second-hand Peugeot 106 in which I would trawl around London late at night and into the early hours when the sodium-lit streets were relatively empty.

This could be a little unsettling at times. On numerous occasions I had drunks attempt to enter the car, I had projectiles thrown at me and, on one particular evening in Hammersmith, I was chased by a gang of boozed-up thugs. All very character-building . . .

After slogging through the 320 runs it was time to begin my 'appearances'.

An examiner can ask you anything on an appearance. After completing the Blue Book, a student is expected to have a good working knowledge of the city and the ability to mentally calculate the straightest distance between any two points. Appearances are effectively an emulation of the job itself.

They are also terrifying; I found that the butterflies began fluttering in my guts the night before. When an appearance goes well though, it can be a source of great elation.

Most of my appearances took place at Penton Street. This involved climbing a staircase to the dentist-like waiting room. Here the mental torture began, for on the wall there was a huge map of London, artfully placed as a reminder of how much you still needed to learn.

The other candidates, all smartly suited, would sit in silence, knees jangling nervously, chins cupped, mouths anxiously stroked. You could feel the tension. If it became unbearable, the toilets were conveniently located opposite – but if you happened to be caught short when your name was called, you were liable to be refused your appearance that day.

When the time came, your allotted examiner would appear at the door and call you by your surname. Then you would follow them to their office along what we students called the 'Corridor of Fear'.

The examiners – all of whom have themselves undergone The Knowledge – are a varied bunch. Some are delightful, others are downright terrifying. But what you do come to realise is that they are testing your temperament, for it's important to maintain your cool if you wish to convey random strangers through the streets of London.

On several occasions this test of character began in the Corridor of Fear itself.

All students are issued a score card which must be presented at each appearance. Naturally I wanted to keep this safe and so fashioned a plastic protective wallet for it. One day after being called, the examiner asked for my card and, noticing the cover, slid it off. As we walked along the corridor, he proceeded to scrape the unguarded, precious document all the way along the wall. What could I say?

The corridor also had several fire doors along it and as I was led to another appearance, the examiner made sure that each set unceremoniously swung back in my face.

On yet another occasion, the examiner walked painfully slowly – so slowly that I ended up treading on his ankles. Needless to say I was mortified.

Once in the office, a student must sit in a chair – which is not to be moved under any circumstance. I remember one instance when my examiner for that day had placed my perch right at the other end of the room and as he asked me runs from a distance, I could barely hear him. In hindsight, however, this was an excellent training tool – for there are plenty of occasions when you meet a passenger whose voice is so soft you do indeed struggle to understand their requests.

In all I had to sit twenty-seven appearances. Thankfully my very first was with one of the kinder examiners, although she did make it clear that 'Today we'll go easy on you . . . be warned, it will become tougher.' And my, was she right.

On an appearance, the examiner asks several runs of their own choosing. First comes a point and you must name the road it's on.

'We'll start at Grafton Square.'

I froze and my spirits sunk. For the life of me I couldn't see it (and have kicked myself ever since; it's just north of Clapham Common).

'No . . . sorry, ma'am.'

'Okay. How about Maritime House?'

Suddenly it clicked.

'Maritime House is on Old Town, Clapham, ma'am.'

'Yes. And from there, we'll run it to the Caesar Hotel.'

'The Caesar Hotel is on Queens Gardens, ma'am.'

'Off you go.'

The idea now is to describe the most direct route between those two points, naming every turn and street name and describing the links between them in The Knowledge's own special verbal shorthand (see the Glossary at the back of this book for how to interpret this). So my answer in this case, as the examiner peered over her glasses at a map mounted on a wooden board in front of her, was as follows:

> *Leave Maritime House on right, comply roundabout, leave by North Street, forward Silverthorne Road, left Broughton Street, right Queenstown Road, comply Queen's Circus, leave by Queenstown Road continued, forward Chelsea Bridge, forward Chelsea Bridge Road, left Royal Hospital Road, right Franklin's Row, left St Leonard's Terrace, right Walpole Street, cross King's Road, forward Anderson Street, forward Sloane Avenue, forward Pelham Street, right Thurloe Square, left Thurloe Place, right Exhibition Road, forward Alexandra Gate, forward Serpentine Road, forward Serpentine Bridge, forward The Ring, forward Victoria Gate, left Bayswater Road, right and left Lancaster Gate, right Leinster Terrace, forward Leinster Gardens, right Queen's Gardens . . . set down Caesar Hotel on left.*

The rest of that very first appearance is something of a blur but fortunately I was awarded a 'C'. This means I scored 3 points. The other marks available are: A (6 points), B (4 points) and D (no points).

To get their 'drop' and progress to the next stage, a student must acquire 12 points within seven attempts – failure to do so results in the dreaded 'red line'; any points acquired are wiped out and it's back to the beginning of the stage (or the stage before that if you have the misfortune to acquire two red lines). In my first appearance I was fortunate that the examiner was encouraging and accommodating. Not all exams were so pleasant, however; in fact some were downright intimidating.

Feeling relatively confident, I attended my second appearance 56 days later.

I was called, followed the examiner to his office and was invited to sit down. And then I waited . . . and waited and waited while he drummed his fingers and stared at his computer, clicking his mouse idly as if he were shopping online and I was invisible. Finally the first question came.

'What's my name?'

It took a moment for me to register. Having never met this gentleman, I had no idea whatsoever what his name was.

'I'm sorry, sir . . . I don't know,' I mumbled.

'Okay,' my tormentor smiled. 'Rule number one on The Knowledge: I'll never ask you anything you don't know.'

I nodded eagerly.

'So,' he continued. 'What's my name?'

By now my mind was fogging and I uttered a further apology. But it didn't matter, the examiner had already moved on.

'Highgate Private Hospital?'

I rejoiced. A nice, straightforward point.

'View Road, sir.'

There was no reply. The examiner simply stared at me, wobbling a pen between his thumb and forefinger. I took his lengthy silence as an indication that I'd given the wrong answer.

'No . . . not View Road,' I muttered. 'Erm . . . Denewood Road? No . . . North Hill.' My brain scrambled, I began to name numerous roads around Highgate.

Still silence.

'Sorry, sir. I don't know.'

'You said it,' he finally chuckled. 'View Road.'

'Oh . . .'

At the time this exchange baffled me. But, just like my experiences in the Corridor of Fear, it was in fact excellent training – for it taught me to trust my instinct. There have been a number of instances in which a passenger is convinced their destination is at a completely different location but, using tact, I've been able to get them to the correct place.

While this appearance was benignly perplexing, there were others when the examiner was just plain hostile. On one particularly ghastly appearance, the examiner ignored me while I recited my given runs, flicking through a newspaper before leaning back in his chair with a pained look.

Finally, pinching the bridge of his nose, he looked at me and, with great weariness, said: 'You're not very good, are you, Mr Lordan?'

'No, sir . . . sorry, I'm having a bad day.'

'If I were a passenger in your cab I'd be pretty dizzy by now, wouldn't I?' he sighed. 'You're going around in circles.'

On another appearance the same examiner pretended to fall asleep. On another he decided to hurl a book across the room. But, again, it was effective training, because a tiny percentage of cab passengers do indeed treat you like dirt.

Once the Blue Book has been completed and a student has proceeded to appearances, their exploration of London should intensify. It's now up to the apprentice cabbie to concentrate on any places they may have missed, sharpening their mental map, keeping as up-to-date as possible with any new or changing points and chanting the 320 runs every day like a child learning their times tables.

Revision is key. Most students, usually through one of London's numerous Knowledge schools, find a 'callover partner', a fellow sufferer with whom they can practise random routes, penning them onto a large laminated map and then poring over what went wrong and what would work better.

It was during this period that I participated in a study led by Professor Eleanor Maguire at University College London's Institute of Neurology who was attempting to discover whether the oft-stated claim that London cabbies' brains are larger than average was true. As part of a wider study, it was hoped that the findings could help those suffering from Alzheimer's.

For this I was asked to carry out a number of spatial awareness tasks before undergoing a brain scan. I received copies of the images which showed the interior of my head from several angles – quite an uncanny experience. I was then asked to return shortly before passing The Knowledge for a second scan.

It turned out that my brain had indeed experienced some cell growth (albeit microscopic!). The part of the brain in question was the hippocampus, a curled section of grey matter which resembles a sea horse (hence the name, which is Greek for 'sea monster'). The hippocampus deals with memory and navigation. Qualified cabbies who'd been driving a taxi for a number of years also took part in the study and they too had considerably greater density of cells in their hippocampus.

The study concluded that it is possible for individuals to alter the structure of their brain if they train it hard enough – rather like muscles in your arms and legs. This is important to consider because, in this era of rapidly increasing technology, it can be easy to forget just how truly magnificent the brain is. And exercising it makes it all the better.

It has also become fashionable of late to criticise The Knowledge, because 'we all have SatNav now'. Such comments overlook the complexity of what driving a taxi in London – and dealing with the public – entails.

As we've seen, London's streets have developed organically; there is little rhyme or reason to them and this can bamboozle some SatNavs. And even if they can cope, what happens if you lose the signal or the battery goes flat?

London's a busy place, and the moment a fare climbs into your cab you must be prepared to set off immediately. Pausing to prod away at a screen will cause traffic to build up behind you. Moreover, it's illegal to interact with any electronic device while moving.

In some cases the spelling and pronunciation of London's streets are ambiguous. If you heard 'Jermyn Street' or 'Beauchamp Place', for example, without seeing them written down, how would you go about tapping in such names? German? Jermin? Bochamp? Beecham?

Some passengers get areas and street names mixed up. A good example I once had was 'Covent Garden, please; King William Street.' After checking with the passenger, I ascertained they in fact meant William IV Street – King William Street is near London Bridge.

There are plenty of occasions when a passenger is unsure of their destination and can only give the approximate area or a rough description of what the building looks like. Other folk throw colloquial terms at you such as the 'hole in the wall' (a drop-off point for Victoria station), change their destination halfway through or require multiple drops in a roundabout order.

There are the excited visitors who ask for tours, recommendations and local knowledge and the seasoned regulars who demand an unorthodox route; indicating so with just one or two waypoints before flicking off the intercom and busying themselves with paperwork.

I've even picked up people with chronic back injuries who've begged me to avoid speed bumps and, on more than one occasion, been asked to act as an ambulance.

A brain, programmed with The Knowledge of London, is able to cope with all of these scenarios. It's the best SatNav you can get.

After what seemed like an eternity I finally made it to 21s and was being examined every three weeks. The end felt like it was in sight.

By now, the Knowledge HQ had moved to a more modern office; the Palestra in Southwark. In some ways, this was worse than Penton Street as the high security necessitated a stint in two separate waiting rooms: one in the lobby and the other upstairs.

Soon, I was up for my 'req' (short for 'required standard', the moment when you pass).

Over six appearances I'd managed to scrape 9 points; all I needed was a 'C' to make it up to 12 and I'd be done. Since most people, like I had, have built up points in previous appearances before the req, it is generally considered to be a formality; on my four years on The Knowledge I'd never heard of anyone not scoring on it.

I must've been a first.

I was booked in early; 8.30 a.m. In the waiting room I met another Knowledge student who was also approaching the finishing line. We wished each other good luck in hushed tones.

'Mr Lordan, please.'

Once in the new, fresh-smelling office there was no 'hello' or 'good morning'; the examiner launched straight into it.

'Tenbury Court?'

'Sorry, sir.'

'The Linnean Society?'

'No . . . sorry, sir.'

It grew worse and worse; the most obscure points I'd ever been asked. One of them, the 'Prince of Knowledge apartments', I've still yet to discover.

I was given a D. Redlined; back to the beginning of the stage. Years later, I found out that my mum had baked a celebration cake which had to be quietly binned.

I walked out in a daze and bumped into the student I'd met in the waiting room. When I told him what had happened he assumed I was joking.

And so it was back to it, studying, exploring and calling over. Once again I was taken to the limit; over six appearances I gained 3 Ds and 3 Cs. I had one chance left.

Fortunately on this occasion I passed and I'm not ashamed to admit there were tears in my eyes. (If you want to know which route it was, you can find out later on in this book . . .)

I apologised to the examiner – the same one who'd previously told me I was 'not very good'. By now his stern persona – which had all been an act – was replaced with kindness; he assured me strong emotions were quite normal and that he believed I would 'make an excellent cabbie'. And that choked me up all the more.

In this book, I've selected 50 of the 320 Blue Book runs that will hopefully provide an insight into what it's like to study The Knowledge of London. Along the way I've highlighted various aspects of history and trivia that I've discovered on my own travels, along with a few tricks and tips for those wishing to brave the streets themselves.

The runs have been divided into groups of ten, with each collection based on a certain memory technique to help you give your own hippocampus a workout.

The first set looks at acronyms and mnemonics; short, snappy words and phrases which are ideally suited for recalling certain road groups.

Secondly, I've compiled ten short stories where characters, objects and events are employed as cues for roads and area names. While far from the calibre of Hans Christian Andersen, it's hoped that these curious little tales will help nudge your brain in the right direction.

The third batch uses 'memory champion' techniques, as employed by people who compete in tests of memorisation; namely the 'memory palace' and the 'method of loci' in which your mind is encouraged to wander around various surreal environments, focusing upon certain objects and characters along the way as an aide-memoire.

The fourth group presents a collection of runs through which specific threads of London lore and history flow; the interconnections of which provide a useful tool for recalling the order of streets and districts.

The final set of runs are ones which are personal to me; an insight into the memories which I have accumulated as both a Knowledge student and London cabbie.

Please note (especially if any of my old Knowledge examiners are reading) that although nothing is wildly off course, one or two routes may take the odd wee diversion, purely for the purpose of including an interesting point!

RUNS USING MNEMONICS & ACRONYMS

Over the years Londoners – particularly cabbies – have gained a reputation for cultivating a quick wit and snappy dialogue. The most famous example is probably Cockney rhyming slang, but younger groups within the capital continue to be inventive with language today.

This culture of having a playful way with words makes much use of acronyms and mnemonics. An acronym is the process of combining the first letters of a series of words into a separate, stand-alone term, and a mnemonic (from the Greek *mnemon*, meaning 'mindful') is a similar device in which the first letters of a string of words are this time employed to conjure up a catchy little phrase – an ideal tool when faced with having to memorise the long, daunting groups of streets and roads required for The Knowledge.

A classic example of an acronym would be 'BBC' (for British Broadcasting Corporation), while 'Never Eat Shredded Wheat' is a mnemonic for recalling the points of the compass in the right order (north, east, south, west).

In terms of The Knowledge, students do not shy away from being creative when making up their own acronyms and mnemonics and there's good fun to be had in swapping their latest gems with fellow trainee cabbies.

There are two particular examples that are universally known throughout the London taxi trade:

The mnemonic '**little apples grow quickly please**', which helps recall the order of theatres – Lyric, Apollo, Gielgud, Queen's and Palace – in the order they stand when heading north along Shaftesbury Avenue, is a very useful tool when contending with the chaos of the West End.

Secondly, there is the acronym '**WASP**', which stands for Walpole Street, Anderson Street, Sloane Avenue and Pelham Street, a handy shortcut which runs between Chelsea and South Kensington.

Funnily enough, the ruder or more vulgar an acronym or mnemonic is, the better it tends to stick in the mind . . . For this section, however, I have striven to provide clean examples and will leave it up to readers to formulate any naughtier terms within their own minds!

EUSTON STATION NW1 → BRIXTON PRISON SW2

Euston station and Brixton prison are essentially on the same longitude, making this a useful run for orientation. A good acronym to begin with is 'MEG', which helps recall Melton Street, Euston Road and Gower Street.

After passing through Bloomsbury and touching upon Shaftesbury Avenue, the run then cuts through Covent Garden and the heart of government, where the acronym '**SOAM**' takes us along St Margaret Street, Old Palace Yard (the site where Guy Fawkes and his fellow conspirators faced a grisly execution), Abingdon Street and Millbank before heading south of the river – although Lambeth Bridge actually runs from west to east; you don't technically aim south until exiting Lambeth Circus.

Once over the Thames, the acronym '**LAKSS**' (Lambeth Circus, Albert Embankment, Kennington Lane, South Lambeth Road and Stockwell Terrace) directs us towards Stockwell and Brixton, areas whose previous residents have included Vincent Van Gogh and David Bowie.

1 EUSTON STATION

The entrance to Euston was originally flanked by a grand doric arch, but this was controversially demolished in the 1960s to make way for today's modern building, which is more akin to an airport than a traditional railway station.

2 GOWER STREET

Gower Street is home to University College London. When founded in 1826, one of the university's biggest champions was philosopher Jeremy Bentham whose preserved corpse is (rather unsettlingly) displayed inside the campus. The university's equally disturbing Grant Museum of Zoology and Comparative Anatomy is also on Gower Street.

3 SEVEN DIALS

This area is named after the seven sundials which top the

column at the centre of this compact roundabout. The monument was originally built in the late 17th century and soon became a focal point for crime thanks to the lawless maze of surrounding streets. Today's column is a modern reconstruction.

4 KING CHARLES ISLAND

The junction which forms Trafalgar Square's southern point is called King Charles Island, named after the bronze statue of Charles I that stands in the shadow of Nelson's Column. This is London's official centre, the point from which all distances to the city are measured. The statue was forged during Charles I's lifetime but following the English Civil War and his subsequent beheading it was deemed an unwanted relic. According to legend, the statue was buried for safekeeping by metalsmith John Rivet and presented to Charles II upon the monarchy's restoration.

5 WHITEHALL

The only remaining building from the former Palace of Whitehall, Banqueting House, was where James I and Charles I came to party. Pocahontas was once a guest here and the ceiling is adorned with a stunning Rubens commission. Ironically it was outside Banqueting House that Charles I was executed in 1649.

6 DOWNING STREET

Famously home to the British Prime Minister, Downing Street is named after Irish-born Sir George Downing who built the property in the 1600s. As a young man, Downing spent time in America and was among the first batch of students to graduate from Harvard University.

7 LAMBETH BRIDGE

Lambeth Bridge is painted red, a reference to the House of Lords who sit upon red leather benches in Parliament's southern chamber. Similarly, Westminster Bridge to the north is coloured green in line with the House of Commons' seats.

8 SOUTH LAMBETH ROAD

The squat, round building on the junction with Clapham Road was once the entrance to a WWII shelter. It's now decorated by a peace mural featuring local heroine Violette Szabo. The daughter of a London cabbie, Szabo grew up on nearby Burnley Road and served with the Special Operations Executive in WWII, parachuting into occupied Europe to liaise with the French Resistance. She was captured in 1944 and executed aged just 23.

Leave by left: Melton Street
Right: Euston Road
Left: Gower Street
Forward: Bedford Square
Forward: Bloomsbury Street
Forward: Shaftesbury Avenue
Right: Prince's Circus
Left: Shaftesbury Avenue continued
Left: Monmouth Street
Comply: Seven Dials
Leave by: Monmouth Street continued
Forward: Upper St Martin's Lane
Right: Cranbourn Street
Left: Charing Cross Road
Forward: St Martin's Place
Forward: Trafalgar Square
Forward: Whitehall
Forward: Parliament Street

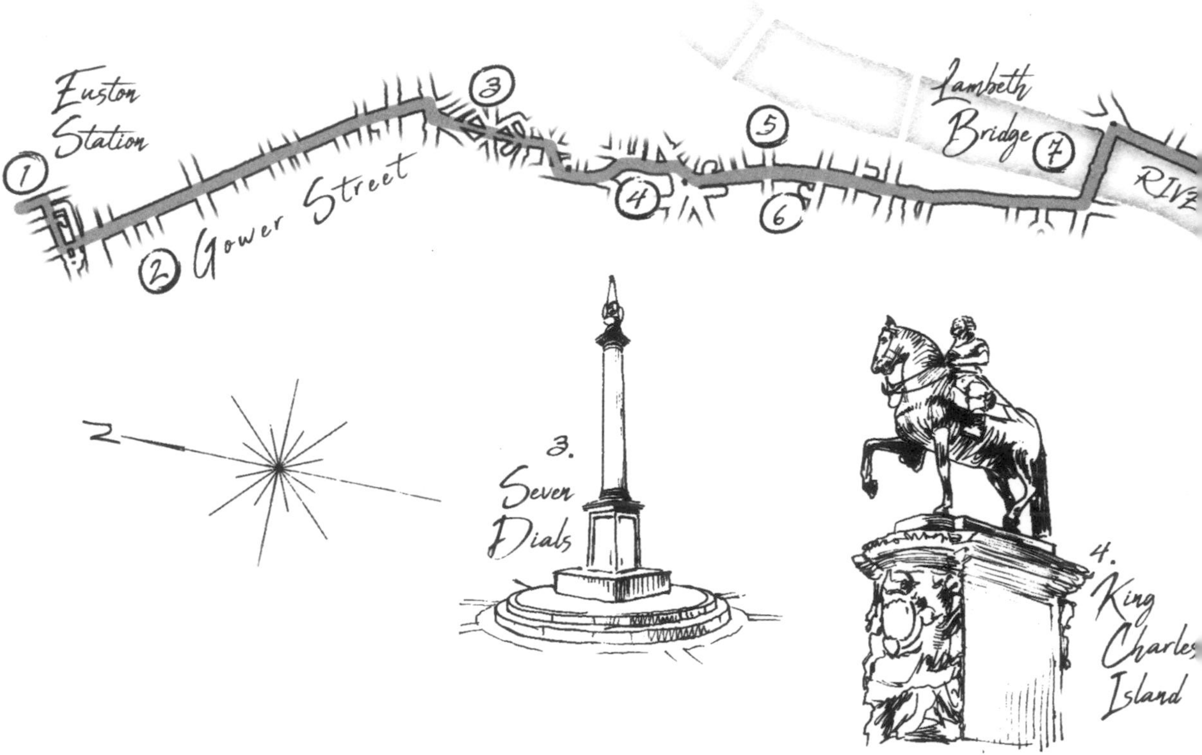

Euston Station
Gower Street
Lambeth Bridge

3. Seven Dials

4. King Charles Island

Forward: Parliament Square
Forward: St Margaret Street
Forward: Old Palace Yard
Forward: Abingdon Street
Forward: Millbank
Comply: Millbank Circus
Leave by: Lambeth Bridge
Comply: Lambeth Circus
Leave by: Albert Embankment
Left: Kennington Lane
Right: South Lambeth Road
Left: Stockwell Terrace
Right: Clapham Road
Left: Stockwell Road
Left: Stockwell Park Walk
Right: Brixton Road
Forward: Brixton Hill
Right: Jebb Avenue
Brixton prison on left

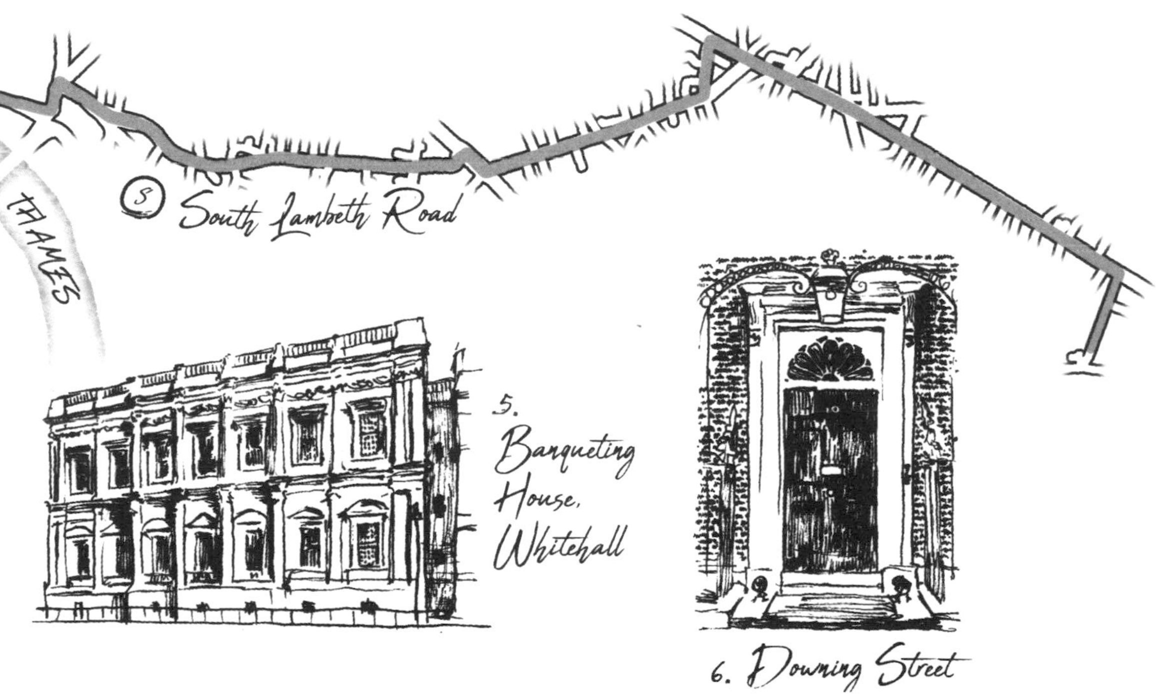

STAMFORD STREET SE1 → STAMFORD HILL N16

This run links two Stamfords: Stamford Street and Stamford Hill which, despite sounding similar, are on completely opposite sides of the city.

Near the beginning of the run, the mnemonic '**bask under nice fair weather**' is handy for remembering Blackfriars Bridge, Unilever Circus, New Bridge Street, Farringdon Street and West Smithfield.

Although the idea of sunbathing by the Thames may seem farfetched, the city did once have an artificial beach located beside Tower Bridge. This 'tolerable Cockney imitation of the seaside', as one paper described it, was hugely popular until it closed in 1971 over pollution fears.

The next memory prompt is the rather inelegant '**GOB**', which gives us Goswell Road, Old Street and Bath Street; a good cut-through from the City to Hoxton.

Goswell Road is of particular interest as it's the only 'road' to appear within the boundaries of the historic Square Mile – all other thoroughfares in the City are dubbed streets, lanes, alleys and so on.

Lastly we have the mnemonic '**now bring some big kippers**', which can be used to recall New North Road, Baring Street, Southgate Road, Ball's Pond Road and King Henry's Walk. In January and February you'll often hear cabbies grumbling about the 'kipper season', the dreaded time of year when work levels fall flat due to much of the public being short of cash following the excesses of Christmas.

1 BLACKFRIARS BRIDGE

Blackfriars Bridge has several pulpits along each side, a homage to the Blackfriars Monastery which stood beside the Thames until it was dissolved by Henry VIII. Also on the bridge is a statue of Queen Victoria (who opened the bridge in 1869) and the Temperance fountain which originally stood outside the Royal Exchange before making way for the London Troops Monument shortly after WWI. In 1982, the body of Roberto Calvi – aka 'God's Banker' – was discovered hanging beneath Blackfriars Bridge. His mysterious death has been a cause of great debate ever since.

2 CHARTERHOUSE SQUARE

During the Black Death this area was used as a mass burial-pit. Charterhouse Square is now noted for Florin Court, a beautiful art deco block which starred as Hercule Poirot's apartment in the long-running TV adaptation of Agatha Christie's stories.

3 SHEPHERDESS WALK

In Victorian times, The Eagle on Shepherdess Walk inspired a variation of the children's rhyme, 'Pop! Goes the Weasel':

Up and down the City Road,
In and out the Eagle,
That's the way the money goes.
Pop! Goes the weasel!

These lyrics refer to cash-strapped locals who'd pawn items in shops along the City Road and then waste whatever cash they'd accumulated in the pub.

4 NEW NORTH ROAD

Gainsborough Studios are named after the Gainsborough Pictures film studio that once occupied the site. Many productions were shot at Gainsborough between the 1920s and '50s, including twelve Alfred Hitchcock films. An Easter Island-esque bust of the famous director now looms over a courtyard within the complex.

5 STOKE NEWINGTON HIGH STREET

Established in 1840, Abney Park Cemetery had become overgrown and derelict by 1979. It was purchased by Hackney Council for £1 and has since been transformed into a nature reserve. Famous people buried here include Salvation Army founder William Booth and Joanna Vassa – daughter of anti-slavery campaigner, Olaudah Equiano – whose grave was rediscovered in 2005. In 2006 the cemetery featured in Amy Winehouse's 'Back to Black' video.

Leave by left: Blackfriars Road
Forward: Blackfriars Bridge
Comply: Unilever Circus
Leave by: New Bridge Street
Forward: Farringdon Street
Right: West Smithfield
Left: East Poultry Avenue
Right: Charterhouse Street
Forward: Charterhouse Square
Forward: Carthusian Street
Left: Aldersgate Street
Forward: Goswell Road
Right: Old Street
Left: Bath Street
Cross: City Road
Forward: Shepherdess Walk
Right: Eagle Wharf Road
Left: New North Road
Right: Baring Street
Left: Southgate Road

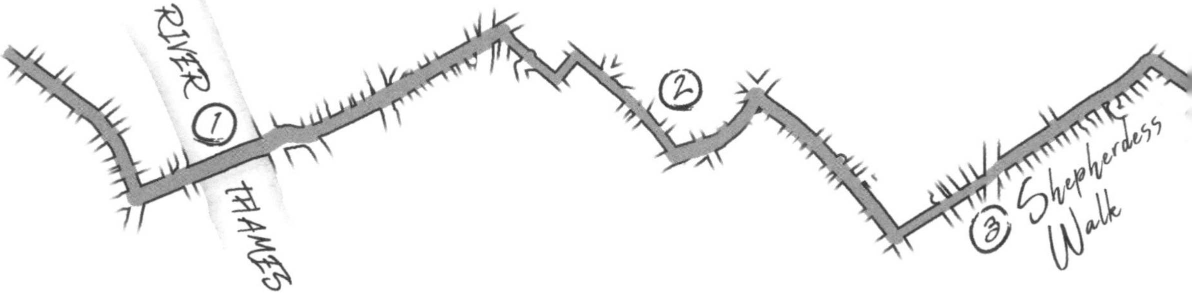

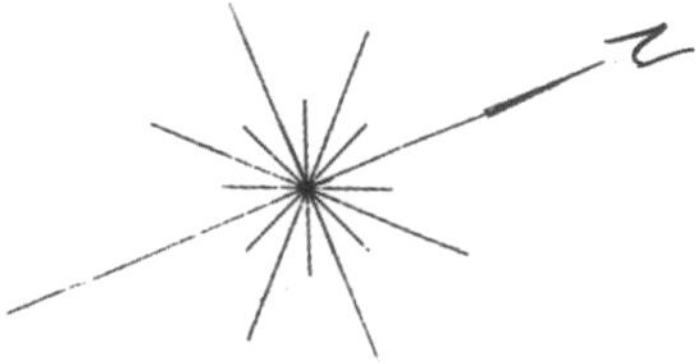

RIVER THAMES
1
2
3 Shepherdess Walk
N

1. Blackfriars Bridge

Right: Ball's Pond Road
Left: King Henry's Walk
Right: Mildmay Road
Forward: Crossway
Left: Stoke Newington Road
Forward: Stoke Newington High Street
Stamford Hill facing

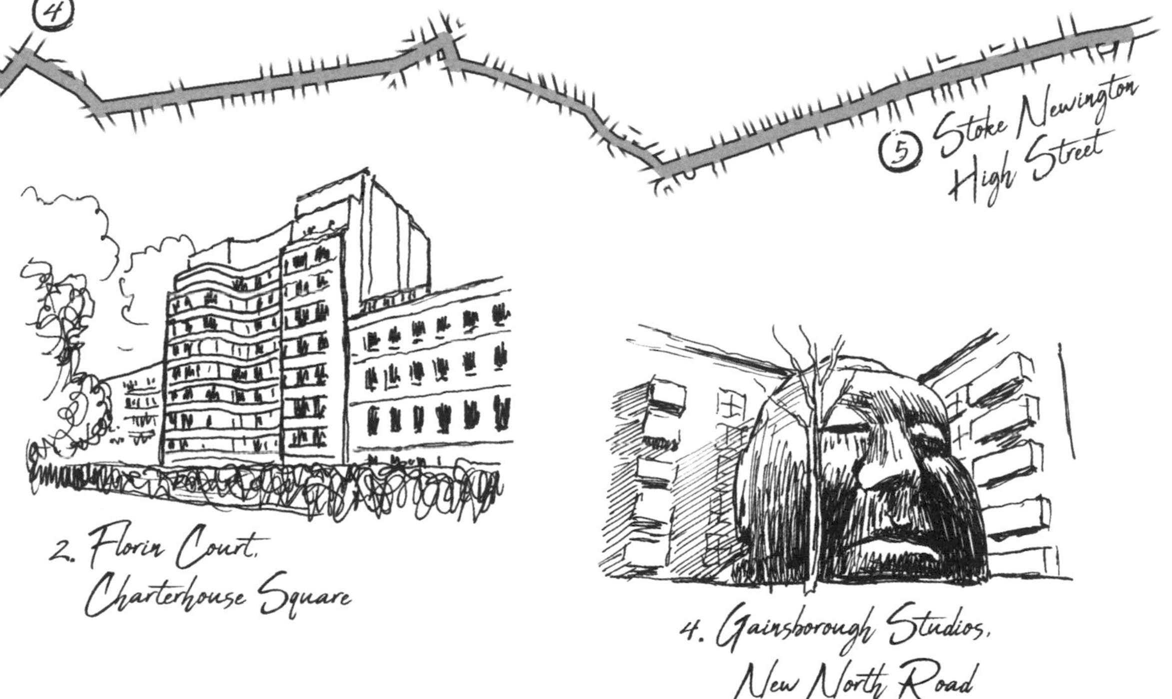

WARWICK GROVE E5 → ANGEL STATION N1

This run commences in an area clustered with residential streets and one-way systems, a jumble I personally found very tricky to learn when studying The Knowledge. The acronym 'MESS' therefore seemed rather appropriate; it helps call Manse Road, Evering Road, Stoke Newington High Street and Stoke Newington Road.

In the middle of the route we encounter Crossway, Mildmay Road and King Henry's Walk. This is an important Dalston cut-through, which can be remembered with the mnemonic '**collect my keys**' – think of it as unlocking a secret.

King Henry's Walk refers to a hunting lodge which Henry VIII is said to have owned in the vicinity. Although no evidence of this building is known to exist, there is a Boleyn Road nearby too.

1 STOKE NEWINGTON COMMON

Mark Feld – later known as Marc Bolan, frontman for glam-rock band T-Rex – was raised at 25 Stoke Newington Common. A plaque commemorates his childhood home.

2 STOKE NEWINGTON ROAD

On Stoke Newington Road is the Turkish Aziziye Mosque. This glittering blue and gold building was originally a picture palace when first opened in 1913 but had fallen into disrepair by the 1970s. It was converted into a mosque in 1983, the former cinema's twin domes being ideally suited for the purpose. Stoke Newington Road is well served by Turkish restaurants, one of the most popular of which is Mangal 2; particularly famous for being a favourite haunt of artistic duo Gilbert and George, who can be spotted dining here almost every evening, their knowing regularity being something of an art installation in itself.

3 ESSEX ROAD

161–169 Essex Road is home to the former Carlton Cinema which, like the Turkish mosque on Stoke Newington Road, has quite an exotic appearance – ancient Egyptian in this case, no doubt influenced by the excavation of Tutankhamun's tomb which occurred eight years before the cinema opened in 1930. After years of decay the cinema was restored and reopened in 2015 as Gracepoint.

4 ISLINGTON GREEN

This patch of land was originally a place where farmers could freely graze their livestock. The statue here is of Sir Hugh Myddelton who played a major role in bringing fresh drinking water to London. The north side of Islington Green was once dominated by Collins' Music Hall where comic actor Sir Norman Wisdom made his stage debut in 1946. The former theatre is now a Waterstones bookshop.

5 UPPER STREET

Just off Upper Street on Berners Road is the Business Design Centre; a major exhibition venue. The building dates back to the 1860s when it opened as the Royal Agricultural Hall; a centre for showcasing livestock. During the 2012 Olympics, Czech sculptor David Cerny exhibited his London Booster artwork outside the centre: a full-sized red double-decker bus which, with human-like arms attached, grunted away as it did press-ups.

6 ANGEL STATION

The tube station (which opened in 1907 and now boasts the longest escalator on the network) is named after the historic Angel Tavern where the radical activist Thomas Paine began writing *The Rights of Man*.

Leave by left: Upper Clapton Road
Right: Rossington Street
Right: Northwold Road
Left: Stoke Newington Common
Left: Rectory Road
Right: Manse Road
Forward: Evering Road
Left: Stoke Newington High Street
Forward: Stoke Newington Road
Right: Crossway
Forward: Mildmay Road
Left: King Henry's Walk
Right: Balls Pond Road
Left: Essex Road
Forward: Islington Green
Bear left: Upper Street
Forward: Islington High Street
Angel station on left

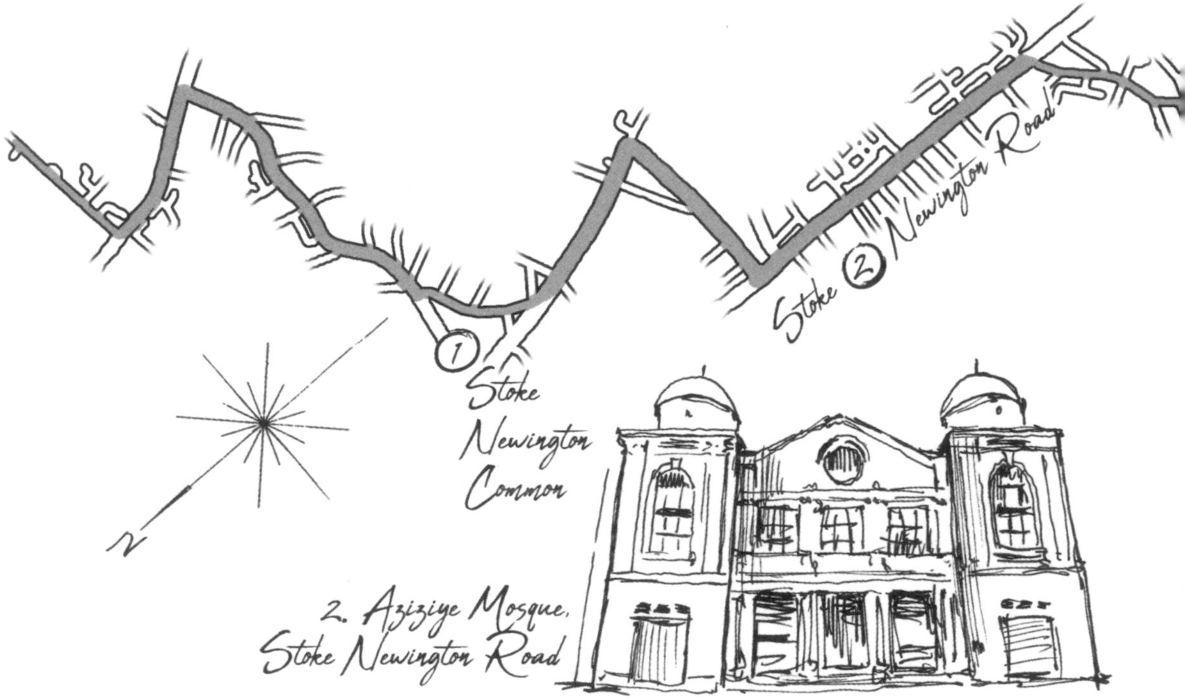

3. Carlton Cinema, Essex Road

THE BOLTONS SW10 → CAMPDEN HILL SQUARE W8

This run mainly nips through quieter back streets, venturing on to two main roads, Cromwell Road and Kensington High Street, only very briefly.

The early part of the route passes through an area nicknamed 'The Gardens' which can feel like something of a maze at first as many streets in the area bear the same suffix: Bolton Gardens, Courtfield Gardens, Collingham Gardens, Harrington Gardens and so on. A neat acronym to help you on your way is **'BBC'** for Boltons Place, Bolton Gardens and Collingham Road.

Cromwell Road was named by Prince Albert, an odd choice considering the connotations it has with one of the monarchy's darker episodes. But this does provide us with a useful mnemonic for remembering a good chunk of the run: **'Cromwell madly chopped when King Charles appeared here.'** This gives us Cromwell Road, Marloes Road, Cheniston Gardens, Wrights Lane, Kensington High Street, Campden Hill Road, Aubrey Walk and Hillsleigh Road.

1 THE BOLTONS

Shaped like a needle's eye, The Boltons has long been one of London's most prestigious addresses. Previous residents have included the American actor Douglas Fairbanks Jr. and composer Lionel Bart, best known for the 1960s musical *Oliver!*

2 BOLTONS PLACE

Beatrix Potter was born here in 1866. Her childhood home was destroyed in the Blitz and the site is now occupied by Bousfield Primary School. A plaque commemorating the author can be seen around the corner on Old Brompton Road, further along which is Brompton Cemetery where names including 'Peter Rabbett' and 'Jeremiah Fisher' can be glimpsed upon fading gravestones . . .

3 MARLOES ROAD

The deaths of two hard-living legends are linked to this road. On the corner of Marloes Road and Cromwell Road is Cromwell Hospital where, in 2005, Northern Irish footballer George Best passed away after a long battle with alcoholism. Further along, on the east side of Marloes Road, is the erstwhile St Mary Abbot's Hospital, which closed in 1992 and now forms the Stone Hall Gardens apartments. On 18 September 1970, guitarist Jimi Hendrix was pronounced dead at St Mary Abbot's after being rushed there from the Samarkand Hotel, Notting Hill.

4 CAMPDEN HILL ROAD

Situated between Campden Hill Road and Hornton Street is the imposing Kensington and Chelsea Town Hall, which was designed in the brutalist style by Sir Basil Spence, the same architect who created Coventry's post-war cathedral. Spence died shortly before the project was completed. On the summit of Campden Hill Road is the Windsor Castle pub, which dates from the early 19th century. Before London's expansion, it was apparently possible to spy Windsor Castle in the distance on a clear day from this spot, hence the pub's name.

5 AUBREY WALK

Squeezed between the houses on Aubrey Walk is St George's Church, which opened in 1864 and was described at the time as being 'Continental Gothic'. Also on Aubrey Walk is an art deco style building that was once home to Dusty Springfield at the height of her fame. The singer is commemorated by a blue plaque.

Leave by: Boltons Place
Forward: Bolton Gardens
Forward: Collingham Gardens
Forward: Collingham Road
Left: Cromwell Road
Right: Marloes Road
Right: Cheniston Gardens
Left: Wrights Lane
Left: Kensington High Street
Right: Campden Hill Road
Left: Aubrey Walk
Right: Hillsleigh Road
Campden Hill Square on left

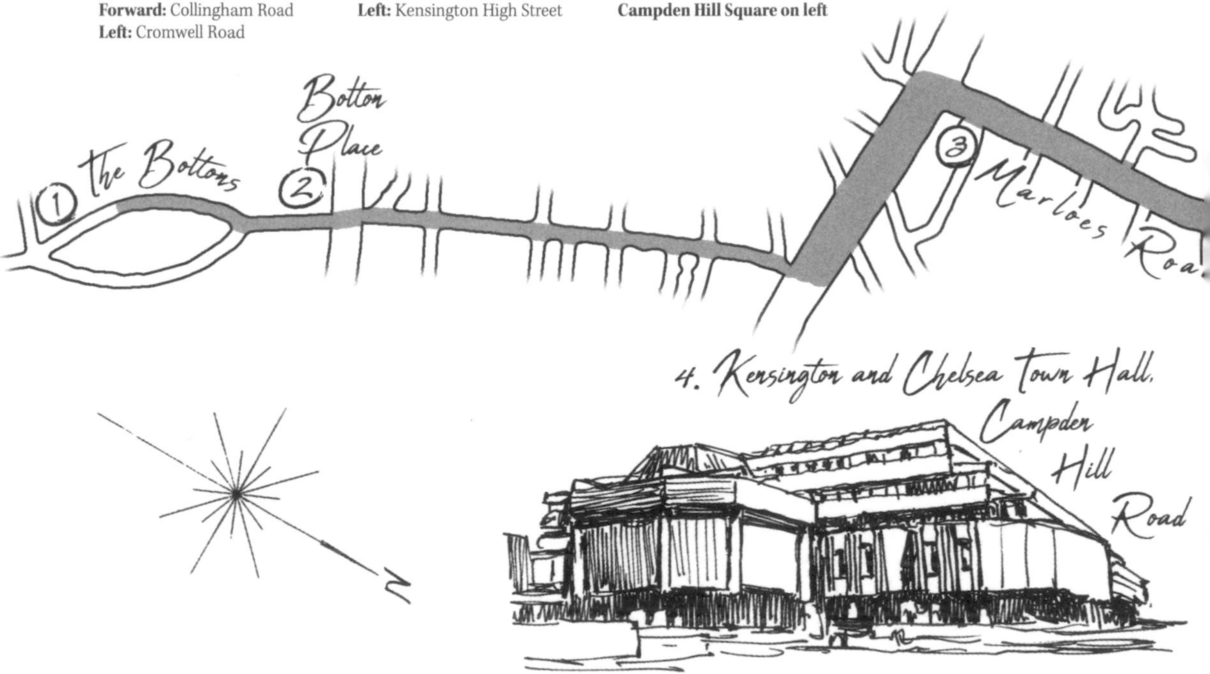

1 The Boltons
2 Bolton Place
3 Marloes Road
4. Kensington and Chelsea town Hall,
Campden Hill Road
N

4
Campden Hill Road
Aubrey Walk
5
WINDSOR CASTLE
5. St George's Church, Aubrey Walk
4. Windsor Castle Pub, Campden Hill Road

OXFORD SQUARE W2 → LATIMER ROAD STATION W10

An important west London run, this route begins in an area close to Paddington station (or 'Padders' as cabbies call it) meaning Knowledge students should pay extra attention when studying the surrounding streets – jobs to mainline stations are bread and butter to a taxi driver and mastering the nifty cut-throughs can make all the difference to a passenger who's running late.

Station jobs can be particularly stressful, so perhaps a cheeky mnemonic to start off with is '**have some gin**' – not recommended in reality if you're behind the wheel, of course, but it does help with calling Hyde Park Crescent, Somers Crescent and Gloucester Square.

The run then cuts through Bayswater en-route to Portobello Road (named after the city of Portobelo in Panama where a battle in the curiously named 'War of Jenkins' Ear' occurred). This stretch can be revised with the mnemonic '**beware wild pigeons**' for Bishop's Bridge Road, Westbourne Grove and Portobello Road.

For the final leg of the run, the acronym '**KELLS**' is handy for remembering the order of Kensington Park Road, Elgin Crescent, Ladbroke Grove, Lancaster Road and Silchester Road.

1 BISHOP'S BRIDGE ROAD

The original Bishop's Bridge was a stone structure built upon land belonging to the Bishops of London. When Paddington station first opened in 1838 the ticket office and waiting rooms were incorporated into the bridge's arches. The arrival of the railway also necessitated a new bridge across the Grand Union Canal. For this, engineer Isambard Kingdom Brunel erected a pioneering iron design which was forgotten after being encased in brick. This piece of industrial history was rediscovered in 2004, narrowly avoiding demolition.

2 WESTBOURNE GROVE

In 1863, Yorkshireman William Whiteley opened a small shop on Westbourne Grove which quickly burgeoned into London's first true department store. As Whiteley's business grew, neighbouring businesses along Westbourne Grove began to suffer, leading other disgruntled shopkeepers to nickname the road 'Bankruptcy Row' – they certainly felt no sympathy when Whiteley's store was razed by fire in 1887. After the blaze, Whiteley rebuilt his emporium on nearby Queensway where, in 1907, he was shot dead in his office by a young man claiming to be his illegitimate son. The store has since been remodelled into Whiteleys Shopping Centre.

3 PORTOBELLO ROAD

As well as the famous antiques market, Portobello Road is also home to the Electric Cinema, one of the UK's earliest, dating back to 1910. It still screens films today.

4 BLENHEIM CRESCENT

Number 13 Blenheim Crescent is home to the Notting Hill Bookshop, which gained fame in Richard Curtis' 1999 film *Notting Hill.*

5 LADBROKE GROVE

Stretching for 1½ miles, Ladbroke Grove is one of London's liveliest streets. It's named after Sir Richard Ladbroke, a former Lord Mayor of London who owned the land and bequeathed it to his nephew, James Weller Ladbroke. In the 1950s, Ladbroke Grove became a focal point for immigrants from the West Indies, a period atmospherically evoked in the 1956 novel *The Lonely Londoners* by Trinidadian author Sam Selvon. Music groups Aswad and The Clash were both formed around Ladbroke Grove and the road is now at the centre of the annual Notting Hill Carnival, the UK's biggest festival of Caribbean culture.

6 LATIMER ROAD STATION

In late August and early September 1958, Latimer Road was at the epicentre of the Notting Hill race riots which are generally believed to have started at the tube station when a group of white youths became antagonistic towards a mixed-race couple, Majbritt and Raymond Morrison. This period of unrest was dramatised a year later in the Colin MacInnes novel *Absolute Beginners.*

Leave by right: Hyde Park Crescent
Left: Somers Crescent
Forward: Gloucester Square
Right: Sussex Place
Left and right: Sussex Gardens
Left: Westbourne Crescent
Right: Gloucester Terrace
Left: Bishop's Bridge Road
Forward: Westbourne Grove
Right: Portobello Road
Left: Blenheim Crescent
Comply: Roundabout
Leave by: Blenheim Crescent continued
Right: Ladbroke Grove
Left: Lancaster Road
Bear right: Silchester Road
Left: Bramley Road
Latimer Road station on left

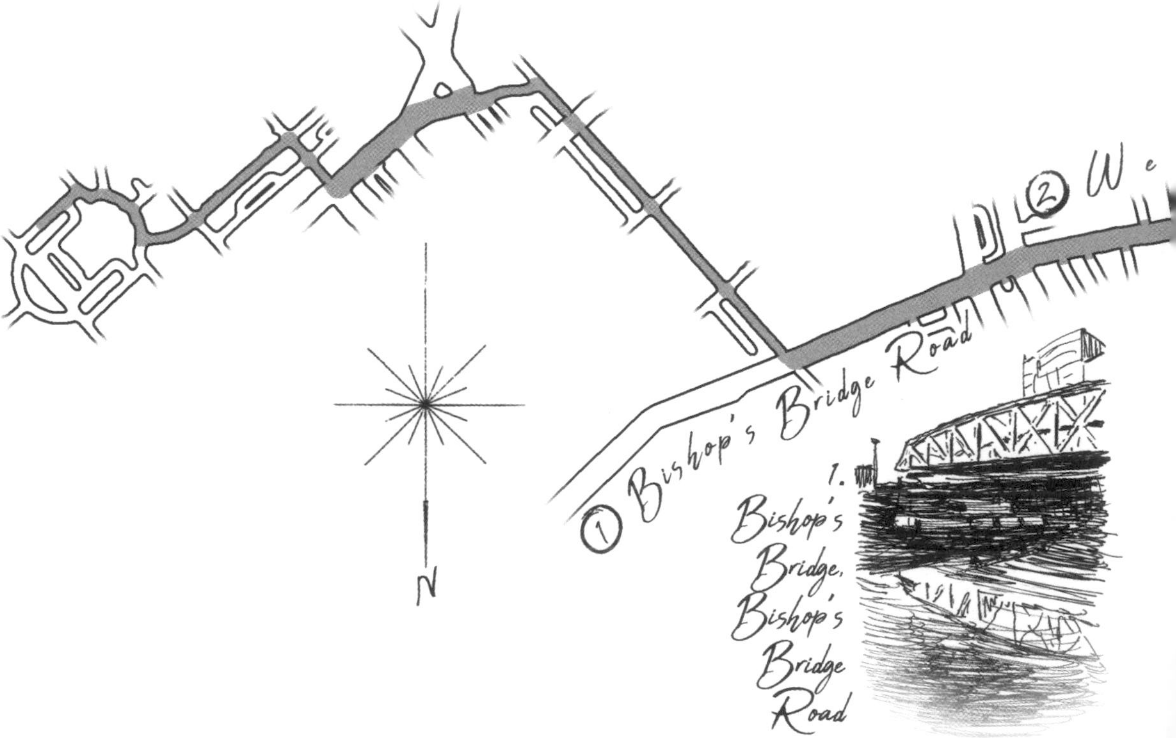

① Bishop's Bridge Road

② We

N

1. Bishop's Bridge, Bishop's Bridge Road

3. Electric Cinema, Portobello Road

LOWNDES SQUARE SW1 → THE HURLINGHAM CLUB SW6

Starting in the heart of Knightsbridge, probably London's poshest shopping street, a good way to memorise the first set of roads on this run is with the mnemonic 'Harriet splashed profuse cash'.

After heading through Cadogan Square (where horror film legends Boris Karloff and Christopher Lee once happened to be neighbours), the run makes steps towards the King's Road, which was originally a private track laid out for Charles II – any other traveller wishing to use it required a special token.

Sprimont Place, Elystan Place and Markham Street form part of this cut-through. A good mnemonic for this is '**see elephants march**', which can be enhanced further if you imagine said pachyderms trudging towards Chelsea.

The last few roads on this run are residential and nondescript which can make it tricky for the brain to latch on to. A good mnemonic though is '**Ben Hur's nag ran**', an allusion to the fictitious Roman chariot racer, which gives us Broomhouse Road, Hurlingham Road, Napier Avenue and Ranelagh Gardens. Again, imagine the chariots rushing down the posh London streets . . .

1 LOWNDES SQUARE

In 1968, scenes for the controversial film *Performance* starring Mick Jagger were shot at an apartment on Lowndes Square. The flat used belonged to politician and businessman Leonard Plugge, a pioneer of commercial broadcasting who is said to have inspired the promotional term 'give it a plug'.

2 SLOANE STREET

On the corner of Sloane Street and Pont Street is the Cadogan Hotel (now the Belmond Cadogan) which first opened in 1887. It was here, on 6 April 1895, that Oscar Wilde was arrested after being found in a relationship with Lord Alfred Douglas. For this 'gross indecency', Wilde received two years' hard labour.

3 PONT STREET

It's likely that Pont Street is named after an old bridge which once crossed the now subterranean River Westbourne. Today's Pont Street is distinctive for its grand, red-brick buildings and for St Columba's Scottish church, which has its own Scottish dance club, the 'London Reels'.

4 CADOGAN STREET

On Cadogan Street is St Mary's Church, one of the first Catholic chapels to be built in England after the Reformation. It was founded by a Frenchman, Abbé Jean Voyaux de Franous, primarily for the use of ex-soldiers resident at the nearby Royal Chelsea Hospital.

5 KING'S ROAD

The former World's End pub (now a restaurant called The World's End Market) is one of the King's Road's best known landmarks and lends its name to the surrounding area. In the late 1960s, two Australians named Ace and John opened a furniture shop called Sophisticat on the World's End section of King's Road. When they first arrived in London, the pair visited Harrods – which then had an exotic pets department – and were dismayed to see a lion cub for sale. After raising enough money, Ace and John purchased the little big cat who they named Christian, and he soon became a well-known sight at their boutique. Christian was later released into the wild in Kenya and a video of him recognising and lovingly embracing Ace and John years later has since become one of the internet's most viewed clips.

6 THE HURLINGHAM CLUB

This exclusive 42-acre club dates back to the late 19th century and was a popular place for pigeon shooting until 1906, hence the club's logo. Today, the Hurlingham is renowned for croquet, bowls and tennis.

Leave by: Harriet Street
Left: Sloane Street
Right: Pont Street
Left and comply: Cadogan Square
Leave by: Cadogan Street
Forward: Whiteheads Grove
Left: Sloane Avenue
Right: Sprimont Place
Right: Elystan Place
Left: Markham Street
Right: King's Road
Forward: New King's Road
Left: Broomhouse Road
Right: Hurlingham Road
Left: Napier Avenue
Left: Ranelagh Gardens
Hurlingham Club facing

Road
6
5. World's End, King's Road
6. The Hurlingham

HUGUENOT PLACE SW18 → SLOANE SQUARE STATION SW1

The starting point for this run refers to an old Huguenot burial ground, established in the 17th century by refugees who'd fled persecution in France.

Once we arrive at Bridgend Circus (beneath which director Stanley Kubrick filmed the notorious opening scene for *A Clockwork Orange*) we can employ the mnemonic '**big yellow lorry**' to cite Bridgend Circus, York Road and Lombard Road.

Next is another mnemonic: '**very big bloated blimps**' for Vicarage Crescent, Battersea Square, Battersea Church Road and Battersea Bridge Road. The airship reference is somewhat apt as the route passes the London Heliport, the city's only dedicated chopper terminal.

A cheeky traffic-dodge on this run uses Howie Street, Elcho Street and Parkgate Road. This can be remembered with the acronym '**HEP**'.

1 BATTERSEA CHURCH ROAD

This street refers to St Mary's, Battersea, the historic Thameside church in which the poet and artist William Blake married Catherine Boucher. St Mary's is also the final resting place of Benedict Arnold; a general who's widely considered to be one of America's most notorious traitors after his plot to surrender West Point Fort to the British during the War of Independence was uncovered.

2 ALBERT BRIDGE

Coloured in pastels of pink, green and blue, many regard Albert Bridge to be London's most beautiful crossing, especially when lit at night.

In its early days, troops from Chelsea Barracks would often march across which, alarmingly, would cause the structure to tremble. To overcome this, a sign requesting soldiers to 'Break step when marching over this bridge' was installed.

3 CHELSEA EMBANKMENT

Opposite the northern end of Albert Bridge is the *Boy with a Dolphin* sculpture, created by David Wynne in the mid-1970s. The boy featured was modelled on Wynne's son, Roland, who died aged 35. The statue is now dedicated to his memory. The sculpture has a twin, *Girl with a Dolphin*, which can be found beside Tower Bridge.

4 ROYAL HOSPITAL ROAD

On the corner of Royal Hospital Road and Swan Walk is the Chelsea Physic Garden which was founded in 1673 to train apothecaries in the use of medicinal plants. In the 1730s, cotton seeds from the garden were sent to Georgia, thus kickstarting the cotton industry in America's Deep South.

5 SLOANE SQUARE

Before being developed in the 18th century, this once rural area was known as the Great Bloody Field (or in some cases, Bloody Bridge). The origin of this gruesome name has long been forgotten although it has been speculated that it referred to the crimes of certain highwaymen. The iconic 1930s Peter Jones department store is on Sloane Square, as is the Royal Court Theatre, where both *Look Back in Anger* and *The Rocky Horror Show* made their debuts. Sloane Square station opened in 1868 and is notable for the large iron pipe which channels the subterranean River Westbourne above the heads of commuters.

Leave by right: East Hill
Left: Trinity Road Slip
Forward: Trinity Road
Comply: Bridgend Circus
Leave by: York Road
Left: Lombard Road
Forward: Vicarage Crescent
Forward: Battersea Square
Bear left: Battersea Church Road
Right: Battersea Bridge Road
Left: Howie Street
Right: Elcho Street
Left: Parkgate Road
Left: Albert Bridge Road
Forward: Albert Bridge
Right: Chelsea Embankment
Left: Royal Hospital Road
Left: Franklin's Row
Right: Turk's Row
Left: Lower Sloane Street

1. St Mary's, Battersea Church Road

2. Albert Bridge

Comply: Sloane Square
Sloane Square station on left

DOVER HOUSE ROAD SW15 → BROMPTON SQUARE SW3

This run begins at the centre of the Dover House Estate, an area defined by quaint, cottage-like homes built just after WWI. Once we reach Queen's Ride the mnemonic 'Queen Liz poked Prince Philip' can be used for Queen's Ride, Lower Richmond Road, Putney High Street, Putney Bridge and Putney Bridge Approach.

After crossing the Thames there are four roads to call which all have 'Fulham' as their prefix (Fulham High Street, Fulham Road, Fulham Broadway and Fulham Road continued). A useful way to remember this number is to think of *Jack and the Beanstalk* and adapt the old line '**Fee-fi-fo-fum**' as a mnemonic.

1 QUEEN'S RIDE

Glam-rock icon Marc Bolan was killed here in a car crash during the early hours of 16 September 1977. His partner and fellow performer Gloria Jones, who was at the wheel, survived but was badly injured. Today, the tree where their vehicle came to rest provides fans with a shrine that is always adorned with notes, pictures and ribbons.

2 LOWER RICHMOND ROAD

Close to the Star and Garter pub, on 31 March 1953, a patrolling bobby apprehended the notorious serial killer John Christie who'd been responsible for the deaths of at least eight women – including his own wife – at his home, 10 Rillington Place, Notting Hill. Christie's evil deeds have been dramatised for film and television with acclaimed actors Sir Richard Attenborough and Tim Roth both tackling the challenging role.

3 PUTNEY BRIDGE

There has been a bridge at Putney since the 1720s. It's believed the crossing was instigated by Prime Minister Robert Walpole who'd suffered a frustrating experience when, after returning from a visit to King George I in

Kingston, found he couldn't hail a ferry at Putney as the watermen were all making merry in a tavern. The first Putney Bridge was wooden; the current stone structure opened in 1886. In 1795, writer and pioneering feminist Mary Wollstonecraft attempted suicide by jumping from the bridge, but was pulled from the river. Since 1845, Putney Bridge has been the starting point for the Oxford and Cambridge Boat Race.

4 FULHAM ROAD

Running parallel to Chelsea FC is a section of the London Overground that follows the course of the submerged Counter's Creek river. In the 15th century, a pontoon named 'Samfordesbrigge' was laid across the stream. This evolved into 'Stamford Bridge', thus giving Chelsea's home ground its name. On the junction of Sloane Avenue is the quirky Michelin House, built for the French tyre company in 1911. The building, which is now a restaurant, is topped with stone wheels and tyres and also has impressive stained glass windows featuring the 'Bibendum' ('Michelin Man') mascot.

5 BROMPTON ROAD

Brompton Oratory was consecrated in 1884 and contains marble statues of the Apostles which were once housed in Siena Cathedral, Tuscany. During the Cold War, Soviet spies used the Oratory as a 'dead letter drop'; a secret space where they could tuck documents and other information for their handlers to collect. One of London Underground's many 'ghost stations' lurks beneath Brompton Road. The station closed in 1934 but its red-tiled entrance can still be seen on Cottage Place, just opposite Brompton Oratory.

ROUTE

Leave by right: Upper Richmond Road
Left: Gipsy Lane
Right: Queen's Ride
Forward: Lower Richmond Road
Left: Putney High Street
Forward: Putney Bridge
Forward: Putney Bridge Approach
Forward: Fulham High Street
Comply: Roundabout
Leave by: Fulham Road
Forward: Fulham Broadway
Forward: Fulham Road continued
Forward: Brompton Road
Brompton Square on left

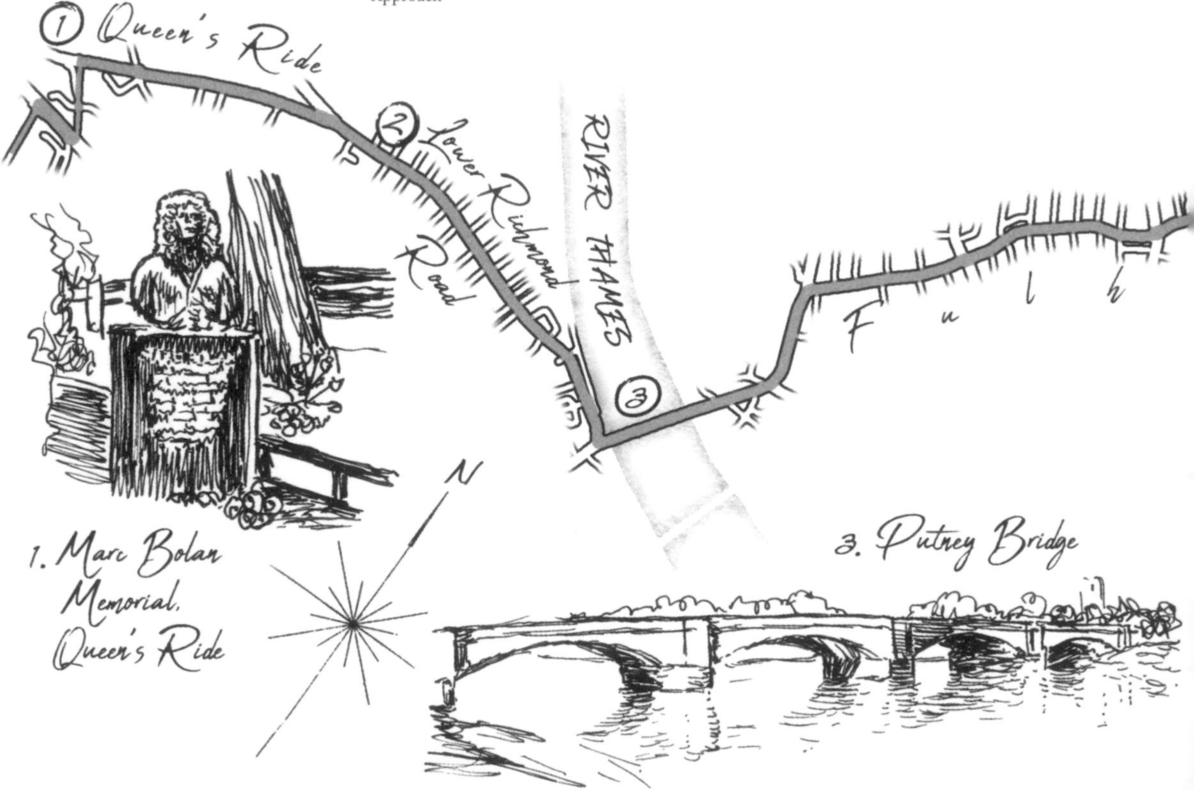

① Queen's Ride

② Lower Richmond Road

RIVER THAMES

③

N

1. Marc Bolan Memorial, Queen's Ride

3. Putney Bridge

Road
Brompton
5
4
Road
4. Michelin House,
Fulham
Road
5. Brompton
Oratory,
Brompton
Road

OVERHILL ROAD SE22 → MARYLEBONE STATION NW1

This is one of the longest runs in The Knowledge, so we'll need several mnemonics! The southern end of Overhill Road is one way, meaning we have to use Belvoir Road, Underhill Road and Melford Road to access Lordship Lane. This sequence can be recalled using the rather immature acronym, 'BUM'.

Once through Dulwich the run winds its way to Brixton via Red Post Hill, Herne Hill Road, Coldharbour Lane and Loughborough Road. A good mnemonic for this section is '**rump hamburgers cost lots**'.

'**Have some pie with beer**' is another food-themed mnemonic. It can be used to learn the roads around the Vauxhall Cross gyratory: Harleyford Road, South Lambeth Road, Parry Street, Wandsworth Road and Bridgefoot.

From the Thames to Victoria, the mnemonic '**vain vampires nibble when vexed**' helps learn Vauxhall Bridge, Vauxhall Bridge Road, Neathouse Place, Wilton Road and Victoria Street.

Finally, towards the end of the run, the acronym '**GUS**' can help recall Great Cumberland Place, Upper Berkeley Street and Seymour Place.

1 DULWICH VILLAGE

This long road has existed as a track since medieval times but was not given its present name until 1913. The area's most notable attraction is Dulwich Picture Gallery, the oldest in England.

2 KENNINGTON OVAL

It was at The Oval cricket ground in 1882 that The Ashes were created after Australia's first Test victory on English soil. As well as cricket, The Oval has also played an important part in football, hosting England's first international game (against Scotland) in 1870 and the first FA Cup final in 1877.

3 VAUXHALL BRIDGE

Cabbies know this as the place where 'London's smallest cathedral' is hidden: a miniature model of St Paul's, held in the hands of a carved, stone figure attached to one of the bridge's columns.

4 WILTON ROAD

In front of Victoria station you'll find Little Ben, a small clock tower dedicated to Franco-British friendship. During the Battle of Britain, a German bomber crashed directly onto Victoria's forecourt after being rammed mid-air by Hurricane pilot Sergeant Ray Holmes in a successful attempt to prevent the enemy craft attacking Buckingham Palace. Sgt Holmes' plane was forced down too, but he bailed out safely and caught a taxi back to his base at RAF Hendon.

5 GROSVENOR PLACE

The Royal Artillery Memorial which stands at Hyde Park Corner was erected to commemorate those killed in WWI and was controversial when unveiled due to its realistic depiction of dead and exhausted soldiers. The stone howitzer on top of the monument points in the direction of the Somme.

6 PARK LANE

At the southern end of Park Lane is the statue of Achilles which, being London's first public nude artwork, raised quite a few eyebrows when it was installed in 1822. Further up on Brook Gate, which links Park Lane's two carriageways, is the Animals in War Memorial, a moving testament to the countless horses, dogs, pigeons and other creatures drafted into 20th century conflicts.

7 CUMBERLAND GATE

Cumberland Gate forms the southern length of the Marble Arch junction and borders an area of Hyde Park known as Speakers Corner; a designated spot where folk can legally gather on a Sunday to debate – and heckle – any topic they wish.

8 MARYLEBONE STATION

Marylebone is the smallest and youngest of London's main railway terminals. It featured in the opening to The Beatles' 1964 film *A Hard Day's Night*, when the Fab Four are chased through the station by a crowd of screaming fans.

ROUTE

Leave by: Belvoir Road
Right: Underhill Road
Right: Melford Road
Right: Lordship Lane
Left: Court Lane
Left: Calton Avenue
Right: Dulwich Village
Forward: Red Post Hill
Forward: Herne Hill Road
Left: Coldharbour Lane
Right and left: Loughborough Road
Right: Brixton Road
Left: Camberwell New Road
Forward: Harleyford Street
Forward: Kennington Oval
Forward: Harleyford Road
Left: South Lambeth Road
Right: Parry Street
Right: Wandsworth Road

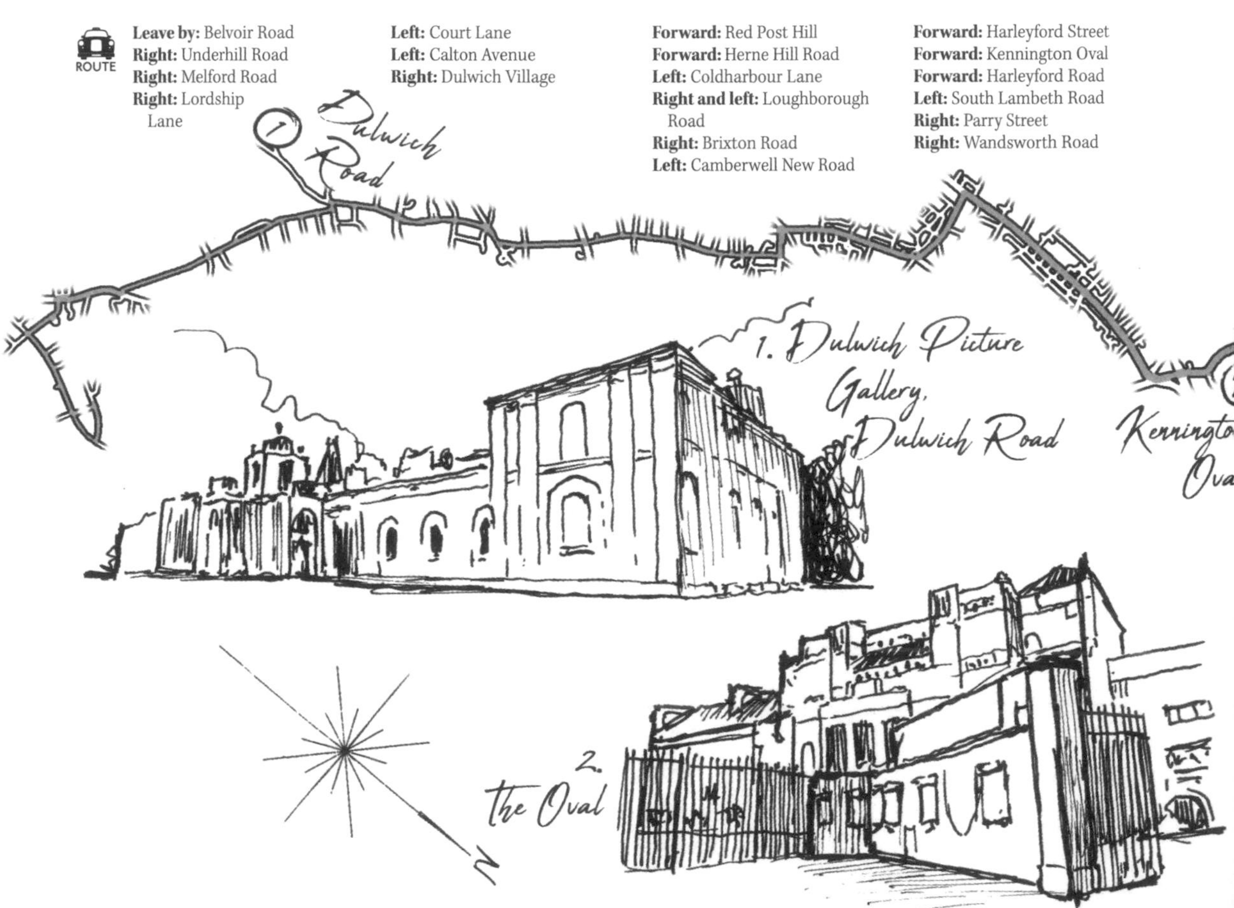

Left: Bridgefoot
Forward: Vauxhall Bridge
Forward: Vauxhall Bridge Road
Left: Neathouse Place
Right: Wilton Road
Left: Victoria Street

Forward: Grosvenor Gardens
Forward: Grosvenor Place
Comply: Hyde Park Corner

Leave by: Park Lane
Left and right: Cumberland Gate
Right: Bayswater Road
Forward: Marble Arch

Left: Great Cumberland Place
Left: Upper Berkeley Street
Right: Seymour Place
Forward: Lisson Grove
Right: Harewood Row
Forward: Melcombe Place
Marylebone station on left

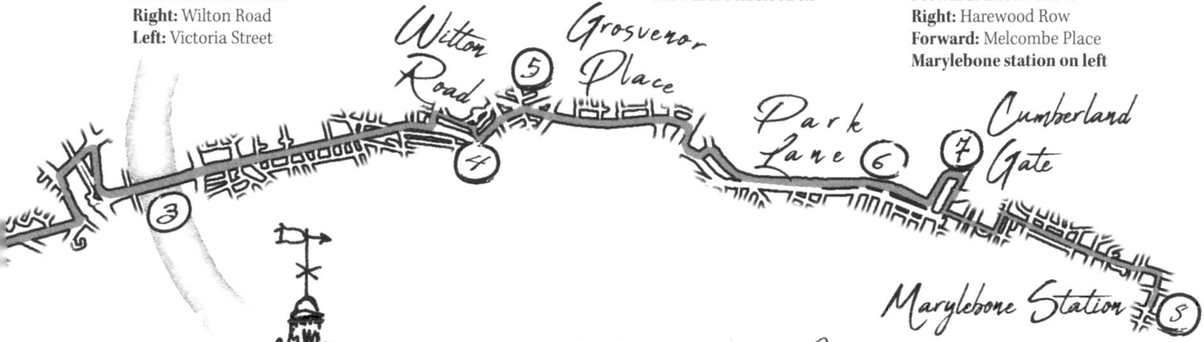

Wilton Road
Grosvenor Place
Park Lane
Cumberland Gate
Marylebone Station

4. Little Ben, Wilton Road

6. Animals in War Memorial, Park Lane

ABBEY ROAD E15 → BALLS POND ROAD N1

It's not unknown to find bewildered tourists wandering around Abbey Road E15 who've become lost while searching for the fabled Abbey Road Studios – which are in fact on the opposite side of town in St John's Wood. As with Stamford Street to Stamford Hill, this is a good example of the pitfalls which can occur when dealing with London street names: exactly the kind of thing you need a cabbie's brain for!

After skirting the perimeter of the huge 2012 Olympic Park, the run heads into Bow via the Old Ford Slip Road, Wick Lane and Tredegar Road. '**OWT**' is a good acronym here and is perhaps appropriate considering it's preceded by the Blackwall Tunnel Northern Approach ('owt' being a slang term commonly used in northern England).

The next series of roads – Parnell Road, Old Ford Road and Crown Gate Roundabout – can be remembered with the mnemonic '**penguins openly chill**', closely followed by '**gorillas love wandering freely**' for Grove Road, Lauriston Road, Well Street and Frampton Park Road. It may help further to imagine these creatures conducting said activities in Victoria Park.

1 OLD FORD ROAD

In 1915 a pub called The Gunmakers Arms (then based at 438 Old Ford Road) was taken over by the East London Federation of Suffragettes who were led by Sylvia Pankhurst. The group renamed it The Mothers Arms, transforming into a refuge for poverty-stricken women and children. The site is now commemorated by a plaque.

2 GROVE ROAD

Grove Road passes through Victoria Park ('Vicky Park' to locals), which was the East End's first public green space when opened. Within the park are two stone alcoves from the old London Bridge, the rest of which now stands at Lake Havasu in Arizona.

3 MARE STREET

Mare Street's most prominent landmark is the Hackney Empire, which opened as a music hall in 1901. It was one of the first theatres lit by electricity and in its early days, both Charlie Chaplin and Stan Laurel performed here. From the 1950s onwards the building was used as a TV studio, then a bingo hall before being threatened with demolition in the 1980s. Thankfully Hackney Empire was saved and has since gone on to become one of London's most cherished venues.

4 GRAHAM ROAD

Connected to Graham Road is Fassett Square which was the basis for the layout for the fictional Albert Square in the BBC's long-running soap opera *EastEnders*. The crossroads where Graham Road meets Dalston Lane is colloquially known as Red Cross Corner after the Victorian house which once provided the humanitarian organisation's London HQ. A large representation of the Red Cross symbol remains a notable landmark on the side of the building.

5 DALSTON LANE

Outside the Dalston Eastern Curve Garden is the three-storey high Dalston Peace Mural, depicting an anti-nuclear march that occurred locally in 1983. The mural was designed by artist Ray Walker who died aged 39. His wife Anna and their friend Mike Jones completed the painting in 1985.

6 BALLS POND ROAD

One of London's quirkier road names, Balls Pond Road refers to John Ball who owned a pub here during the early 19th century. Outside Ball's tavern was a pond where drinkers would goad dogs into catching ducks whose wings had been clipped – a cruel game that gave rise to the common pub name, 'The Dog and Duck'.

ROUTE

Leave by forward: Rick Roberts Way
Left: High Street Stratford
Comply: Bow Flyover Roundabout
Leave by: Blackwall Tunnel Northern Approach Slip Road
Forward: Blackwall Tunnel Northern Approach
Bear left: Old Ford Slip Road
Left: Wick Lane
Forward: Tredegar Road
Right: Parnell Road
Left: Old Ford Road
Comply: Crown Gate Roundabout
Leave by: Grove Road

Forward: Lauriston Road
Left: Well Street
Right: Frampton Park Road

Left: Brenthouse Road
Right: Mare Street
Left: Graham Road
Forward: Dalston Lane
Balls Pond Road facing

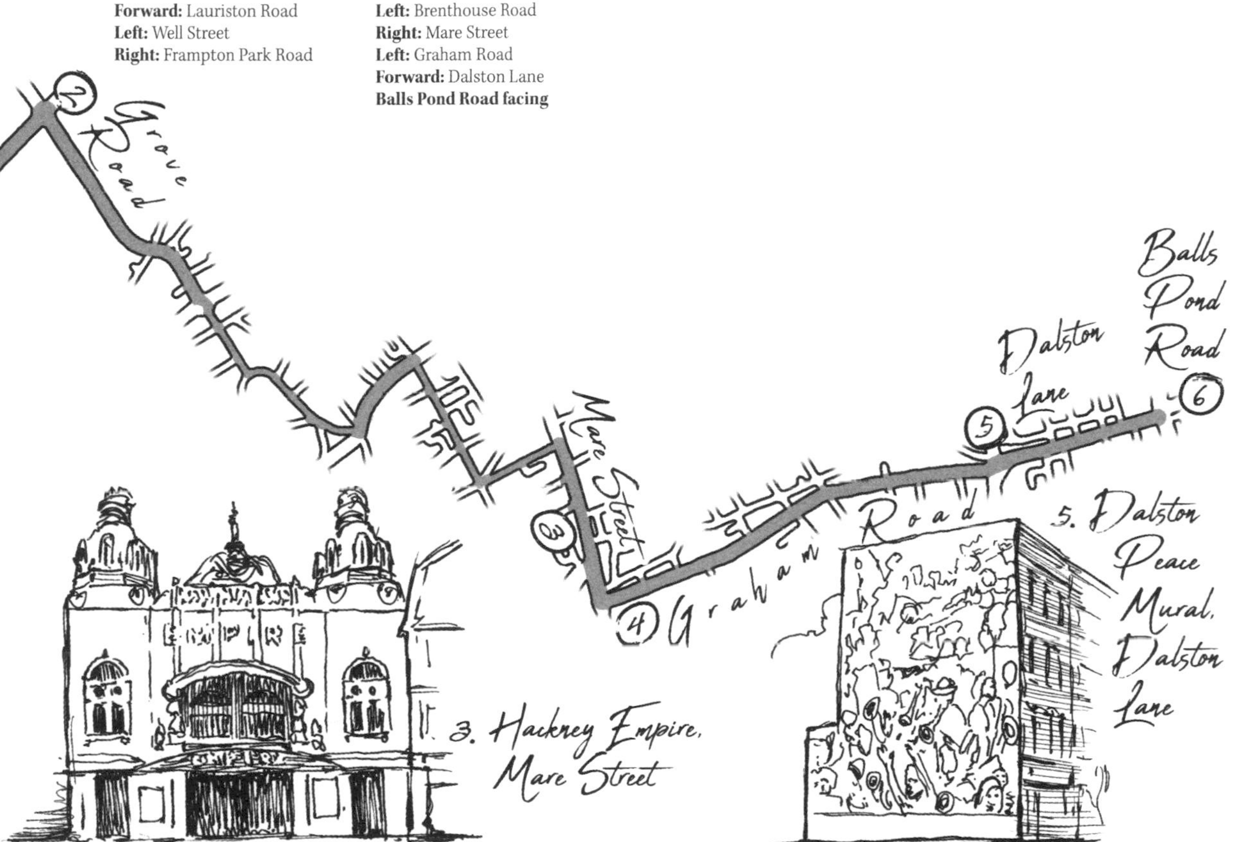

RUNS USING SHORT STORIES

The art of storytelling stretches back to prehistoric times and has long been a key medium for cultures wishing to share and preserve collective histories and memories.

Most people today still love a good story and, whether they be printed or cinematic, certain events and imagery in these tales – such as Cinderella's glass slipper or the huge stone ball that rumbles towards Indiana Jones – are guaranteed to stick in our minds.

Like many students commencing The Knowledge, I initially found the amount of information that the brain was expected to grapple with overwhelming; page after page, list after list, it was quite demoralising.

The idea of creating short stories to sum up each run – in which the names of streets and roads acted as prompts for characters and plot twists – was the first memory technique I turned to and I found it to be most effective. Had it not been for this method of consolidating routes into memorable blocks, I might have been forced to throw in the towel or, at the very least, would've torn out a lot more hair.

Due to the variety of London's street names and the order in which runs flow, it is not always possible to create the perfect plot – these tales are certainly not in the league of Aesop or the Brothers Grimm – and the imagery is often bizarre. But in a way this helps: once dreamt up, the imagery is hard to forget.

As an example, here's the story I use for the run Wapping Lane E1 to Canning Town station E16, which appears in List 9 of the Blue Book (but not in this book: it's here just as an example).

For this route, the story is called . . .

THE HIGHWAYMAN

The Highwayman (1) was a nasty piece of work; bitter as lime (2) and sneaky as an asp (3). He was galloping towards the River Lea where he knew the circus (4) was camped out on the bank; he was sure there would be rich pickings there.

As he approached, however, he noticed troops from the East India Company (5) were guarding the tent. When they spotted the highwayman, the soldiers released their hounds who gave chase, snarling and barking (6) all the way.

The highwayman turned and fled the circus as bullets whizzed past him, ringing out like metal cans (7). He cursed as he slipped (8) down an embankment, knowing there would be no silver for him tonight (9).

Here is a key to the roads prompted by the story:

1. The Highway
2. Limehouse Link
3. Aspen Way
4. Leamouth Circus and Leamouth Road
5. East India Dock Road
6. Barking Road Slip
7. Canning Town Circus
8. Station Road Slip
9. Silvertown Way

For me, a by-product of the short story method is that my mind has generated a cast of characters who now occupy various parts of the city; from the highwayman mentioned above, to various royal figures and a grubby butcher who catches rats down in the East End. Here then are 10 more such routes and stories.

GROSVENOR SQUARE W1 → AMELIA STREET SE17

Grosvenor Square to Amelia Street is a run of contrasts. On the first half is Mayfair and St James's, areas defined by plush hotels, exclusive clubs and some of London's most bespoke boutiques.

Once across Westminster Bridge it's into Lambeth, Kennington and Elephant and Castle which are traditionally among London's most working class districts, although inevitably these are now becoming moneyed too.

MOUNTAINS & MALLS

Carlos (1) was climbing a mountain (2) with his dog, David (3), who'd often bark (4) to demand a lick of piccalilli (5).

When they reached the summit the pair bumped into a fellow mountaineer called James (6) who was peering through his binoculars while puffing on a cigarette (7).

'Look down there,' he said. 'They've built a new shopping mall (8). Let's check it out.'

They scrambled down, but upon arrival the adventurers found the mall's gate was blocked by a guard on horseback (9). A large badge indicated his name was George (10).

'Can't let you in, I'm afraid,' George explained. 'Strict orders from Parliament (11). But see that bridge? If you cross that you should be able to get in via the west entrance (12). Ken will let you in. Can't miss him; massive bloke; weighs at least a ton (13).'

The group followed George's directions, crossing the bridge which swayed over a babbling brook (14).

'Dante (15) had an easier time in the inferno,' grumbled James.

Carlos agreed. 'Yep . . . we should've kicked George right up the butt (16), the worthless wally (17).'

1. Carlos Place
2. Mount Street
3. Davies Street
4. Berkeley Square & Street
5. Piccadilly
6. St James's Street
7. Marlborough Gate and Road
8. The Mall
9. Horse Guard's Road
10. Great George Street
11. Parliament Square
12. Westminster Bridge
13. Kennington Road
14. Brook Drive
15. Dante Road
16. Newington Butts
17. Walworth Road

1 GROSVENOR SQUARE

Grosvenor Square has long been associated with America; a link dating back to the 1780s when Founding Father John Adams lived here, although it wasn't until 1938 that the US Embassy itself was established on the square. The most famous incarnation – the large, purpose-built block on the western side topped by an eagle – opened in 1960. Following 9/11, however, the site posed various security issues and this diplomatic behemoth relocated to a new, heavily guarded location near Battersea in 2018.

2 BERKELEY SQUARE

Legend has it number 50 Berkeley Square is the capital's most haunted spot, where a number of folk have suffered grisly fates after allegedly encountering a screaming entity on the upper floor.

3 ST JAMES'S STREET

In a little nook off the east side of St James's Street is Pickering Place, the capital's smallest square. The former Republic of Texas once squeezed their embassy in here. The courtyard was also the site of London's last duel.

4 MARLBOROUGH ROAD

St James's Palace – now the home of Princess Anne – was built by Henry VIII in the 16th century. Before then the site had been occupied by a medieval hospital for lepers.

5 HORSE GUARDS ROAD

Tucked away here is the entrance to the Churchill War Rooms, a sprawling bunker from which the government conducted much of WWII.

6 WESTMINSTER BRIDGE

Opened in 1750, this was the capital's second bridge; for many centuries before then, the only crossing had been London Bridge. The present Westminster Bridge dates from the mid-19th century.

On the eastern end stands the Southbank Lion which is made from 'Coade Stone', a special material created by Eleanor Coade in the early 19th century that is miraculously immune to the effects of pollution.

7 WESTMINSTER BRIDGE ROAD

At number 121 is Westminster Bridge House; a rather morbid-looking building and with good reason – it was once the terminal for the Necropolis Railway, a company that transported coffins to Brookwood Cemetery in Surrey on special funeral trains. Even in death, bodies were arranged into first, second and third class. The last service steamed out of here in 1941.

Leave by: Carlos Place
Left: Mount Street
Right: Davies Street
Comply: Berkeley Square

Leave by: Berkeley Street
Left: Piccadilly
Right: St James's Street
Left: Pall Mall

Right: Marlborough Gate
Forward: Marlborough Road
Left: The Mall
Right: Horse Guards Road

Left: Great George Street
Forward: Parliament Square
Forward: Bridge Street
Forward: Westminster Bridge

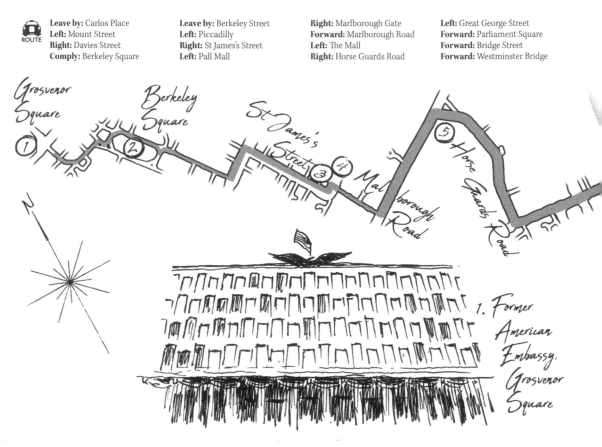

Grosvenor Square
Berkeley Square
St James's Street
Marlborough Road
Horse Guards Road
N

1. Former American Embassy, Grosvenor Square

Forward: Westminster Bridge Road
Right: Kennington Road
Left: Brook Drive
Right: Dante Road
Left: Newington Butts
Comply: Newington Butts Roundabout
Leave by: Walworth Road
Amelia Street on right

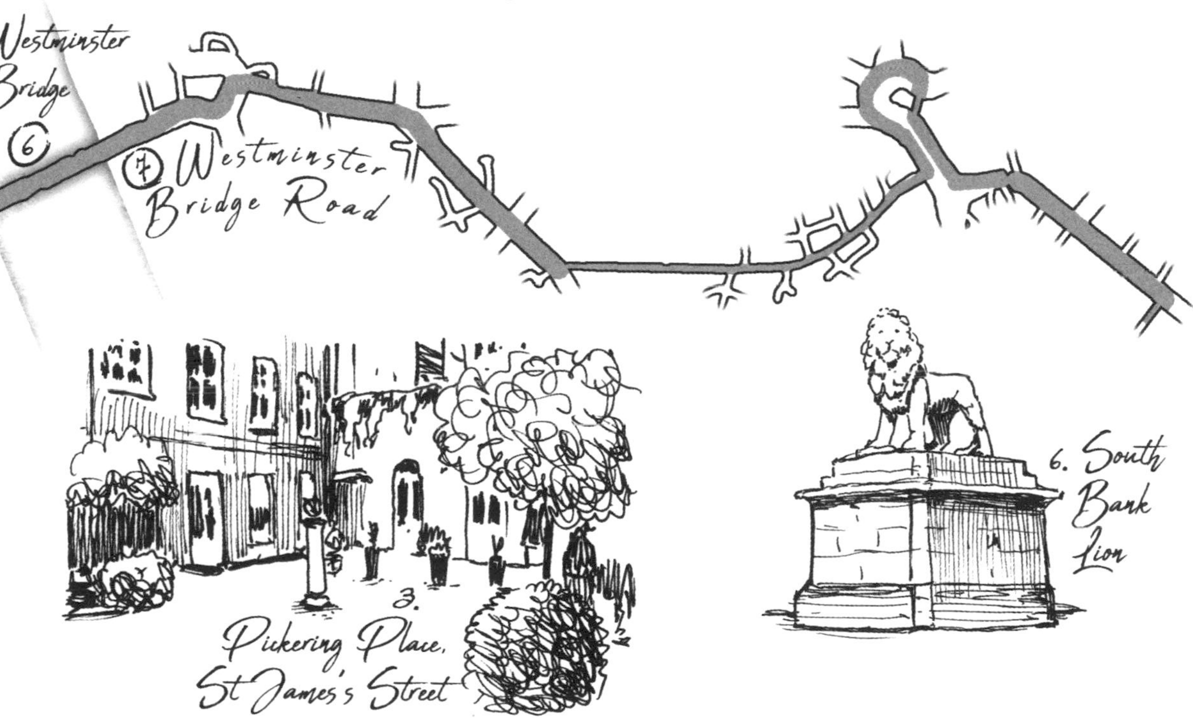

ST JOHN'S WAY N19 → WOODSTOCK AVENUE NW11

When exploring the quarter-mile radius around St John's Way, it's interesting to note that a number of roads in the vicinity are named after Shakespearean characters: Miranda Road & Prospero Road (*The Tempest*), Lysander Grove (*A Midsummer Night's Dream*) and Cressida Road (*Troilus and Cressida*).

Once off, the run trundles high across north London, offering one of the best views of the city via the dizzyingly high bridge on Hornsey Lane.

After leafy Highgate the run winds through Hampstead Garden Suburb, a vital shortcut which shaves off considerable distance and avoids a narrow bottleneck (a remnant from the days of toll gates) at the Spaniards Inn pub.

CRESSIDA'S SNAPSHOT

Cressida White (1) was honking her horn (2) all the way as she drove through Highgate (3). She was heading to Hampstead (4) to collect a prize after winning (5) first place in an *Instagram* (6) competition. The photo entered had been of a wild wood (7) up north (8). As soon as Cressida had snapped it she knew it would do well and would be sure to win gold (9).

1. Cressida Road and Whitehall Park
2. Hornsey Lane
3. Highgate Hill and High Street
4. Hampstead Lane
5. Winnington Road
6. Ingram Avenue
7. Wildwood Road
8. North End Road
9. Golders Green Road

1 HIGHGATE HILL

In folklore, it was while heading away from London on Highgate Hill that Dick Whittington heard the distant chime of Bow Bells, thus encouraging him to turn back and work his way to becoming Lord Mayor of London. Whittington was indeed a real person who did much for the city, although his life has become steeped in mythology over the years. The Whittington Stone is located on Highgate

Hill as a memorial to him, complete with a sculpture of his fabled cat – which many Knowledge students like to pat for good luck.

2 HIGHGATE HIGH STREET

Just off of the High Street is Pond Square which is said to harbour one of London's most bizarre ghosts – a phantom chicken. This odd tale originated in January 1626 when the philosopher Francis Bacon purchased a chicken on Highgate High Street for the purpose of conducting an early experiment in preserving meat. He took the bird to Pond Square where he slaughtered and plucked it before proceeding to stuff the carcass with snow. Since then there have been sporadic sightings of a ghostly bird, scurrying around Pond Square, flapping its wings in a frenzy. Francis Bacon didn't fare too well in this procedure either – he developed pneumonia after being out in the cold and died soon after.

3 THE GATEHOUSE

In the past, both Lord Byron and Charles Dickens have enjoyed a drink at this site. On the pub's upper floor is a small, fringe theatre, Upstairs at the Gatehouse, which, at 446 feet above sea level, is officially London's highest theatre.

4 HAMPSTEAD LANE

On Hampstead Lane is Kenwood House, a Georgian-era mansion whose beautiful gardens and impressive art collection – including masterpieces by Rembrandt, Gainsborough and Vermeer – are open to the public. Kenwood's grounds also host concerts and open-air cinema events.

5 HAMPSTEAD WAY

Near Mountview Close is an unassuming, fenced-off building which resembles an electricity substation. This is in fact an access point to North End (or, more commonly, Bull and Bush, named after a nearby pub), a tube station that never was. Construction on North End began in 1903 but was soon abandoned, leaving behind a cavernous space – the deepest point on the network – through which Northern Line trains still rumble between Golders Green and Hampstead. In the 1950s this space was converted into London Underground's very own nuclear bunker, a nerve centre from which the system's floodgates could be controlled in the event of an atomic attack.

Leave by: Cressida Road
Forward: Whitehall Park
Left: Hornsey Lane
Right: Highgate Hill
Forward: Highgate High Street
Comply: Roundabout
Leave by: Hampstead Lane
Right: Winnington Road
Left: Ingram Avenue
Left: Wildwood Road
Bear right: Hampstead Way
Left: Wellgarth Road
Right: North End Road
Forward: Golders Green Road
Comply: Roundabout
Leave by: Golders Green Road continued
Woodstock Avenue on left

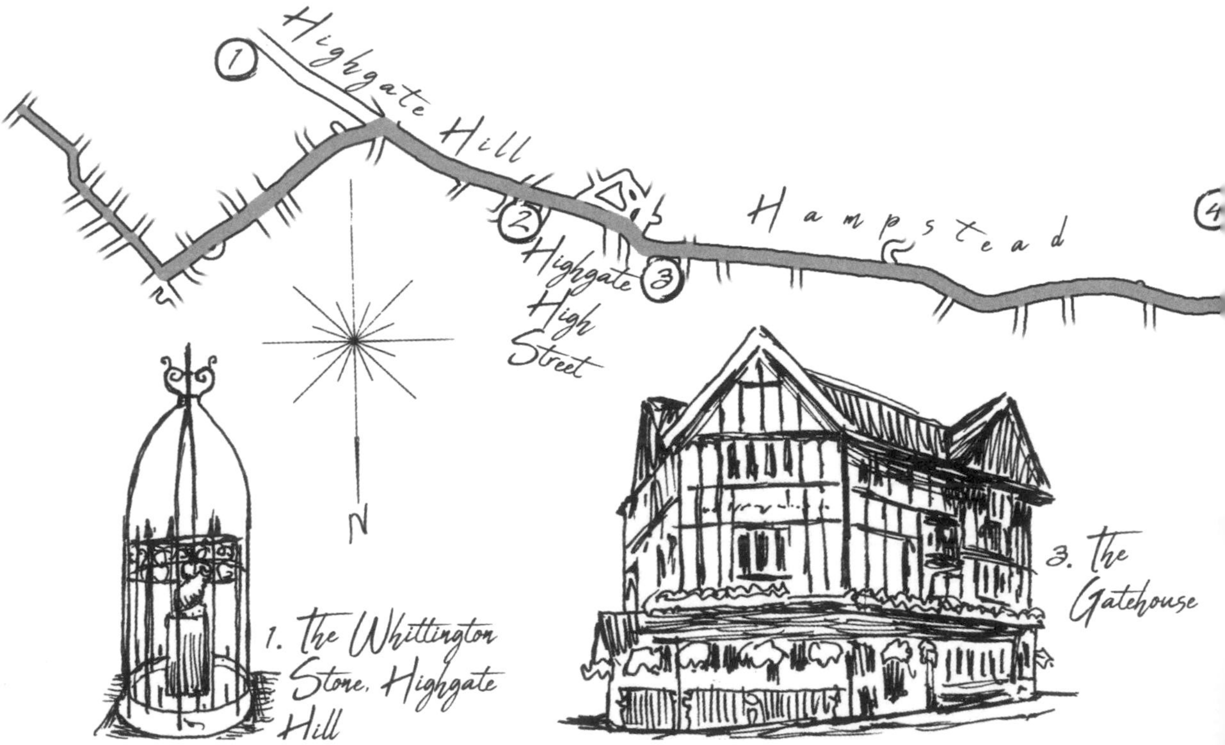

Highgate Hill

Hampstead

Highgate High Street

N

1. The Whittington Stone, Highgate Hill

3. The Gatehouse

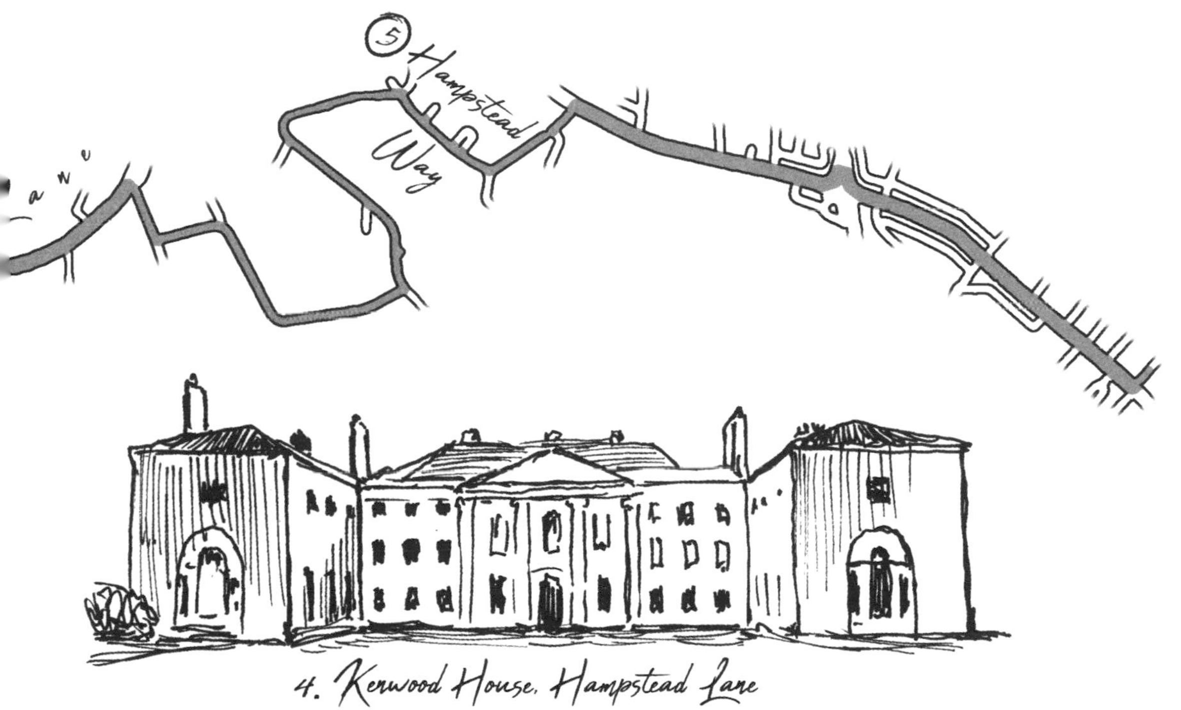

4. Kenwood House, Hampstead Lane

ROYAL COLLEGE OF MUSIC SW7 → CROUCH HILL STATION N4

There's some beautiful scenery on this run as it includes both Hyde Park and Regent's Park. It wasn't always so genteel though. In centuries past, Hyde Park in particular was a favourite haunt of highwaymen, making it dangerous to traverse after dark. Because of this, 300 oil lamps were installed, making it the first road in England to be lit at night.

The end point, Crouch Hill, is commonly seen as one of London's most confusing roads due to the fact it runs parallel to Crouch End Hill. Luckily the station is a good landmark to latch onto.

THE ROGUE'S PROPOSAL

The Prince (1) always enjoyed making an exhibition (2) of himself and when he spotted Alexandra (3) he decided to show off by diving into the Serpentine (4).

When he emerged he clambered onto the bridge (5) soaking wet and produced a diamond ring (6) from his trunks.

'Will you marry me?'

'I will,' blushed Alexandra.

'Great! Let's get hitched up north (7) – in Cumberland (8). And you must meet my parents, George and Mary (9), who live in York (10).'

'Certainly,' said Alexandra. 'I wouldn't want to be an outsider; I'd like to become acquainted with your family circle (11). But do you mind if we go to Gloucester (12) first? There's a park (13) hosting a music festival; one of the bands does a good rendition of "Rule Britannia (14)"; I've seen them gig in Camden (15).'

'I'd rather not. Had a bit of trouble last time I was there; ended up doing time in Parkhurst and Holloway prison (16).'

'What for?'

'Oh, you know . . . not paying road tolls, selling rhino horns, taking backhanders . . . (17)'

The Prince crouched down.

'Will you forgive me?'

'Not likely!' snapped Alexandra and she booted her fiancé down the hill (18).

1. Prince Consort Road
2. Exhibition Road
3. Alexandra Gate
4. Serpentine Road
5. Serpentine Bridge
6. The Ring
7. North Carriage Drive
8. Cumberland Gate
9. George Street and Marylebone Road
10. York Gate
11. Outer Circle
12. Gloucester Gate
13. Parkway
14. Britannia Junction
15. Camden Road
16. Parkhurst Road and Holloway Road
17. Tollington Way, Hornsey Road and Hanley Road
18. Crouch Hill

1 PRINCE CONSORT ROAD

Prince Consort Road backs onto the Royal Albert Hall, which was originally going to be named the Hall of Arts and Sciences. When Queen Victoria laid the foundation stone, however, she announced an impromptu change, stating her wish that the prefix 'Royal Albert' be added in honour of her late husband.

2 SERPENTINE ROAD

Two buildings either side of the Serpentine Bridge collectively form the Serpentine Gallery. The northern branch was formerly a gunpowder store. Its unusual, wavy roof was added by Zaha Hadid Architects.

3 MARBLE ARCH

This spot was once the site of the dreaded Tyburn Tree, a large three-legged scaffold that could hang multiple criminals in front of baying crowds. The famous arch after which this hectic junction is now named was originally built as an entrance to Buckingham Palace. By the time it was completed, however, the arch was deemed too diminutive and was therefore dismantled and rebuilt here.

4 MARYLEBONE ROAD

Madame Tussaud's was established in the 1830s by Marie Tussaud, an expert wax sculptor who narrowly avoided execution in Revolutionary France.

5 OUTER CIRCLE

Despite being some distance away, the Danish Church of Saint Katharine lends its name to St Katharine's Dock near Tower Bridge. The church once stood at the east London site and was demolished to make way for the basin. It's been in Regent's Park since 1952.

6 PARKWAY

The Dublin Castle pub is one of London's best known small-gig venues. Many bands have launched their careers here including quintessential London groups Madness and Blur.

Leave on right: Prince Consort Road
Left: Exhibition Road
Forward: Alexandra Gate
Forward: Serpentine Road
Forward: Serpentine Bridge
Forward: The Ring (West Carriage Drive)
Right: North Carriage Drive
Left: Cumberland Gate
Right: Marble Arch
Left: Great Cumberland Place
Right: George Street
Left: Gloucester Place
Right: Marylebone Road
Left: York Gate
Right and left: Outer Circle
Right: Gloucester Gate
Forward: Parkway
Forward: Britannia Junction

Prince Consort Road
1
2
Serpentine Road
3
4
Marylebone Road
5
Outer Circle
N

1. Royal Albert Hall

Forward: Camden Road
Bear left: Parkhurst Road
Left: Holloway Road
Right: Tollington Way
Left: Hornsey Road
Right: Hanley Road
Left: Crouch Hill
Crouch Hill station on right

LANCASTER GATE W2 → THE ROYAL FREE HOSPITAL NW3

After leaving Lancaster Gate (which, having four branches, is one of London's most oddly shaped addresses), this corkscrew of a run twists through Bayswater, Little Venice, St John's Wood and Swiss Cottage – all very charming areas.

The only blight is the Lower Westway, a grim road beneath a road where the exit to Warwick Avenue can be easily missed.

THE STRICKEN LANCASTER

The Lancaster (1) bomber had taken a hit and smoke was streaming from its stricken engines. Captain Lee was battling with the steering (2) column, grappling with it as a butcher would a meat cleaver (3). But it was no good: they were barrelling down quicker than a roll of Gloucester cheese (4).

'If ever we needed a bishop (5), it's now, lads,' he grimly joked. The stricken craft lurched, plunging lower towards the west (6). 'Damn this wicked war (7).'

Lee turned to his co-pilot.

'Any ideas?'

'Plenty of fields (8) near Edgware (9), Skip; we could aim there. We want something clear, not a wood or grove (10); there's an Abbey (11) down there too; don't want to crash into that.'

'Clever thinking, Lou (12), looks like College (13) wasn't wasted on you; your brain's quite a size (14).'

'Yep, had to study hard,' laughed the co-pilot, 'or my nan would've killed me (15).'

Suddenly a hill loomed ahead and Captain Lee took stock (16) as his life flashed before his eyes. He thought of Rosslyn (17) . . . would he ever see her again? He gave the order.

'Everyone bail out!'

The crew leapt from the plane, parachutes popping one by one. With sheer good fortune there happened to be a pond (18) below and they all splashed down safely.

1. Lancaster Gate
2. Leinster Terrace and Gardens
3. Cleveland Gardens and Terrace

4. Gloucester Terrace
5. Bishop's Bridge Road
6. Lower Westway
7. Warwick Avenue
8. Blomfield Road
9. Edgware Road
10. St John's Wood Road and Grove End Road
11. Abbey Road
12. Loudoun Road
13. College Crescent
14. Belsize Lane
15. Ornan Road
16. Haverstock Hill
17. Rosslyn Hill
18. Pond Street

1 LEINSTER GARDENS

The white stuccoed townhouses along this road hide a secret: numbers 23 and 24 are in fact fake, built to hide a ventilation shaft which was originally intended for steam engines puffing along the early underground railway. Today, electric trains on the Circle Line still rattle behind the two follies.

2 BISHOP'S BRIDGE ROAD

Paddington Station was established in the 1830s as London's rail link with the West Country, a project overseen by Isambard Kingdom Brunel when he was just 27 years old. Brunel returned in the 1850s to build the station that still stands today, the roof of which was inspired by the Great Exhibition's Crystal Palace.

3 ABBEY ROAD

The famous recording studios were established inside a large Georgian house in 1931 and opened with a session in which Sir Edward Elgar conducted the London Symphony Orchestra. Many famous artists have worked here over the years including Pink Floyd, Kate Bush, Radiohead and of course, The Beatles, whose presence made the zebra crossing outside very famous indeed.

4 FINCHLEY ROAD

The triangle that forms the hectic junction at Swiss Cottage is named after Ye Olde Swiss Cottage, the chalet-like pub that stands marooned in the middle of the gyratory. The tavern (which wouldn't look out of place in the Alps) is also one of a handful in London that lend their name to a tube station (the others being Angel, Elephant and Castle, Manor House and Royal Oak).

5 ROYAL FREE HOSPITAL

The Royal Free Hospital was founded by surgeon William Marsden who came to London from Sheffield in 1816. His idea for a practice offering free treatment came from an experience in which he discovered a young girl collapsed and dying outside St Andrew's Church, Holborn. Marsden's practice had humble beginnings near Hatton Garden and later moved to a larger hospital on Gray's Inn Road. The modern Royal Free has been in Hampstead since the 1970s.

Leave by: Leinster Terrace
Forward: Leinster Gardens
Right: Cleveland Gardens
Forward: Cleveland Terrace
Left: Gloucester Terrace
Right: Bishop's Bridge Road
Comply: Roundabout
Leave by: Lower Westway
Comply: Roundabout
Leave by: Warwick Avenue
Right: Blomfield Road
Left: Edgware Road

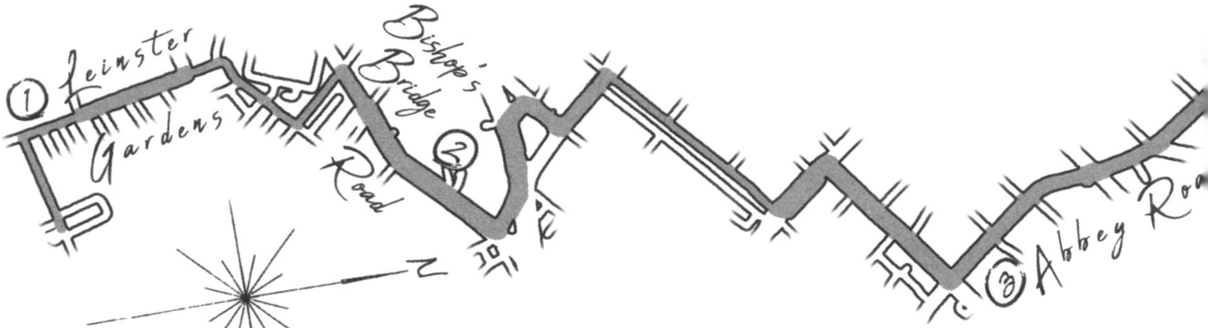

1 Leinster Gardens
Bishop's Bridge Road
2
3 Abbey Road

2. Paddington Station

3. Abbey Road

Right: St John's Wood Road
Left: Grove End Road
Forward: Abbey Road
Right: Langford Place
Left: Loudoun Road
Right: Marlborough Place
Left: Finchley Road
Bear right: College Crescent
Right: Belsize Lane
Forward: Ornan Road
Left: Haverstock Hill
Forward: Rosslyn Hill
Right: Pond Street
Royal Free Hospital on right

4. Swiss Cottage, Finchley Road

KIRKDALE SE26 → SOUTHWARK CROWN COURT SE1

Kirkdale is Sydenham's main road; the area flourished in the mid-1850s after the Great Exhibition's Crystal Palace was re-erected nearby. The ornate High Street Buildings at 134 Kirkdale are a good example of that era's grandeur.

After leaving Kirkdale the run heads towards Lordship Lane – birthplace of the children's author Enid Blyton – before winding through a large swathe of Peckham, the setting for one of Britain's best-loved comedies, *Only Fools and Horses*.

After Peckham the run turns on to the Old Kent Road, famously the cheapest property on the 'Monopoly' board (although it's unlikely you'd bag a bargain in today's market) and then towards Bermondsey Street.

The section of Bermondsey Street between Crucifix Lane and Magdalen Street is a good contender for one of London's creepiest roads as it runs for a considerable length through a gloomy, brick tunnel.

OLD SCHOOLMATES

Kirk and Sid (1) were off to London (2) to meet Barry (3) for a day at Lord's (4) cricket ground.

The friends had grown up together in Peckham Rye (5) where they'd all attended the same school. Their headmaster had been the stern (6) Mr McDermott (7), a man so tough he used to chew (8) tobacco in the assembly hall.

The friends also hoped to see Chad (9) and Lyn (10) who'd been inseparable sweethearts back then, always wandering around Peckham hand-in-hand, from the high street to the hill (11). They'd married beneath a weeping willow (12) one summer (13); on the anniversary of the Battle of Trafalgar (14).

The couple had since moved to an old house in Kent (15) where they ran a bricklaying (16) business, specialising in towers and bridges (17). Chad insisted on using the best tools (18) and battled (19) so hard at his job that he was considered the best brickie in England (20).

1. Kirkdale and Sydenham Hill
2. London Road
3. Barry Road
4. Lordship Lane

5. Peckham Rye and Rye Lane
6. Sternhall Lane
7. McDermott Road
8. Choumert Grove
9. Chadwick Road
10. Lyndhurst Way
11. Peckham High Street and Peckham Hill Street
12. Willow Brook Road
13. Sumner Road
14. Trafalgar Avenue
15. Old Kent Road
16. Bricklayers Arms Roundabout
17. Tower Bridge Road
18. Tooley Street
19. Battle Bridge Lane
20. English Grounds

1 PECKHAM RYE

As a child in the 1760s, the artist and poet William Blake claimed to have seen angelic visions on Peckham Rye. Today the area is home to Peckham Rye Park, within which is the beautiful Japanese Garden.

2 PECKHAM HILL STREET

Opened in 2000, Peckham Library is London's least stuffiest, an innovative, award-winning building shaped like an inverted 'L'.

3 OLD KENT ROAD

On the corner of Albany Road is the Thomas A. Beckett pub which for many years ran a boxing gym on the upper floor. Muhammad Ali, Joe Frazier, Sugar Ray Leonard and Henry Cooper all sparred here in their time.

4 TOWER BRIDGE ROAD

At 87 Tower Bridge Road is M Manze; one of London's oldest pie and mash shops. It was opened in 1902 by Italian immigrant Michele Manze and remains a family business to this day. The cafe, famous for its low prices, wooden benches and bright tiled walls, also serves that other London delicacy, jellied eels.

5 BERMONDSEY STREET

At 58,000 square feet the White Cube Gallery on Bermondsey Street is considered Europe's largest commercial art space. Since opening in 2011, this branch has showcased many contemporary artists including Damien Hirst, Antony Gormley and Tracey Emin.

6 ENGLISH GROUNDS

Permanently moored on the Thames beside English Grounds is *HMS Belfast*, a large warship that has been a floating museum since the 1970s. Launched in 1938 and named after the city in which she was constructed, the *Belfast* saw action in the Arctic Convoys, the D-Day Landings and the Korean War.

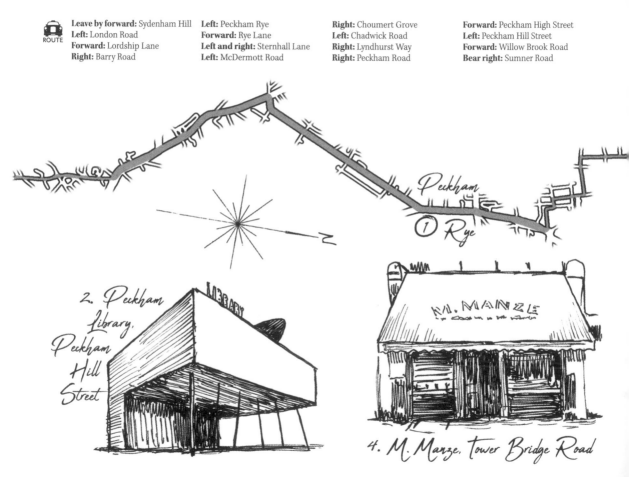

Leave by forward: Sydenham Hill
Left: London Road
Forward: Lordship Lane
Right: Barry Road
Left: Peckham Rye
Forward: Rye Lane
Left and right: Sternhall Lane
Left: McDermott Road
Right: Choumert Grove
Left: Chadwick Road
Right: Lyndhurst Way
Right: Peckham Road
Forward: Peckham High Street
Left: Peckham Hill Street
Forward: Willow Brook Road
Bear right: Sumner Road

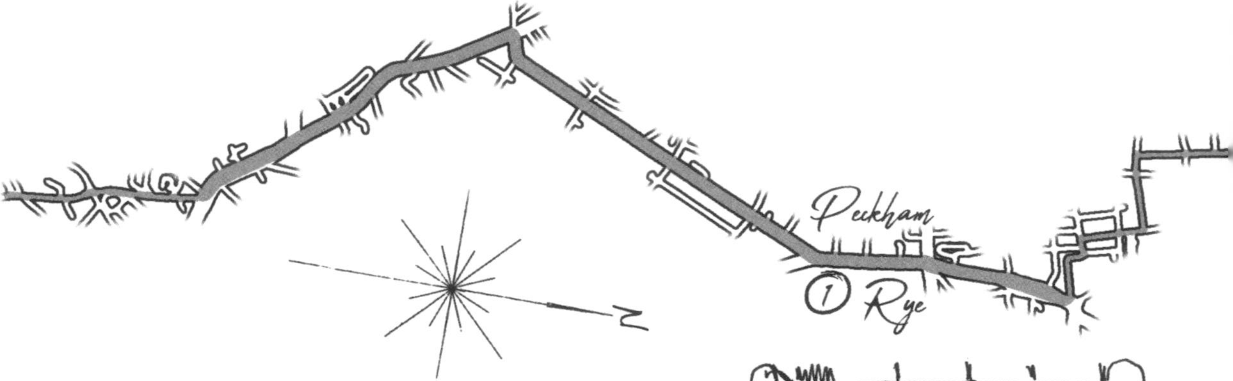

Peckham

1 Rye

N

2. Peckham Library, Peckham Hill Street

4. M. Manze, Tower Bridge Road

Forward: Trafalgar Avenue
Left: Old Kent Road
Comply: Bricklayers Arms Roundabout
Leave by: Tower Bridge Road
Left and bear right: Bermondsey Street
Left: Tooley Street
Right: Battle Bridge Lane
Right: English Grounds
Southwark Crown Court on left

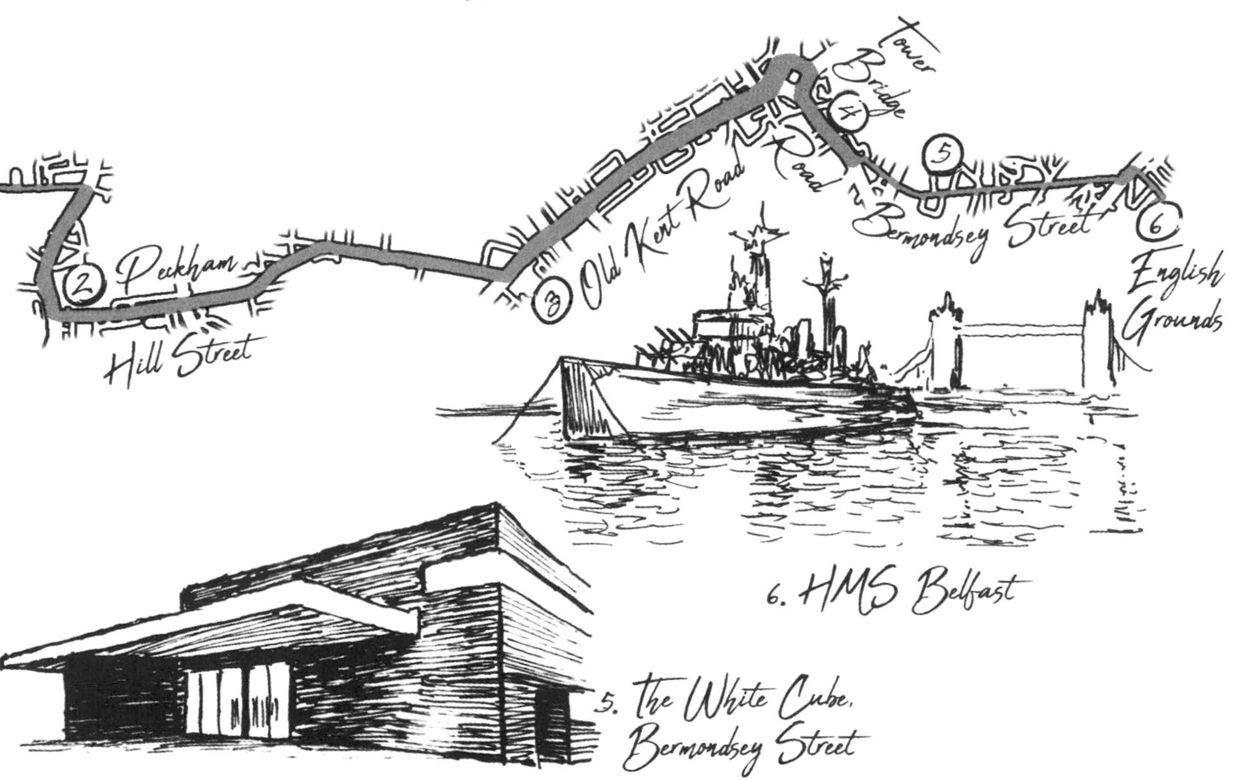

BURLINGTON LANE W4 → WEST HILL SW15

Because of the geography of this area, this run's a tricky one to get straight – essentially Barnes is in the way and a looped route has to be taken around Queen's Ride.

Being deep in south-west London it also has quite a rural feel, skirting the northern end of Putney Heath and also passing one of London's few railway level-crossings at Mortlake.

THE QUEEN'S SOLUTION

Burlington Bertie (1) didn't impress Alexandra (2). She certainly didn't feel obliged to offer him any courtesy (3).

'You get on my wick,' she said. 'Why don't you take a long walk off a short bridge (4)? Or better still, jump off a cliff (5). You're lower and less rich (6) than me; I need someone who can shine (7).'

Upon hearing this, the Queen (8) felt she should take the upper hand (9).

'You two need to spend some time together. Why don't you row down to my place in Hampton (10)? You can picnic in the middle of a field (11), run across the heath (12), go wild (13). And if that doesn't sort the pair of you out, you can do us all a favour and ride off to Tibet (14).'

1. Burlington Lane
2. Alexandra Avenue
3. Great Chertsey Road
4. Chiswick Bridge
5. Clifford Avenue
6. Lower Richmond Road
7. Sheen Lane
8. Queen's Ride
9. Upper Richmond Road
10. Roehampton Lane
11. Medfield Street
12. Putney Heath
13. Wildcroft Road
14. Tibbet's Ride and Corner

1 BURLINGTON LANE

Burlington Lane is named after Lord Burlington who designed Chiswick House, an 18th-century Palladian Villa that stands here. The grand home is surrounded by Chiswick Gardens, which contain a number of Roman-inspired features.

2 CHISWICK BRIDGE

The Chiswick stretch of the Thames is calmer and narrower than in central London, meaning Chiswick Bridge is far more compact than its cousins downriver – it needs only three arches to span the river. The bridge was designed in 1933 by Sir Herbert Baker, an architect whose main body of work is in South Africa.

3 SHEEN LANE

Just across from Mortlake station and its level crossing is a small brick annexe that was built as a private waiting room for Queen Victoria whenever she was travelling by train to Richmond. The structure has since been incorporated into a classic car dealership.

4 ROEHAMPTON LANE

After meeting Private F. W. Chapman, a young man who'd lost both arms in the First World War, Mary Eleanor Gwynne Holford was moved to found Queen Mary's Hospital on Roehampton Lane for soldiers who'd suffered a similar fate. Thousands of men were treated here, receiving pioneering artificial limbs that were crafted at a dedicated workshop in the hospital's basement. Queen Mary's is now a general hospital and in 2010 a small museum dedicated to its history opened within the grounds.

5 WILDCROFT ROAD

The Green Man pub on Wildcroft Road has been in business for over 300 years. When it first opened, this then-remote area was a popular duelling spot and antagonists would retire to the Green Man to prepare for their bout. One such person who participated in a shoot-out here was William Pitt – who happened to be Prime Minister at the time.

6 WEST HILL

The Royal Hospital for Neuro-Disability was founded in the 1850s by Rev Dr Andrew Reed. Charles Dickens helped to raise funds and Florence Nightingale was consulted on the hospital's design. The building in which the hospital is housed is the former Melrose Hall, the gardens of which were landscaped by Capability Brown.

ROUTE

Leave by: Alexandra Avenue
Forward: Great Chertsey Road
Forward: Chiswick Bridge
Forward: Clifford Avenue
Left: Lower Richmond Road
Right: Sheen Lane
Left: Upper Richmond Road West
Bear left and right: Queen's Ride
Right: Upper Richmond Road
Left: Roehampton Lane
Left: Medfield Street
Left: Treville Street
Right: Putney Heath
Comply: Roundabout
Leave by: Wildcroft Road

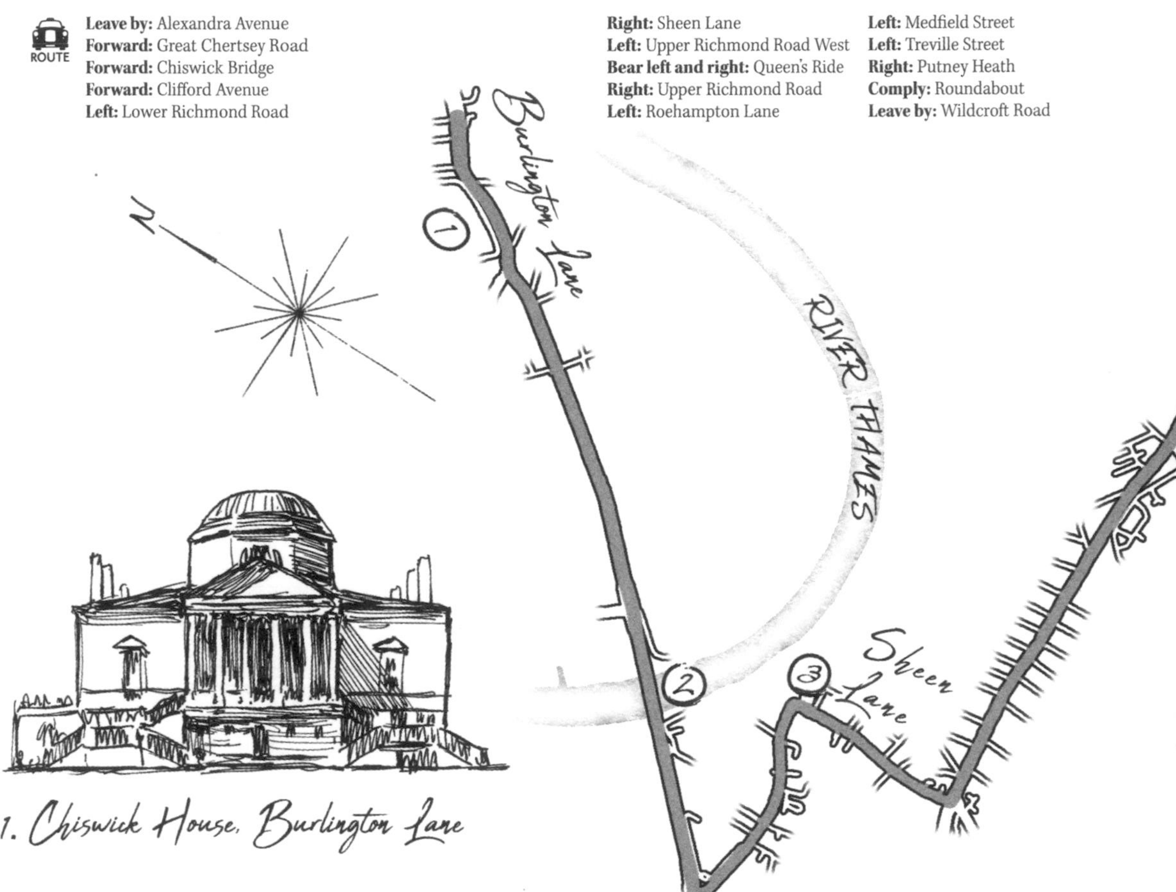

1. Chiswick House, Burlington Lane

Right: Putney Hill
Forward: Tibbet's Ride
Comply: Tibbet's Corner
West Hill on left

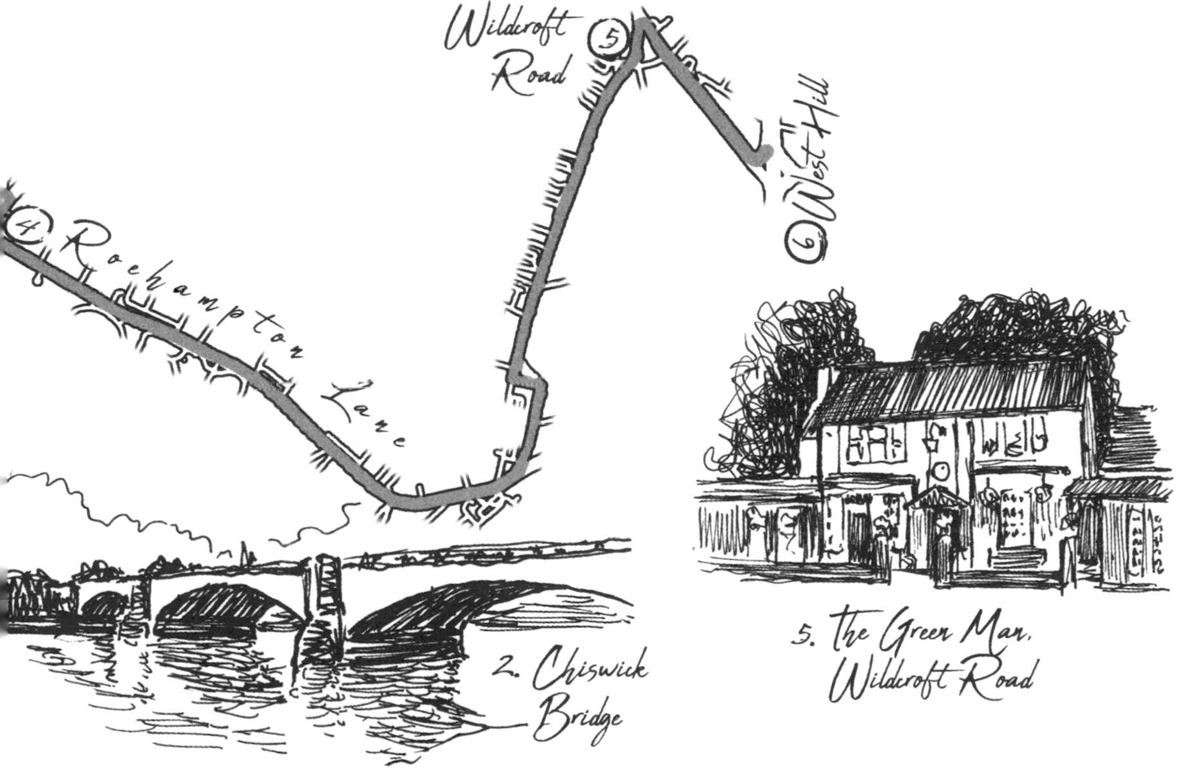

2. Chiswick Bridge

5. The Green Man, Wildcroft Road

HERNE HILL STATION SE24 → WATERLOO STATION SE1

It's difficult to imagine now, but Railton Road was at the epicentre of the 1981 Brixton Riot.

In recent years the road's southern end has been pedestrianised which, coupled with the number of independent shops around the station, gives the area a village-like feel.

A number of roads connected to Railton Road are named after poets: Chaucer, Milton, Shakespeare, Spenser. There is also a Milkwood Road (from which Herne Hill station has a side entrance), which some speculate may have influenced the title for Dylan Thomas' famous work, given he was a regular at the nearby Half Moon pub.

Once the run reaches Atlantic Road we're into the beating heart of Brixton; past the famous market and Electric Avenue – one of the earliest streets in the UK to be lit by electricity. The run is then relatively simple; up through Kennington in a nice straight line.

THE HERON

A heron swooped down and landed on the cold, metal bar for a welcome rest – it didn't realise the peril it was in, for the perch was in fact a railway (1) line and, not too far away, a freight train was thundering towards the spot on its way to the Atlantic (2) docks to offload its cargo which consisted of many tonnes of bricks (3).

Beside the railway line was a park, out of which a young man called Ken emerged (4). When he spotted the heron he became cross (5); how could the silly bird sit in such a dangerous place? Ken clapped his hands and bayed (6) at the bird, 'Shoo . . . get away!'

Spurred on by the warning (7), the heron flapped off, just as the train rounded a corner and began its approach (8). From his cab (9), the engine driver saw the heron flapping away and noted how lucky it was.

1. Railton Road
2. Atlantic Road
3. Brixton Road
4. Kennington Park Road
5. Kennington Cross
6. Baylis Road
7. Spur Road
8. Station Approach
9. Cab Road

1 RAILTON ROAD

Opened in 1862, Herne Hill is one of London's most attractive station buildings. Before the opening of St Pancras International in 2007, Eurostar trains used to trundle through here on their way to the Channel Tunnel, their speed impeded by the line's Victorian layout.

2 ATLANTIC ROAD

The Dogstar is one of Brixton's most famous clubs – Basement Jaxx, The Prodigy and Grandmaster Flash have all played here. The venue was originally a pub known as The Atlantic, which opened in the 1870s. In the late 20th century it was popular with Brixton's West Indian community and features in the 1977 film *Black Joy*, which was set in the area and starred Norman Beaton and Floella Benjamin.

3 BRIXTON ROAD

On the left is Brixton Academy which originally opened as The Astoria cinema in 1929. It is now a major music venue and has hosted many famous acts over the years, including The Clash, Madonna and The Smiths, who played their last ever gig here in December 1986. Further up Brixton Road at number 88 is the vegan Cafe Van Gogh. This name is a reference to the famous painter, Vincent Van Gogh who lived nearby at Hackford Road in the 1870s. While at Hackford Road, Van Gogh fell in love with the landlady's daughter. Sadly his strong emotions were unrequited, which some believe was a catalyst for the decline in his mental health.

4 SPUR ROAD

Situated on Spur Road is a small blue crane. It's sited over the subterranean depot for the Waterloo and City line and is used for hauling tube carriages out whenever the need arises.

5 CAB ROAD

Waterloo is Britain's largest railway station (and one where cabbies feel particularly comfortable ranking up thanks to the namesake road). The terminal originally opened some distance away at Nine Elms, and moved to its current location – once described as being 'occupied by hay-stalls and cow-yards and by dung-heaps and similar nuisances' – in the 1840s. In its early days Waterloo was a haphazard mess; platforms were numbered incoherently and a set of tracks cut right across the pedestrian concourse. The station was smartened up at the turn of the 20th century and gained its famous four-sided clock that is suspended over the concourse. In 1961, director John Schlesinger shot *Terminus* at Waterloo, an early fly-on-the-wall documentary about a day in the life of a station. This little known gem is now public domain and can be viewed online.

Leave on right: Railton Road
Forward: Atlantic Road
Right: Brixton Road
Bear right: Kennington Park Road
Left: Kennington Road
Forward: Kennington Cross
Forward: Kennington Road continued
Forward: Baylis Road
Left: Spur Road
Comply: Roundabout

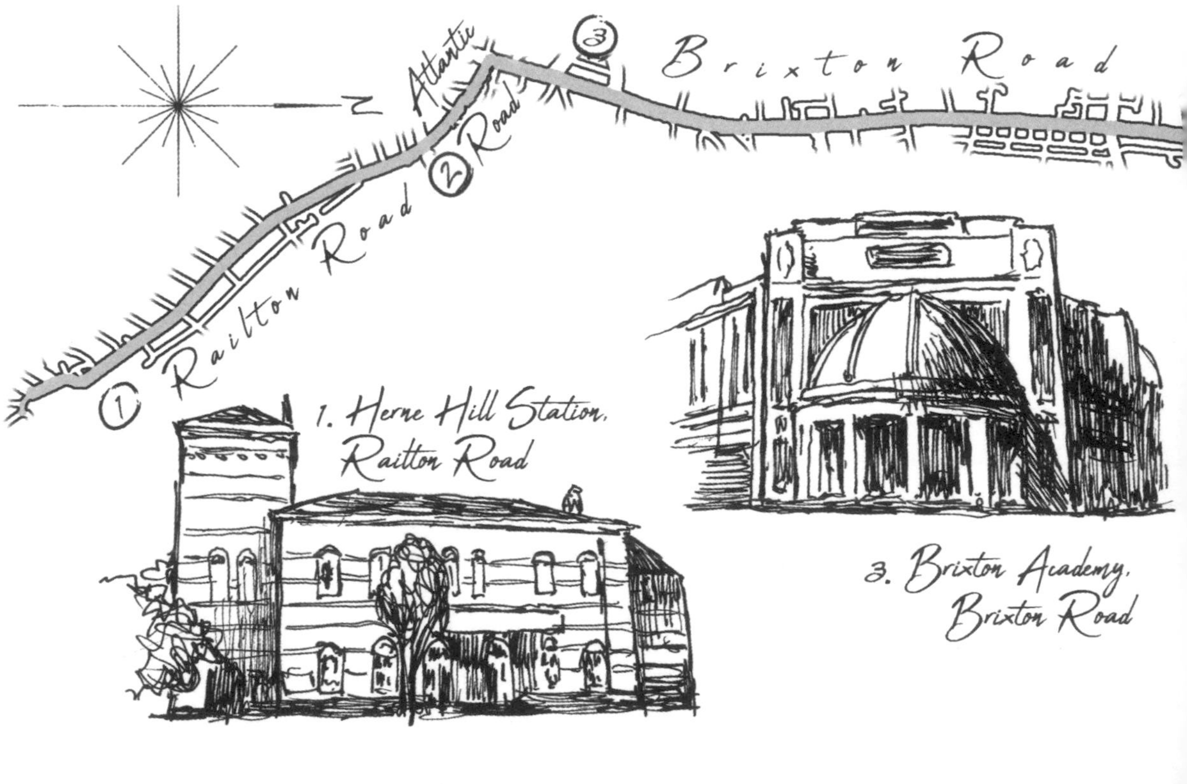

Atlantic Road
Railton Road
Brixton Road

1. Herne Hill Station, Railton Road

3. Brixton Academy, Brixton Road

Leave by: Station Approach
Left: Cab Road
Waterloo station on left

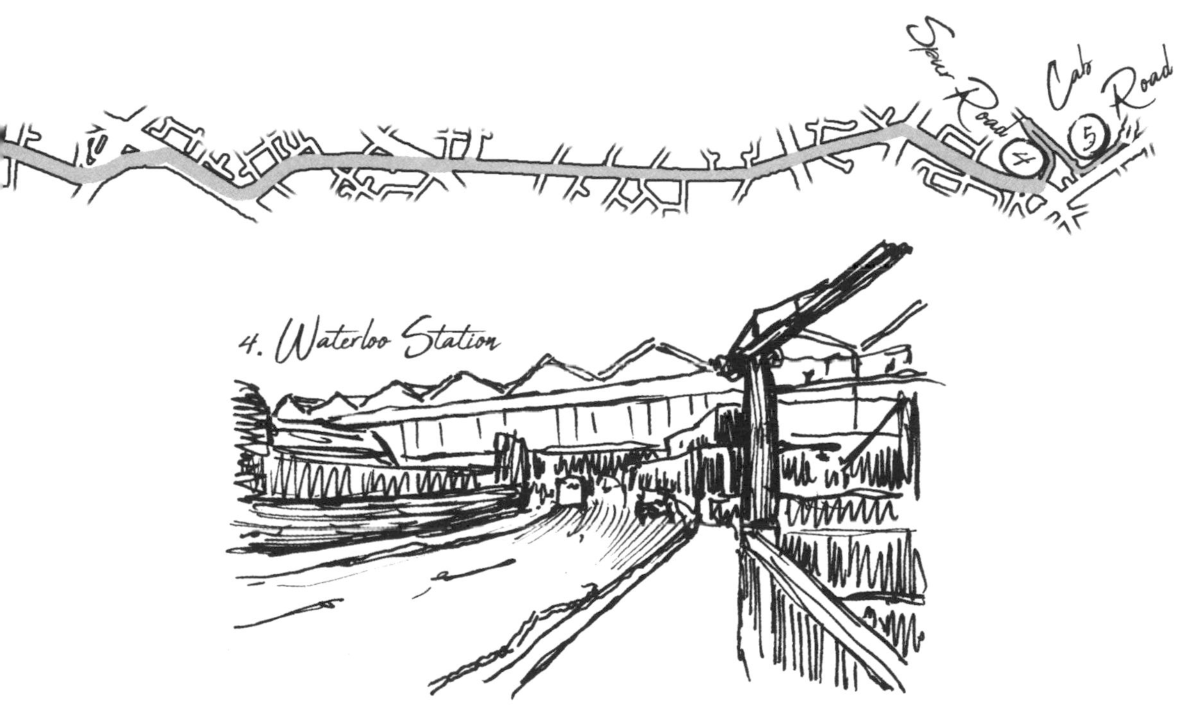

FULHAM HIGH STREET SW6 → POWIS SQUARE W11

The first half of this run snakes through Fulham's dense maze of back streets before crossing the roar of the A4, passing Marcus Garvey Park – named after the Jamaican political leader who lived nearby – and then heading into Kensington and Notting Hill.

It's interesting to note that a number of roads branching off Ladbroke Grove's western side – Cornwall Crescent, Blenheim Crescent and so on – are curved. This is a remnant of the Kensington Hippodrome, a racecourse that once covered the area. The curved roads follow the route of the former racetrack.

THE SCARY FILM

In the scary monster film (1), the creatures burst out from behind closed doors, riling (2) their victims with sheer terror (3).

Lillie (4) enjoyed watching it (although at first she thought she was going to see a drama about Oliver Cromwell) (5) and stuck with it until the end (6), snacking on ham (7) and Melton Mowbray pork pies (8).

Her noisy eating annoyed the Abbot (9) who was sitting behind her, as he'd travelled all the way from Holland (10) to see this. Angered, he left the cinema, and went to The British Museum to view the Elgin Marbles instead (11).

1. Munster Road and Filmer Road
2. Rylston Road and Dawes Road
3. Sherbrooke Road
4. Lillie Road
5. West Cromwell Road
6. North End Road
7. Hammersmith Road
8. Melbury Road
9. Abbotsbury Road
10. Holland Park
11. Elgin Crescent

1 FULHAM HIGH STREET

It's ironic that the Temperance on Fulham High Street is a pub: it was originally a billiard hall, opened by the Temperance Movement in 1910 as a place where the consumption of alcohol was actively discouraged.

2 RYLSTON ROAD

The St Thomas of Canterbury church is by Augustus Pugin, the same architect who designed the finer details on the Houses of Parliament. Buried in the church graveyard is Joseph Aloysius Hansom, the man who invented the horse-drawn Hansom cab, a common sight in Victorian London and an ancestor of today's black taxis.

3 HAMMERSMITH ROAD

Built on the site of what was once, rather curiously, a wine-producing vineyard, Olympia is one of London's oldest and most important exhibition halls. Notable for its incredible iron and glass roof, it first opened in 1884 as the National Agricultural Hall and changed to its current name two years later. The first motor show was held at Olympia in 1905 and in 1937 London's first multi-storey car park opened to serve the centre.

4 ABBOTSBURY ROAD

Holland Park was once home to a Jacobean mansion called Holland House, named after its second owner, the Earl of Holland. Before that it had been known as Cope Castle after Sir Walter Cope, Chancellor of the Exchequer to King James I, for whom it had been originally built. Holland House was destroyed during the Blitz and only a few fragments of it remain today. The surrounding grounds, however, remain popular – especially the beautiful Japanese Kyoto Garden where peacocks roam free.

5 POWIS SQUARE

When it opened in 1888, the twin-spired Talbot Tabernacle was nicknamed the 'Taj Mahal of North Kensington'. The church remained in use until the mid-1970s when it was closed and threatened with demolition. Locals successfully campaigned to save the building and today The Tabernacle is an important community hub, hosting plays, concerts and exhibitions.

Leave by: Fulham Road
Left: Munster Road
Right: Filmer Road
Cross: Dawes Road
Forward: Sherbrooke Road
Left: Rylston Road
Right: Lillie Road
Comply: Roundabouts

Leave by: North End Road
Cross: West Cromwell Road
Forward: North End Road continued
Right: Hammersmith Road
Left: Melbury Road
Right: Abbotsbury Road
Right and left: Holland Park

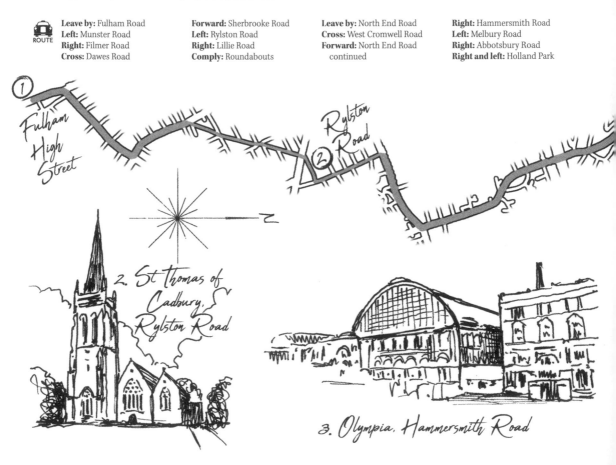

2. St Thomas of Cadbury, Rylston Road

3. Olympia, Hammersmith Road

Right: Holland Park Avenue
Left: Ladbroke Grove
Right: Elgin Crescent
Forward: Colville Terrace
Powis Square on left

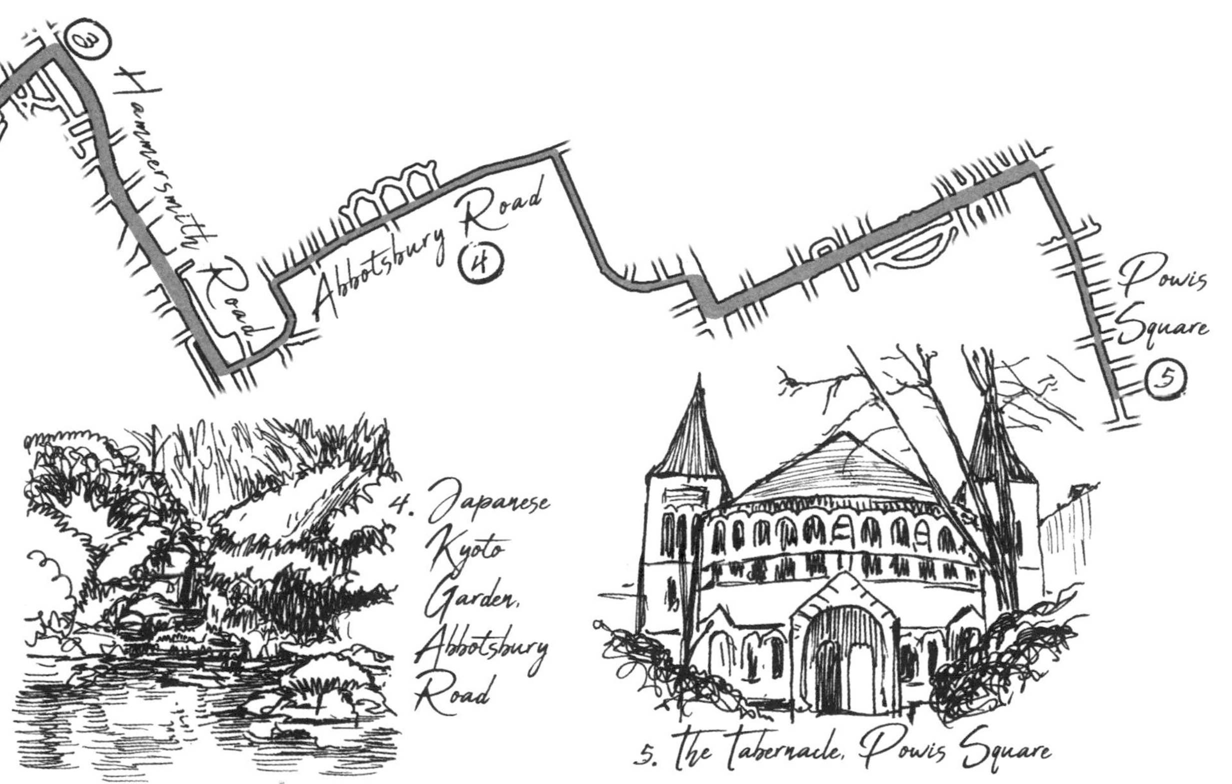

4. Japanese Kyoto Garden, Abbotsbury Road

5. The Tabernacle, Powis Square

PENTON PLACE SE17 → NARROW STREET E14

After heading along Newington Butts – 'Butts' being a reference to the archery once practised here – this run contends with two major south London hubs: Elephant and Castle and Bricklayers Arms. Named after a tavern, Elephant and Castle has a long history and is mentioned in Shakespeare's 'Twelfth Night', while 'The Brick' as it's traditionally known to locals, was once the site of a major railway yard.

At Abbey Street – named after the long-lost Bermondsey Abbey – the route passes beneath the arches (complete with ornate columns) built by the former London and Greenwich Railway, the capital's first passenger service when it began operating in the 1830s.

Once through the Rotherhithe Tunnel, Narrow Street is just to the right, although we're not allowed to access it directly. Instead a 'turn-around' must be employed, an alternative route that spins us back and allows us to approach our destination from the north.

KEN'S ELEPHANT RIDE

After giving it a gentle kick up the backside, Ken (1) clambered upon the elephant (2) and began his long ride down to Kent (3). After passing Tower Bridge, they bumped into Abbey (4) who'd just returned from a trip to Jamaica (5).

'I missed you,' said Ken.

'Sorry,' replied Abbey. 'I tried calling (6) you but I went through a tunnel (7) and lost the signal.'

Ken and the elephant marched on, and as they did a low-hanging branch (8) knocked Ken out cold. When he came to, he was face down on the ground with a big, grisly rat (9) leering right at him.

'Sorry, that's mine,' came a voice. It was a butcher (10) and he plucked the rat up by the tail. 'This fellow's going in the mincer.'

Ken was horrified. 'You turn rats into mincemeat?'

'Yep, it's good commerce (11). I've been using 'em since the scandal with horse meat. I package it up and ship it out on a ferry (12).'

1. Newington Butts and Kennington Park Road
2. Elephant and Castle
3. New Kent Road
4. Abbey Street
5. Jamaica Road
6. Culling Circus
7. Rotherhithe Tunnel
8. Branch Road
9. Ratcliffe Lane
10. Butcher Row
11. Commercial Road
12. Horseferry Road

1 ELEPHANT AND CASTLE

Elephant and Castle is dominated by modern architecture. Of note is the 1960s stainless steel Faraday Memorial (which conceals an electricity substation for the Northern Line and is named in honour of the scientist Michael Faraday who was born on Newington Butts) and the Strata Tower, which has three distinctive wind turbines on its roof and is known colloquially as both The Lipstick and The Razor.

2 JAMAICA ROAD

Inside Bermondsey tube station's ticket hall is a plaque in memory of Dr Alfred Salter who, along with his wife Ada, established a free medical practice on the site at the turn of the 20th century. At the time Bermondsey was an extremely poor area and being the days before the NHS, the Salters' free care was a godsend.

3 ROTHERHITHE TUNNEL

Opened in 1908, it's said that the bends in the white-tiled Rotherhithe Tunnel were incorporated as a preventative measure to stop horses from bolting towards daylight. Still a major river crossing, this is the only tunnel beneath the Thames to share space with cars and pedestrians, although it's very rare to see anyone walking through here due to the noxious vehicle fumes.

4 NARROW STREET

There has been a pub called The Grapes on Narrow Street for over 400 years. The current building is Georgian and is part-owned by the actor Sir Ian McKellen. Charles Dickens knew this pub from his childhood and used it as the basis for 'The Six Jolly Fellowship Porters' in *Our Mutual Friend*.

Leave by right: Kennington Park Road
Forward: Newington Butts
Comply: Elephant and Castle
Leave by: New Kent Road
Comply: Bricklayers Arms Roundabout
Leave by: Tower Bridge Road
Right: Abbey Street
Right: Jamaica Road
Comply: Culling Circus
Leave by: Tunnel Approach
Forward: Rotherhithe Tunnel
Bear left: Branch Road
Left: Ratcliffe Lane
Right: Butcher Row
Right: Commercial Road
Right: Branch Road
Left and right: Horseferry Road
Narrow Street on left and right

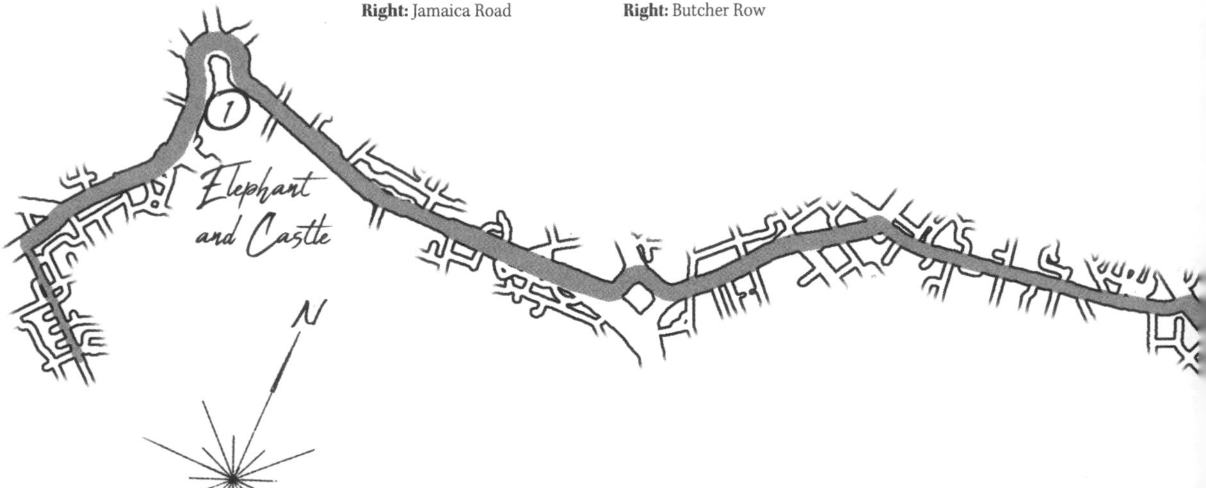

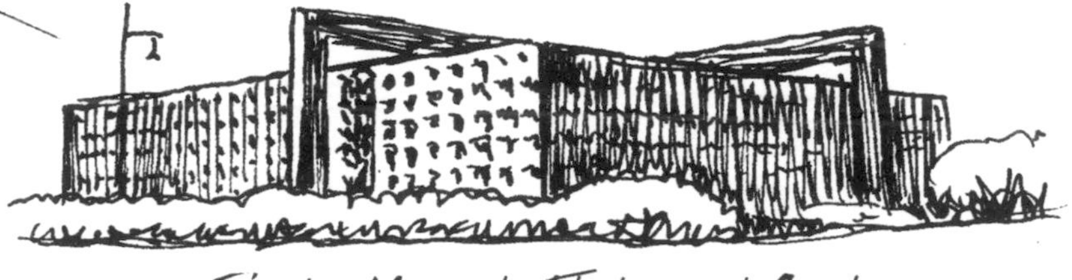

Elephant and Castle

N

1. Faraday Memorial, Elephant and Castle

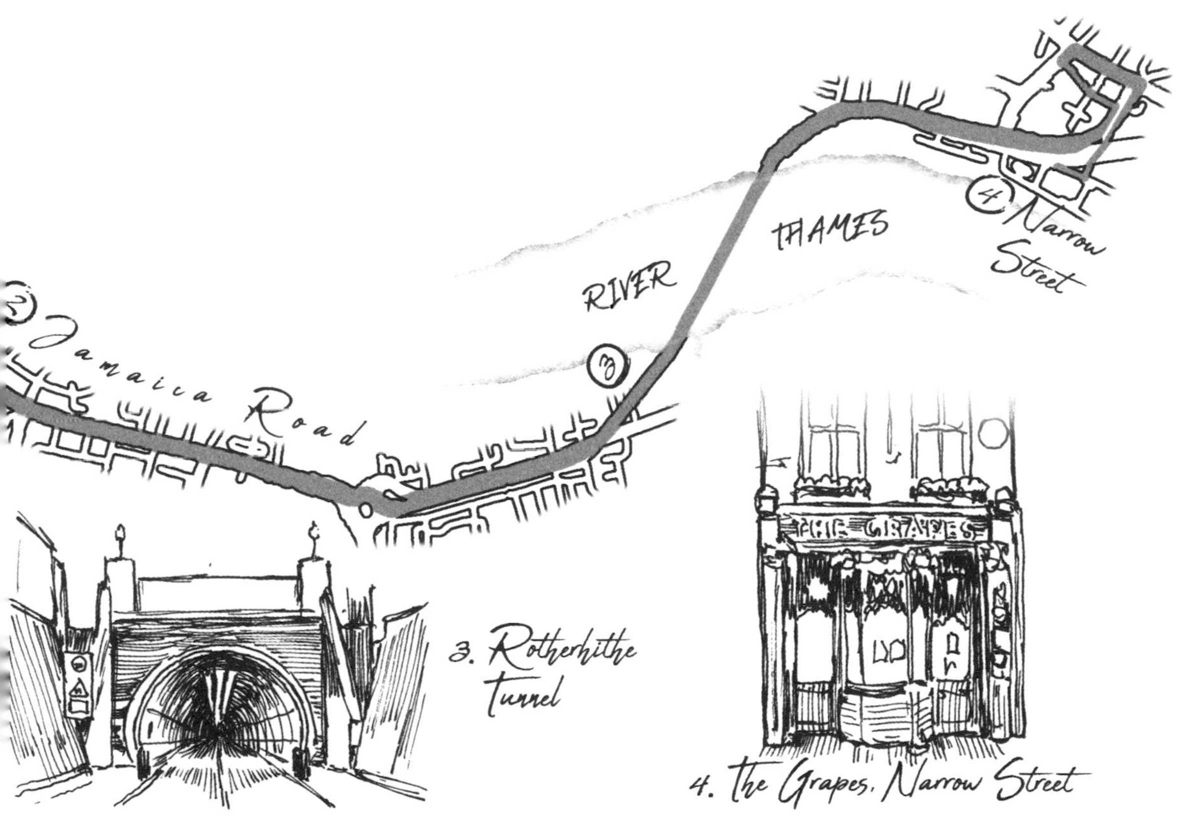

Jamaica Road
RIVER
THAMES
Narrow Street
3. Rotherhithe Tunnel
THE GRAPES
4. The Grapes, Narrow Street

MANOR FIELDS SW15 → BEDFORD HILL SW12

This run, which cuts across south-west London and crosses the River Wandle, can be a tricky one to master due to the twists, turns and predominantly residential streets. Trinity Road is fairly straightforward though – in fact, it's unusually long and straight for a London road.

GRANVILLE'S LONG WALK

It was night and the grove was well-lit (1), you could see it from both the western hills (2) and the neighbouring southern grove (3).

The view put Granville (4) in a merry (5) mood as he gathered up the kimono (6) which he'd purchased in Swaffham (7). It was a present for Ann (8) who lived way over west (9) and Granville was off to meet her; there would be many heaths and fields to cross on his journey (10).

On the way Granville saw a statue of Mary Magdalen (11), which put him in mind of the Holy Trinity (12).

His thoughts then switched to his feet – they were tired and he wished his friend James was there to drive (13). After all, Ann lived well past Nottingham (14), which was an extremely long way. No wonder she'd thought he was being sarcastic (15) when he said he'd walk it.

Before long Granville came across an overgrown park (16) and found his way blocked by a fence (17) and a large chestnut tree (18).

'That settles it,' he said. 'I'll catch a train from the station (19) instead.'

1. Lytton Grove
2. West Hill
3. Sutherland Grove
4. Granville Road
5. Merton Road
6. Kimber Road
7. Swaffield Road
8. St Ann's Hill
9. Westover Road
10. Heathfield Road
11. Magdalen Road
12. Trinity Road
13. St James's Drive
14. Nottingham Road
15. Sarsfeld Road
16. Balham Park Road
17. Boundaries Road
18. Chestnut Grove
19. Balham Station Road

1 MANOR FIELDS

Manor Fields is a neat, private estate of distinctive 1930s apartments. It was on this site that Thomas Cromwell – Henry VIII's chief minister who features in Hilary Mantel's historical novel, *Wolf Hall* – was born into a poor family.

2 HEATHFIELD ROAD

Originally known as the Surrey House of Correction, Wandsworth prison opened in 1851 and remains one of the UK's highest capacity jails. Many notorious criminals were executed at Wandsworth including George Chapman (the 'Borough Poisoner' who was a Jack the Ripper suspect), William Joyce (a.k.a. Nazi propagandist 'Lord Haw-Haw') and John George Haigh (the 'Acid Bath Murderer'). Although capital punishment was effectively abolished in the UK in 1965, it did remain for certain crimes such as treason and as such a fully working gallows was maintained at Wandsworth until the 1990s.

3 ST JAMES'S DRIVE

This was once the site of St James's Hospital (now covered by Old Hospital Close), which closed in 1988. In September 1978, the Bulgarian writer and dissident Georgi Markov was rushed to St James's suffering from a mysterious fever after being stabbed with an umbrella by a mysterious assailant on Waterloo Bridge. The umbrella was in fact a specially-designed Soviet weapon that had injected a tiny ricin pellet into Markov. He died at the hospital hours later.

4 BALHAM STATION ROAD

Balham station serves both the tube's Northern Line and the national rail mainline to Brighton. The tube entrance was architect Charles Holden's first design for a London Underground station – he'd go on to design many more, including Alperton and Rayners Lane, which were celebrated for their modern style. In 1940 Balham tube station suffered a direct hit during an air raid, tragically killing over 60 people sheltering on the deep platforms.

5 BEDFORD HILL

The Bedford is one of south London's best known pubs. It opened in 1931 and is now noted for hosting the regular Banana Cabaret; a comedy club that has hosted many famous acts including Jack Dee, Catherine Tate and Eddie Izzard.

Leave by left: Putney Hill
Right: Lytton Grove
Left: West Hill
Right: Sutherland Grove
Left: Granville Road
Comply: Roundabout
Leave by: Merton Road
Left: Kimber Road
Forward: Swaffield Road
Right: St Ann's Hill
Left: Westover Road
Right: Heathfield Road
Left: Magdalen Road
Right: Trinity Road
Left: Nottingham Road
Right: St James's Drive
Left: Sarsfeld Road
Right: Balham Park Road
Left: Boundaries Road
Right: Chestnut Grove

1 Manor Fields

N

2. Wandsworth Prison, Heathfield Road

Forward: Balham Station Road
Bedford Hill on left and right

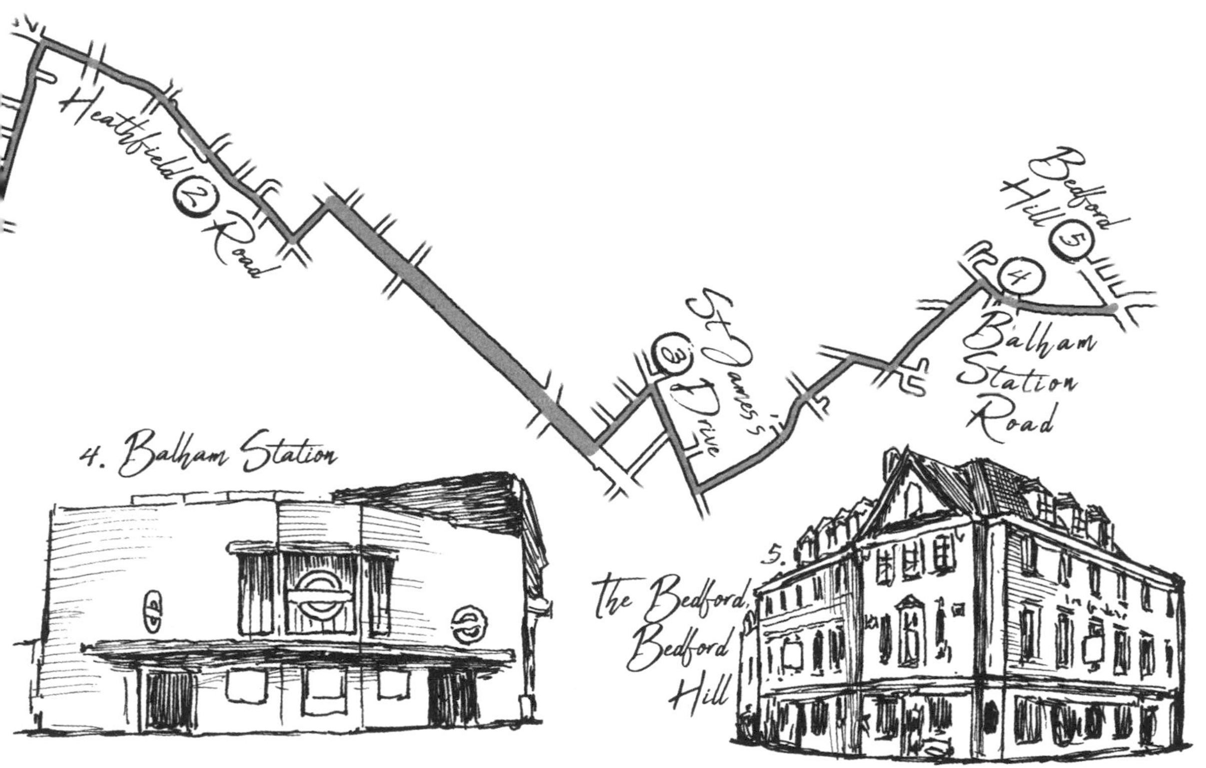

RUNS USING HISTORY

An appreciation of London's long history can be most useful when studying The Knowledge; indeed it was something I was actively encouraged to pursue at the Knowledge school I attended by the college's founder, Malcolm Linskey.

Knowing about an area's past is especially useful when learning the quarter-mile radii at the beginning and end of each run, as it can be common for surrounding street names to reference local history; factual links make for great memory hooks.

Take, for example, the roads clustered north and south of the Strand, many of which are named after places in England – Surrey Street, Exeter Street, Arundel Street, Essex Street. This is a reference to the various members of the nobility associated with these towns and counties who constructed their grand London homes along the banks of the Thames at a time when it was fashionable to do so. Somerset House is the only surviving example of this trend.

Some examples are more subtle, such as Anglers Lane in Kentish Town, so called because the Fleet River used to run above ground through the area (and was no doubt a popular fishing spot), or Bermondsey's Tanner Street and Leathermarket Street; a reference to the foul-smelling tanneries that once churned away there.

An awareness of history is also useful for visualising London's map layout as certain parts have grown in distinct ways. The route from London Bridge, up through Bishopsgate and onto Kingsland and Tottenham for example, is long and straight – a clear Roman route once known as Ermine Street. Just as obvious is the long stretch from Marble Arch, along Edgware Road, up through Kilburn, Cricklewood and beyond – the course of old Watling Street (now the A5) which conveyed ancient travellers all the way to Wales.

Meanwhile, further south, Great Dover Street and the Old Kent Road project an approximate trajectory from the bottom of Borough High Street towards Canterbury, a path that Chaucer and his fellow medieval pilgrims would still recognise today.

In some cases, threads of history run through the Knowledge runs themselves – ten examples of which appear in this section.

Students who immerse themselves in The Knowledge find that it makes the brain buzz and many maintain a passion for learning once they've passed and gained their badge. Because of this, the Worshipful Company of Hackney Carriage Drivers runs a popular course for cabbies who wish to train as taxi tour guides.

THORNHILL SQUARE N1 → QUEEN SQUARE WC1

Kings and Queens — This is the second run on The Knowledge. It begins in Barnsbury, which is an area characterised by fine Georgian squares and terraces: it also has numerous links to royal history along the way.

The first thing to bear in mind is that a tavern and tea-garden called Copenhagen House once stood nearby on a site now occupied by Caledonian Park, approximately half a mile from Thornhill Square.

It's believed Copenhagen House was named either in honour of the King of Denmark or the Danish Ambassador, both of whom stayed there in the 17th century.

Consequently the first roads on this run have a Danish theme. Matilda Street is named after Queen Caroline Matilda who was born in London but became Queen consort to Denmark after her marriage to Christian VII. Copenhagen Street is of course named after Denmark's capital.

The run then heads towards King's Cross Road, the name of which (along with the encompassing area) originates from an 18ft monument to King George IV that was erected in the 1830s on the junction (i.e. cross) where Euston Road, Pentonville Road and Gray's Inn Road meet.

Unfortunately, George IV had been generally despised by the public and his memorial was demolished after just six years. Despite this, the name King's Cross stuck.

Next we have Frederick Street, marking the name of many kings from both Denmark and Prussia. Alternatively you can use Acton Street, which is home to The Queen's Head pub.

Gray's Inn Road is an ancient route named after the Inn of Court that lies at its southern end.

The most curious name on this run is Lamb's Conduit Street. This refers to William Lamb who helped channel fresh water into the city from this spot. He also provided the poor with pails for transporting the water – hence the fountain and statue at the top of Guildford Place depicting a woman holding a jug.

The end point, Queen Square, is named in honour of Queen Charlotte, wife to King George III (their son being George IV after who the erstwhile King's Cross is named).

George III famously suffered from mental illness and it was in a house on this square that he was treated. This historic link helps remember some important points around the square – the National Hospital for Neurology and Neurosurgery and The Queens Larder pub, where Queen Charlotte is said to have stored her husband's food supply.

1 PENTONVILLE ROAD

The Scala has a mixed history. It was designed as a cinema, but this purpose was delayed by the outbreak of WWI when it was commandeered as a makeshift factory for aircraft components. The cinema finally opened in 1920 and by the 1970s was also hosting rock concerts.

2 GRAY'S INN ROAD

The most distinctive building on Gray's Inn Road is the art deco Trinity Court, which was built in the 1930s. It features in the 1986 film *Mona Lisa*, which was set around King's Cross at a time when the area was a notorious red-light district.

3 GREAT ORMOND STREET

Initially known as The Hospital for Sick Children, Great Ormond Street opened on Valentine's Day 1852 and was the first hospital in the UK solely dedicated to treating youngsters.

At first the hospital was based in an old town house and had just ten beds. Charles Dickens – whose former home can be visited in nearby Doughty Street – did much to help the hospital's expansion when he gave a charity reading of *A Christmas Carol* in 1858 which raised enough funds to purchase a second building. By the 1870s the hospital as it appears today was beginning to take shape. Further financial assistance came from J M Barrie who gifted the copyright of *Peter Pan* to the hospital in 1929.

Leave by: Matilda Street
Right: Copenhagen Street
Left: Caledonian Road
Left: Pentonville Road
Right: King's Cross Road
Right: Frederick Street
Left: Gray's Inn Road
Right: Guildford Street
Left: Guildford Place
Forward: Lamb's Conduit Street
Right: Great Ormond Street
Queen Square facing

Gray's Inn ② Road
Great Ormond Street ③
2. Trinity Court, Gray's Inn Road
3. Great Ormond Street Hospital

PARLIAMENT STREET SW1 → GOLDEN LANE EC1

The River — This is a useful run to know if you're heading from Westminster to the City as it provides an alternative to the Strand, Aldwych and Fleet Street.

This route is particularly special at night; the view of the Thames from the illuminated Victoria Embankment is beautiful after dark, and Smithfield Market buzzes with activity as meat traders prepare for their early morning customers.

It also closely follows the most central section of London's lifeblood – the Thames.

The first major site is the Houses of Parliament, Britain's main seat of government. The entire eastern length of this grand building backs directly on to the Thames, an aspect of its design intended to provide defence against the 'mob'.

For much of the 19th century, the Thames was essentially an open sewer and in the summer of 1858 the stench became so horrendous that the government was almost forced to relocate.

Dubbed 'The Great Stink', this event resulted in the construction of a modern sewer network, masterminded by Sir Joseph Bazalgette. Part of this project involved reclaiming land from the Thames in order to build roads, beneath which sewer pipes could be laid. One such road is on this run – Victoria Embankment, which follows the river's curve. A small memorial to Bazalgette can be seen on Victoria Embankment opposite Northumberland Avenue.

One remnant from the pre-embankment era is the York Watergate, a landing point for boats which was formerly part of York House. Since the reclamation of land from the Thames, this stone structure can now be seen marooned among the grass in Victoria Embankment Gardens.

Once the run turns onto New Bridge Street we are once again following the course of a river – this time the subterranean Fleet, a tributary to the Thames that can be seen trickling out beneath Blackfriars Bridge.

New Bridge Street becomes Farringdon Road and the route is relatively straight, running from north to south. Imagining the Fleet's course, which flows down from Hampstead, can be a useful reference when attempting to visualise the map.

1 BRIDGE STREET

Bridge Street offers the most imposing view of the Houses of Parliament clock tower commonly referred to as Big Ben – although this nickname is in fact a reference to the large bell housed within. The tower's official title was originally St Stephen's Tower but it was renamed the Elizabeth Tower in 2012 in honour of Queen Elizabeth II's diamond jubilee. Dating from the 1850s, the bell weighs 13 tonnes and was cast at the Whitechapel Bell Foundry – it took 16 horses to haul it to Westminster. There is no official explanation as to where the name Big Ben originated, although it's believed it's either in honour of a formidable bareknuckle boxer and Covent Garden publican named Benjamin Caunt, or Sir Benjamin Hall who was the Chief Commissioner of works at the time.

2 VICTORIA EMBANKMENT

Both the Royal Air Force Memorial (topped by a large, gold eagle) and the National Submarine War Memorial – which is illustrated with an appropriately claustrophobic relief – stand on Victoria Embankment. There are also three vessels permanently moored here – the *Tattershall Castle*, which was formerly a paddle streamer for the Humber Ferry; the *Hispaniola* (formerly the *Maid of Ashton*), which worked on Scotland's Holy Loch; and the *HQS Wellington*, which saw action both in the Dunkirk evacuation and the Atlantic convoys. The *Tattershall* and the *Hispaniola* are a bar and restaurant while the *Wellington* is now a conference venue.

3 BEECH STREET

Beech Street is a long tunnel, built beneath the sprawling Barbican Estate which is home to both some 4,000 residents and Europe's largest performing arts and conference venue. The estate covers an area once known as Cripplegate, which was entirely wiped out in the Blitz. The Barbican, a classic example of brutalist architecture, was built over a number of decades during the post-war period and was finally completed in 1982. The complex is famous for being tricky to navigate and as such long yellow route markers can be found around the estate's many walkways for those in a hurry to get to one of its numerous theatres, cinemas or conference halls.

Leave by left: Bridge Street
Left: Victoria Embankment
Bear left: Slip road
Left: New Bridge Street
Forward: Farringdon Street
Right: West Smithfield
Left: East Poultry Avenue
Right: Charterhouse Street
Right: Lindsey Street
Left: Long Lane
Cross: Aldersgate Street
Forward: Beech Street
Golden Lane on left

Victoria Embankment
RIVER THAMES
Bridge Street
1
2
N

1. Big Ben

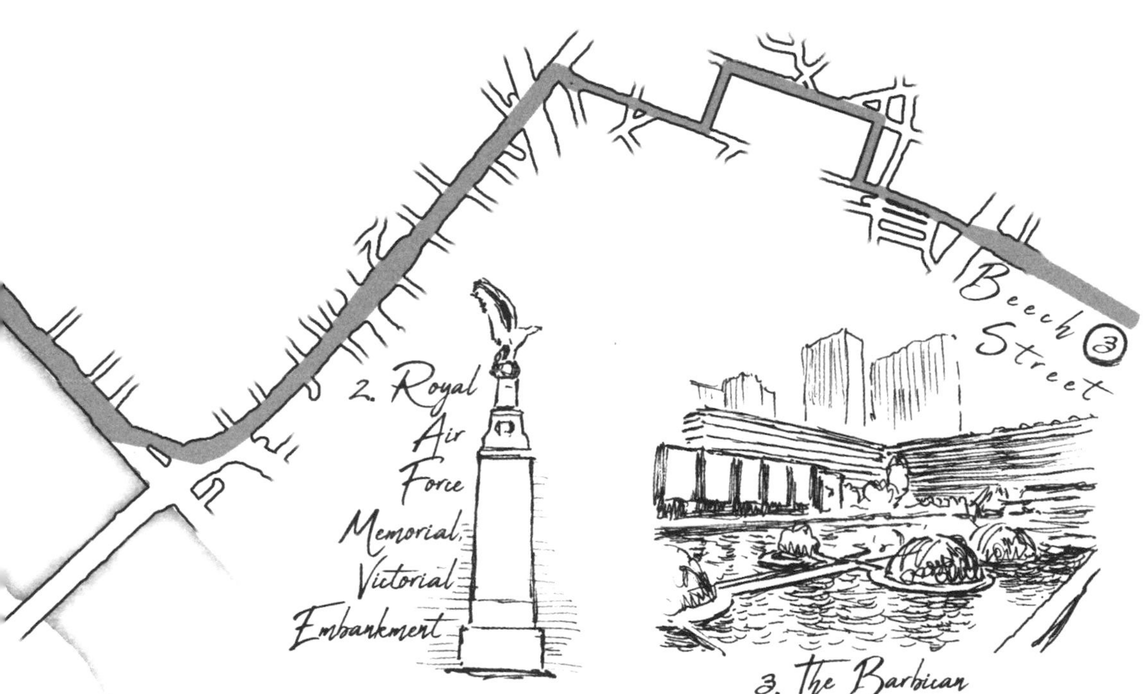
2. Royal Air Force Memorial, Victoria Embankment
Beech Street
3
3. The Barbican

TIMBER POND ROAD SE16 → GROCERS' HALL COURT EC2

Follow the Money — This run involves areas intrinsically linked to trade and commerce; factors that have been instrumental in London's development as a world city.

It begins on the Rotherhithe peninsula where many of the roads are relatively new, built in the 1980s upon what used to be the huge network of quays known as the Surrey Commercial Docks.

Bearing this past in mind helps recall the surrounding streets, as some are named after the former dockyards and the nations with which they traded: Quebec Way, Canada Street, Norway Gate, Russia Dock Road and so on (the same too applies to Jamaica Road further along).

Other roads have similar, maritime-themed names such as Gunwhale Close, Keel Close and Deal Porters Way – deal porters being dockers who dealt with timber.

The run then winds through Bermondsey, passing Shad Thames (where the villainous Bill Sikes meets his end) and on to Tooley Street. Tooley is another named derived from an international link, morphed over a period of many years from St Olave's – a church that was named after King Olaf of Norway, the renowned figure who ordered London Bridge to be physically pulled down in 1015 in order to defend the city against a Danish attack.

Once across London Bridge – the capital's oldest river crossing – we're into the City, the capital's financial heart. It's therefore no surprise to find Lombard Street, a reference to goldsmiths from the Italian region of Lombardy who traded here. Next is Bank Junction, named of course after the Bank of England, which has been here since 1694.

On a more down-to-earth level, Poultry really is a reference to chickens. The street it runs into, Cheapside, was medieval London's main shopping precinct; look out too for Bread Street, Milk Street and Honey Lane.

At Poultry, if you peer up at the building on the junction with Grocers' Hall Court you'll see a statue of a boy hugging a goose. The bird is 'Old Tom', a goose who escaped slaughter at nearby Leadenhall Market and was subsequently adopted by traders as a pet. He lived to the grand old age of 37.

1 TOOLEY STREET

Much of Tooley Street is squeezed between converted warehouses – including the impressive Hay's Galleria which is now a shopping centre – and the imposing, brick arches of London Bridge station, which first opened in 1836 as the terminal for the London and Greenwich Railway; the capital's very first passenger line.

2 LONDON BRIDGE

There have been many bridges at this site, the first dating back to the Roman era when it played a key role in helping the small settlement of Londinium flourish. In the year 1212, one of London's worst disasters occurred on the bridge when crowds flocked to witness a fire. Tragically, sparks lit both ends of what was then a wooden structure and it's estimated around 3,000 souls perished, either through fire or drowning. The most evocative version of London Bridge stood from 1209 to 1831. It had many arches that would cause the Thames to freeze solid during the winter, and was crammed with shops and houses. In 1831 a more orderly stone bridge was erected. This remained until 1967 when the present bridge began to be built. This latest incarnation was officially opened by the Queen in 1973 while its predecessor was famously purchased as the world's largest antique by an American entrepreneur, Robert P McCulloch, who had it rebuilt at Lake Havasu, Arizona, where it can still be seen today.

3 BANK JUNCTION

This major London artery is dominated by three classic buildings: the looming 'curtain wall' of the Bank of England, the Royal Exchange and Mansion House.

4 THE ROYAL EXCHANGE

The Royal Exchange was designed as a place where merchants could meet to do business without having to huddle in alleys and coffee houses. It dates back to the 16th century and was inspired by a similar institution in Antwerp.

5 MANSION HOUSE

Mansion House meanwhile is the official home of the Lord Mayor of London (not to be confused with the more modern city-wide mayor). The building opened in the 1750s and, as the Lord Mayor was the City's chief magistrate, it contained a number of prison cells. One notable person interned here was Emmeline Pankhurst.

Leave by: Poolmans Street
Left: Needleman Street
Right: Surrey Quays Road
Right: Lower Road
Comply: Culling Circus
Leave by: Jamaica Road
Bear left: Tanner Street
Right: Druid Street
Forward: Crucifix Lane
Right: Bermondsey Street
Left: Tooley Street
Forward: Duke Street Hill
Right: London Bridge
Forward: King William Street
Forward: Lombard Street
Comply: Bank Junction
Leave by: Mansion House Street
Forward: Poultry
Grocers' Hall Court on right

N

2. London Bridge

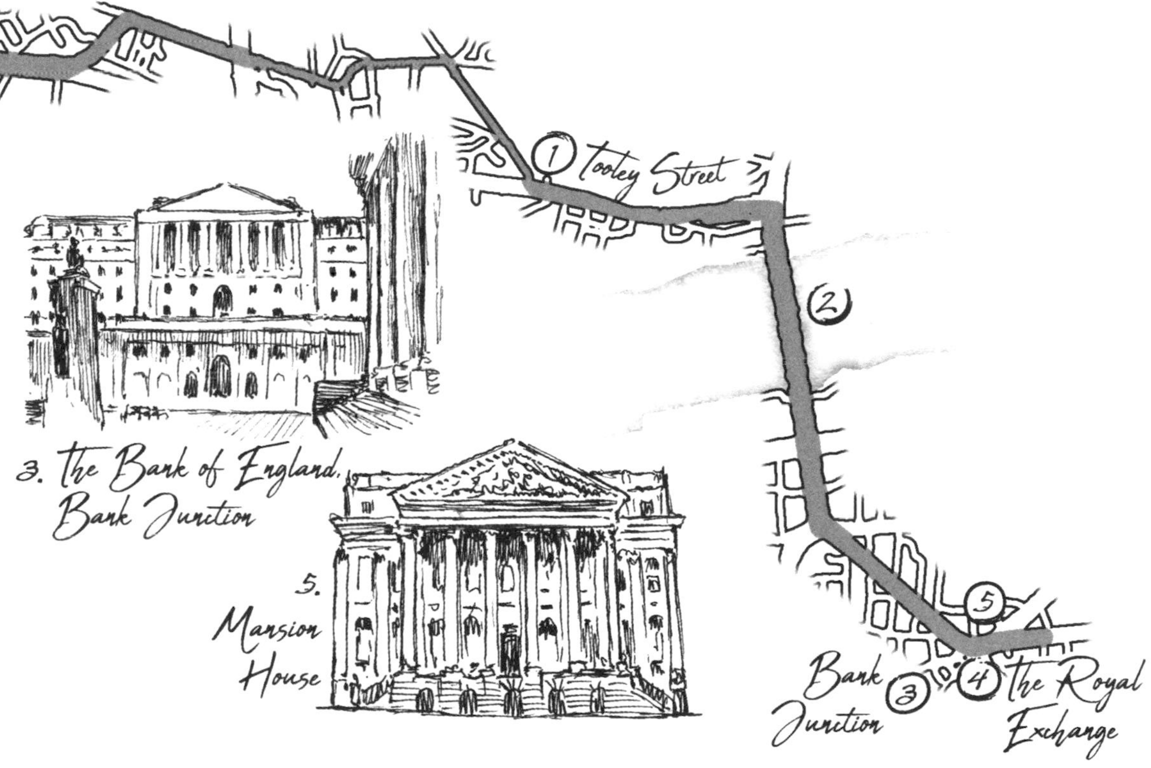
1 Tooley Street
2
3. The Bank of England, Bank Junction
5. Mansion House
5
Bank Junction 3
4 The Royal Exchange

ARBOUR SQUARE E1 → SADLER'S WELLS THEATRE EC2

Communities and Immigrants — London was built on immigration and nowhere is this more apparent than in the lively areas of the ever-changing East End through which this run passes, providing us with some useful shortcuts and intriguing points to discover along the way.

Commercial Road is a good clue as to where much of London's immigration originated from – the sprawling dockyards around which many sailors from abroad decided to settle.

In the late 19th century the main wave of immigration into the East End came from Eastern Europe as Jewish people fled persecution and economic hardship.

Although Jewish communities have now largely moved to areas around north London, a few reminders of their East End heritage do remain, such as The Congregation of Jacob Synagogue on Commercial Road.

Even in London, Jews were still subjected to oppression from certain groups. The western section of Commercial Road (just past the junction with White Church Lane) ends at a point colloquially known as Gardiner's Corner after the former Gardiner's Department store.

It was outside this shop on 4 October 1936 that Jewish protesters gathered with supporters to oppose a fascist march led by Oswald Mosley. As the demonstration pushed back, this became known as the Battle of Cable Street; named after a long road that runs parallel to Commercial Road.

It was on Commercial Road in the early 1940s that London's first mosque opened. Based in three houses, it moved a short distance to Whitechapel Road in 1974 and is now known as the East London Mosque.

The park, which stands on the site of the former church, is called Altab Ali Park in honour of a young Bangladeshi man who was murdered nearby in a racist attack in 1978.

Brick Lane is perhaps the most recognisable thoroughfare in London associated with immigration.

The first group to settle here were the French Huguenots. They specialised in weaving, but such work in London was a closed shop controlled by the guilds. This is why the Huguenots settled around Brick Lane and Spitalfields; they were outside the city's jurisdiction. Looking at a map, it's evident that Commercial Street and Brick Lane very much skirt around the City's boundary.

As well as the curry restaurants and bagel bakeries along Brick Lane, perhaps the most profound symbol of London's immigration is the Brick Lane Mosque, which has also been a protestant church and a synagogue during its lifetime – the only building in the world to have done so.

1 BRICK LANE

Always bustling day and night, Brick Lane is home to the former Truman's Brewery, identifiable by the large chimney that still towers above. In its day, Truman's was London's largest beer producer. It closed in 1989 but has since been reborn on a smaller scale, with production moving to Hackney. The old site is now a major exhibition space complete with clubs, markets and restaurants.

2 OLD STREET ROUNDABOUT

This roaring traffic junction is also known as St Agnes Well, although it's difficult to imagine such an urban site could produce fresh water nowadays. In recent years this area has been dubbed Silicon Roundabout due to the many tech companies that have sprouted around it.

3 SADLER'S WELLS THEATRE

Now one of the world's most important dance venues, this theatre originated in the 17th century when Richard Sadler established a 'Musick House' next to a popular spa. Rather bizarrely, one of its earliest attractions was said to be a singing duck. An early performer here was Joseph Grimaldi, son of an Italian immigrant and grandfather to the modern clown, who made his debut at the theatre when he was just a child. Sadly Joseph's life was a tragic one and he succumbed to alcoholism in 1837. Nearby, both his gravestone and a blue plaque marking his former home can be seen in Joseph Grimaldi Park and Exmouth Market respectively.

Leave by right: Commercial Road
Right: White Church Lane
Cross: Whitechapel High Street
Forward: Osborn Street
Forward: Brick Lane
Left: Quaker Street
Left: Wheeler Street
Right: Commercial Street
Forward: Great Eastern Street
Forward: Old Street
Comply: Old Street Roundabout
Leave by: Old Street continued
Right: Central Street
Left: Lever Street
Right: Goswell Road
Left: Spencer Street
Right: St John Street
Left: Rosebery Avenue
Sadler's Wells Theatre on right

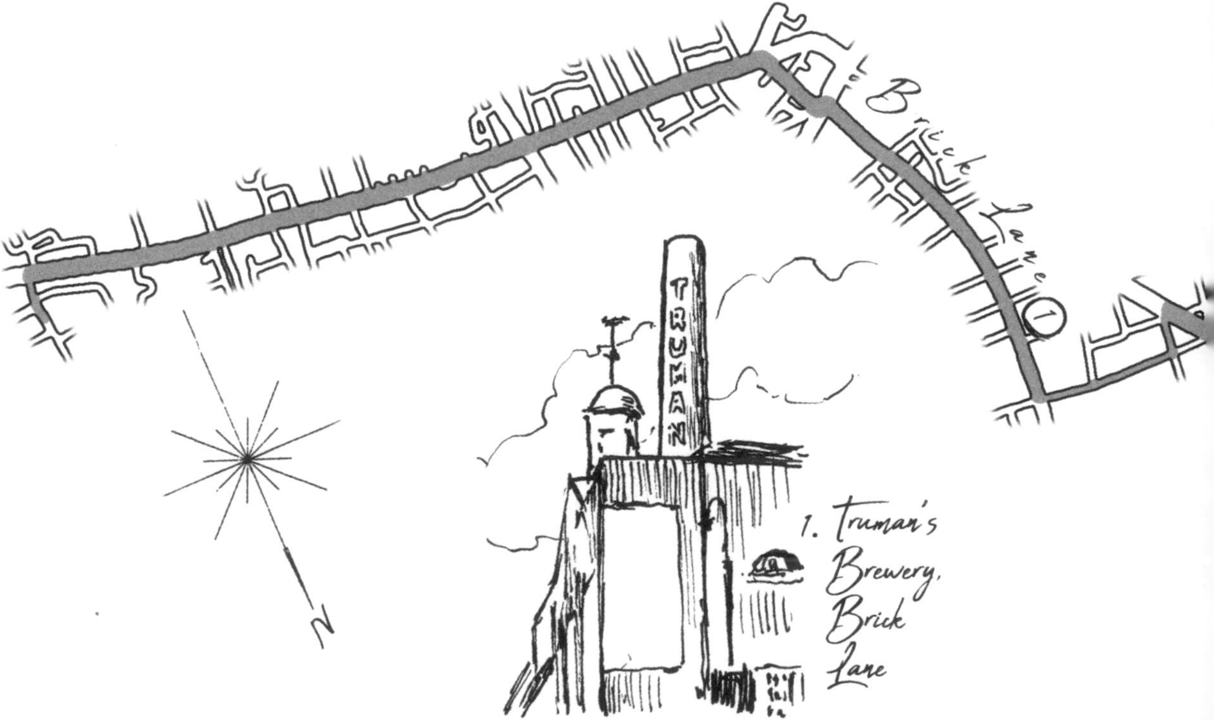

Brick Lane

TRUMAN

1. Truman's Brewery, Brick Lane

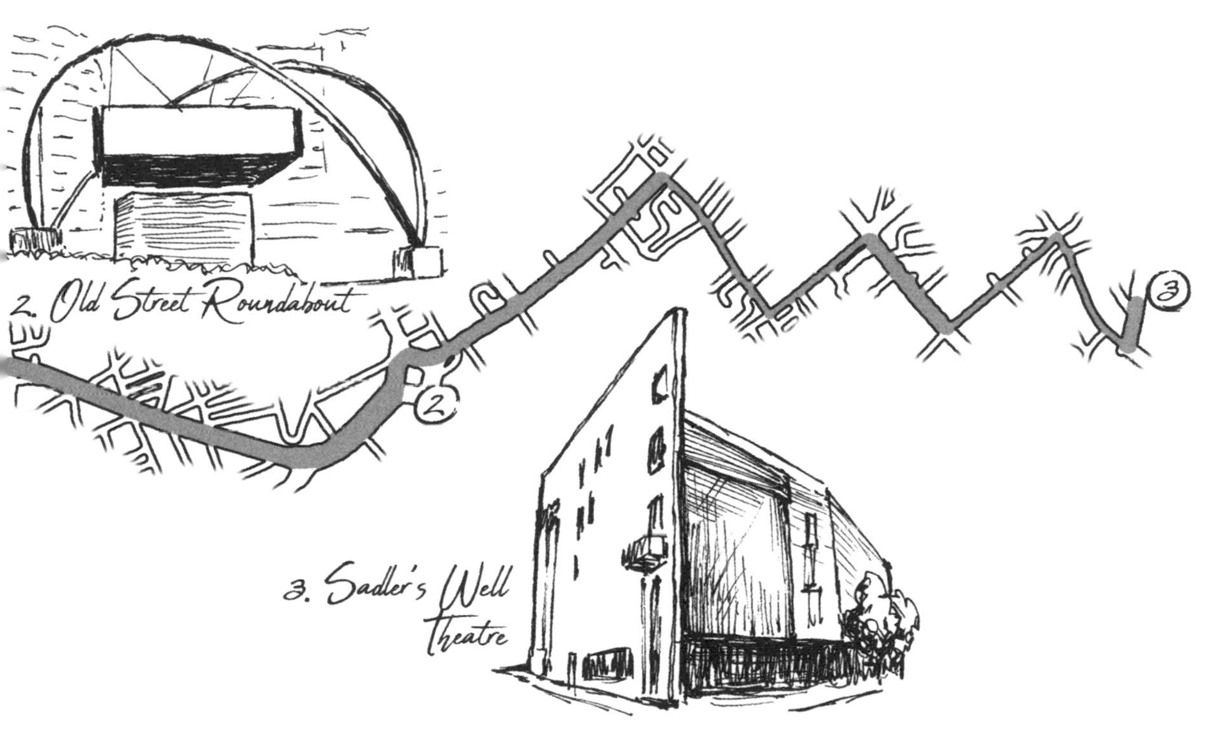
2. Old Street Roundabout
3. Sadler's Well theatre

LEICESTER SQUARE WC2 → THE GUILDHALL EC2

A Tale of Two Cities — Rich in history, this run passes all manner of hotels, galleries and other historic buildings. The first few roads – Orange Street to Bedford Street – are a vital cut-through for any cabbie as they skip out Trafalgar Square.

Angel Street is pretty nifty too as only buses and taxis are permitted to skirt around it.

Historically, London has always been split between two camps: commerce and monarchy, represented by the City and Westminster respectively.

Working backwards, this run traces that relationship and, along with nods to the city's Roman past, is a useful route for visualising central London's topography.

Starting in the West End, Leicester Square dates back to the 1660s. This was a time of upheaval; the Great Fire had devastated London's Square Mile and those who could afford to began to migrate west, carving out new, fashionable areas such as Soho and Mayfair, close to the seat of the newly restored monarchy.

One estate to take advantage of this growth was the Bedford Estate – hence Bedford Street, which takes us down to the Strand.

Since medieval times, the Strand has been the physical connection between Westminster and The City. Its name is an old English term meaning 'land bordering water' because the Thames used to be much wider.

Towards its eastern end the Strand is interrupted by Aldwych. Opened in 1905, this broad, arc-shaped road is relatively recent. Its name, however, is far more ancient, stemming from 'Aldwic' – a nordic term for 'old settlement' – which referred to a small community of Danes who made their home outside the City's old wall.

Just before the Strand becomes Fleet Street, we pass Temple Bar, the official boundary between The City and Westminster.

Traditionally, any monarch wishing to enter the City is expected to pause here and request permission; a symbolic gesture which acknowledges The City's autonomy. The original Temple Bar was a stone gateway which can now be seen in Paternoster Square beside St Paul's Cathedral.

After Fleet Street it's on to Ludgate Circus and Ludgate Hill. These names are intrinsic to the City; Ludgate was an entrance on the old London Wall and the fact that there's a Ludgate Hill is important too because, along with Cornhill, this was a major geographic factor which encouraged the Romans to build a settlement here; hills being vital in terms of defence. Further along, another old gateway is referenced by Newgate Street.

Finally, we come to the heart of the City: the Guildhall, which is the Square Mile's civic centre. This grand building dates back to the 15th century, although fire and bombs have seen it rebuilt over the years.

The gallery also houses what's believed to be the largest painting on public display in Britain: *The Defeat of the Floating Batteries at Gibraltar*. This mammoth artwork was painted by the American artist John Singleton Copley who once lived in . . . Leicester Square.

1 CHARING CROSS ROAD

Opposite the National Portrait Gallery is a memorial to Edith Cavell, a nurse who treated the wounded from all sides in WWI, but was executed in 1915 after assisting in the escape of Allied prisoners.

2 THE STRAND

The Adelphi Theatre opened in 1930, although there have been various venues on this site for over 200 years. In 1897, an infamous murder took place at the Adelphi's stage door when a struggling actor, Richard Archer Price, stabbed fellow actor William Terriss in a jealous rage.

3 FLEET STREET

The figures who ring the chimes on the clock of St Dunstan-in-the-West are Gog and Magog; two giants who, according to legend, are guardians of the City. Another church of note here is St Bride's whose tiered spire is said to have inspired the wedding cake design. Opposite is perhaps the most striking building on Fleet Street – a black and silver art deco office block which is the former office of the *Daily Express*.

4 KING EDWARD STREET

On the corner of Newgate Street stand the ruins of Christ Church Greyfriars, which was designed by Sir Christopher Wren. It was destroyed during the Blitz and its remaining walls now harbour a peaceful garden.

Leave by: St Martin's Street
Left: Orange Street
Right: Charing Cross Road
Forward: St Martin's Place
Left: William IV Street
Left: Chandos Place
Right: Bedford Street
Left: The Strand
Bear left: Aldwych
Forward: The Strand continued
Forward: Fleet Street
Forward: Ludgate Circus
Forward: Ludgate Hill
Left: Old Bailey
Right: Holborn Viaduct
Forward: Newgate Street

1. Edith Cavell Memorial

3. St Bride's Fleet Street

Bear left: King Edward Street
Right: Angel Street
Right: St Martin's-Le-Grand
Left: Cheapside
Left: Wood Street
Right: Gresham Street
Left: Aldermanbury
The Guildhall on right

KENSAL ROAD W10 → KINGS CROSS STATION N1

London Transport — This is a busy, often stressful route that most cabbies will usually encounter at least once during a working shift. But at least it's relatively straightforward, despite the concrete tangle of the double-decked Harrow Road and Westway.

This run goes in tandem with several historic routes that have been key in aiding London's growth.

The first leg runs parallel alongside two other modes of transport – to the north is the Grand Junction Canal (part of the Grand Union Canal) and to the south, the railway line into Paddington station.

Just before Edgware Road, the canal forks north towards Little Venice and Regent's Park and, along with the railway, south towards Paddington Basin. Bearing this layout in mind is a useful tool for map orientation. The railway connection also gives us Great Western Road; named after the company who built the line from London to Bristol.

Originally Marylebone Road and Euston Road were collectively called the New Road when laid out in the 1750s. The track's purpose was to help farmers bypass Oxford Street and Holborn when taking cattle to Smithfield Market, a function it still achieves today, albeit with roaring traffic rather than ambling livestock.

Before London grew, New Road was at the northern edge of the city and this is why Euston, St Pancras and King's Cross stations can all be found here; in the early days, landowners were opposed to having newfangled railways encroaching on their land.

The straightforward route laid out by Marylebone and Euston Roads made it the ideal path to follow when the world's first underground railway was laid beneath in the 1860s. Trains still rumble below today, and stations along the line such as Baker Street, Great Portland Street and Euston Square serve as useful landmarks.

1 MARYLEBONE ROAD

The grand red-bricked Landmark Hotel was originally known as the Great Central Hotel when it first opened in 1899 to serve passengers using Marylebone station. In its early days, guests could exercise on a wooden cycle track that looped around the roof. Old Marylebone Town Hall has long been a popular celebrity wedding venue. Paul and Linda McCartney, Ringo Starr, Chrissie Hynde and Liam Gallagher all said their vows here.

2 EUSTON ROAD

Resembling an abstract, brick ship, the British Library opened at this site in 1998 after transferring from its former home at The British Museum. The huge building plunges five floors below ground and contains over 600km of shelving – a distance that continues to grow every year. As well as various exhibitions, the library also has its 'Treasures' gallery, among which are displayed a priceless array of rare documents, including workbooks by Leonardo Da Vinci and a rare copy of the Magna Carta.

3 PANCRAS ROAD

St Pancras was designed by Sir George Gilbert Scott and opened in 1868. Due to its important trade link with the breweries in Burton-on-Trent, a huge storage area for beer barrels was a key design requirement. These cellars have since been converted into a bustling shopping area. Although it's now one of London's most celebrated buildings, the station narrowly avoided demolition in the 1960s. It was saved largely due to the efforts of the poet Sir John Betjeman, a statue of whom can be seen inside, gazing up in disbelief at the vast, restored roof. For many years, the neighbouring King's Cross station was also neglected with an unsightly, green metal canopy snaking around its front. The station has since been restored to its former glory and is popular with fans of Harry Potter who come seeking the mythical 'Platform 9¾'.

Leave by: Golborne Road
Comply: Roundabout
Leave by: Elkstone Road
Left: Great Western Road
Right: Woodfield Road
Left: Woodfield Place
Right: Harrow Road
Comply: Roundabout
Leave by: Harrow Road continued
Bear right: Marylebone Flyover
Forward: Marylebone Road
Forward: Euston Road
Forward: Euston Underpass
Forward: Euston Road continued
Left: Pancras Road
Right: Station forecourt
Kings Cross station on left

N

2.

The British Library, Euston Road

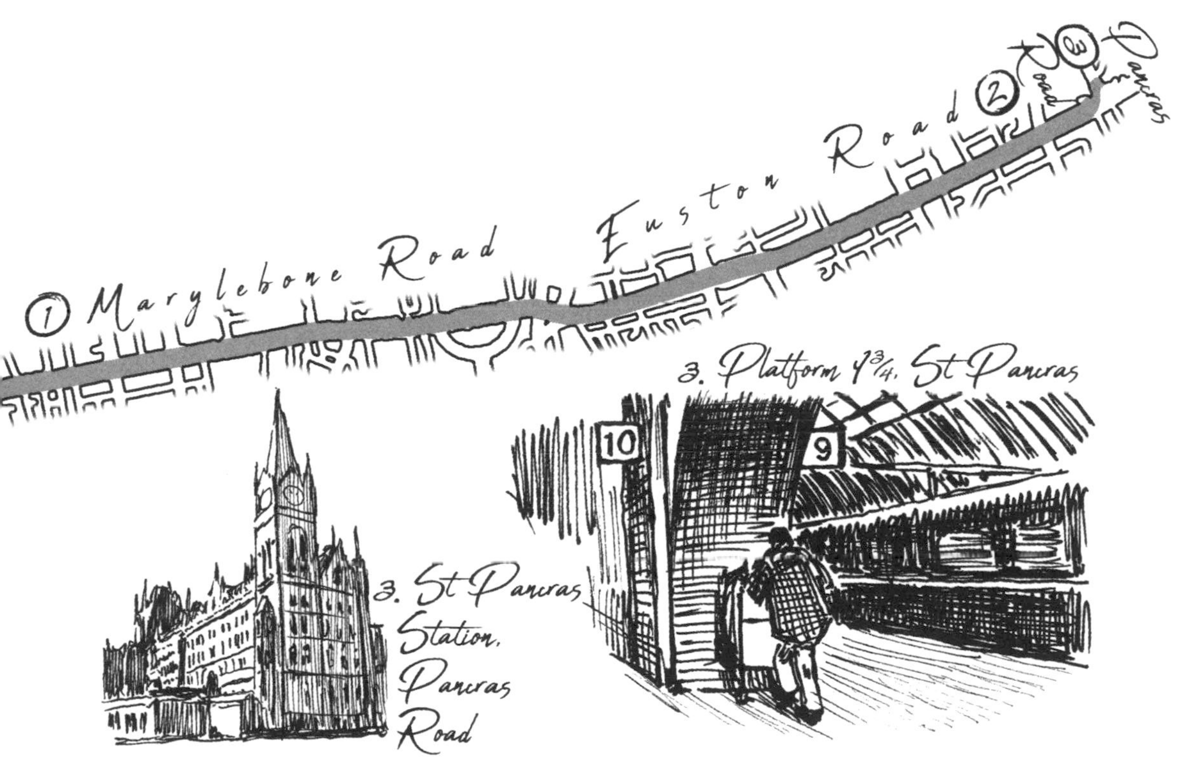
① Marylebone Road
Euston Road
②
Road
③
Pancras
3. Platform 9¾, St Pancras
10
9
3. St Pancras Station, Pancras Road

PARNELL ROAD E3 → NORTH GREENWICH STATION SE10

Rust and Regeneration — This isn't the prettiest of runs. Like its counterpart, the Westway, the Blackwall Tunnel Northern Approach was designed as an inner-city motorway (part of a wider plan which never came to fruition) and the grey swathe it cuts through East London has a dystopian feel.

The Blackwall Tunnel is no fun either, a notorious bottleneck which most cabbies will use only when absolutely necessary. These gripes aside, however, there is some interesting history and architecture along the way that is often overlooked.

This run begins and ends within two former industrial areas, both of which crumbled into dereliction before being successfully regenerated.

On Tredegar Road, we pass Fairfield Road, former site of the Bryant and May match factory. During the Victorian era many women toiled under appalling conditions here, contending with fourteen-hour days and the risk of a dreadful illness known as 'phossy jaw', which was caused by white phosphorus and resulted in jaw-rot and eerily glowing bones.

By 1888 it was decided enough was enough and 1,400 women walked out in what became known as the Matchgirls Strike, a bold action for the time, which secured them more favourable terms. The former factory has since been converted into the Bow Quarter apartments.

Once on the Blackwall Tunnel Northern Approach we pass the vast Queen Elizabeth Olympic Park which was the main site for the 2012 games. This was once an industrial area, formed around the River Lea, which runs parallel to the Blackwall Tunnel Northern Approach on its course to the Thames.

Today, however, you'll find a legacy of Olympic buildings including the London Stadium, The Copper Box, the Velopark and the London Aquatics Centre, as well as Sir Anish Kapoor's Orbit Tower; a twisting 376ft-tall observation platform where those brave enough can now experience the world's longest, fastest tunnel slide. The Tower is also a useful landmark to lock on to if you get lost in the area.

Once through the Blackwall Tunnel, which was built to facilitate commerce between the East End and south London, the run takes a sharp turn towards the Greenwich Peninsula.

Mirroring the start point, this land was formerly occupied by a large gasworks and is now where you'll find the O2 Arena – formerly the Millennium Dome, hence Millennium Way.

1 BLACKWALL TUNNEL NORTHERN APPROACH

Marooned among the dust and thunder of one London's most uninviting roads is Bromley Hall, which dates from the Tudor period and, despite its unlikely location, is believed to be the oldest surviving brick house in London. It was once owned by Henry VIII who entertained his mistress Elizabeth Blount here. As the years went by, Bromley Hall, like much of this part of London, was caught up in industry and for a time served as a gunpowder factory. Further along, motorists are treated to a looming view of Balfron Tower which is the older sibling to the more famous Trellick Tower near Notting Hill. The Balfron was designed in the 1960s by Ernö Goldfinger who himself spent time living there in order to gain feedback from residents. Also visible behind Balfron Tower is Glenkerry House, which was Goldfinger's last tower, completed in 1979.

2 THE BLACKWALL TUNNEL

London's most easterly crossing, the Blackwall Tunnel is in fact two separate tubes. The first was dug in the 1890s, the second in the 1960s. Over the years, there have been numerous ghostly reports of drivers picking up a young hitchhiker at the mouth of the tunnel during the early hours, only to find they've vanished by the time they reach the other end . . .

3 MILLENNIUM WAY

One of London's most famous modern structures, the Millennium Dome was created as a venue to celebrate the year 2000. Famously, it was considered something of a white elephant at the time, but has gone on to be successfully reinvented as the O2 Arena.

Leave by left: Tredegar Road
Forward: Wick Lane
Right: Slip Road
Bear right: Blackwall Tunnel Northern Approach
Forward: Blackwall Tunnel
Forward: Blackwall Tunnel Southern Approach
Bear left: Slip Road
Comply: Roundabout
Leave by: Millennium Way
Right: Edmund Halley Way
North Greenwich station on left

1. Bromley Hall, Blackwell Tunnel Northern Approach

1. Balfron tower, Blackwell Tunnel Northern Approach

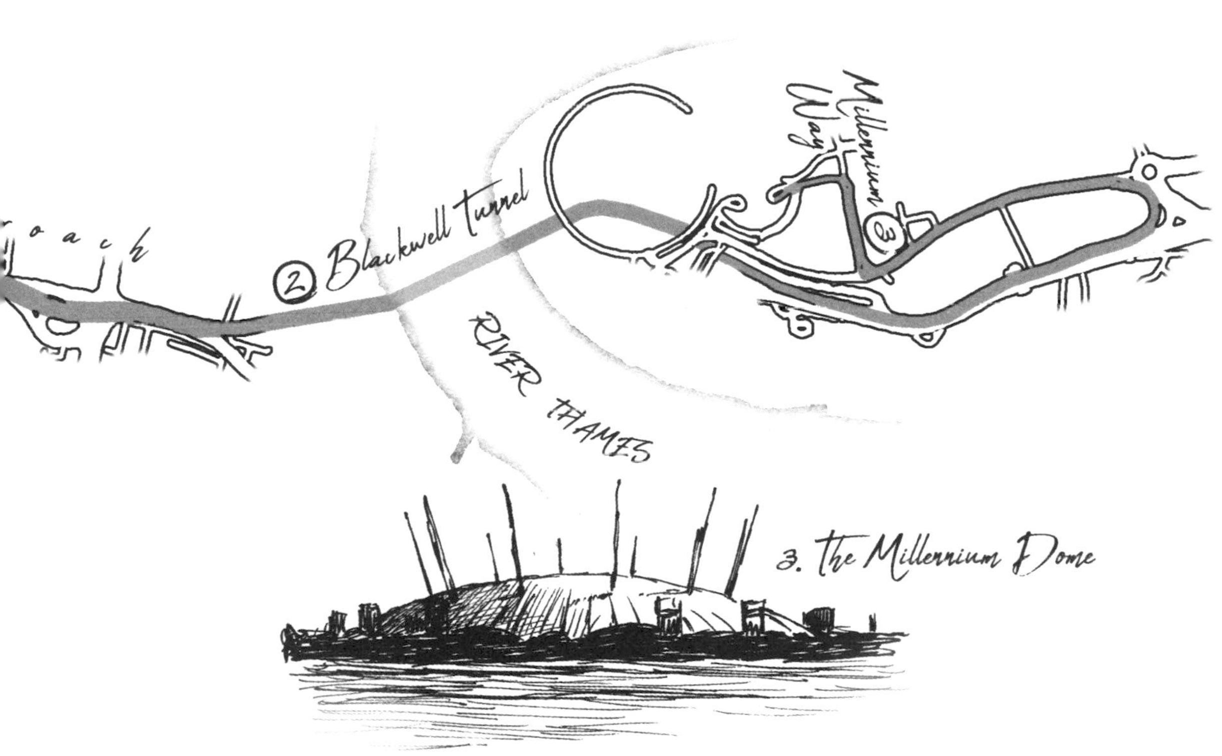

Millennium Way
2 Blackwell tunnel
3
RIVER THAMES
3. The Millennium Dome

HOLLOWAY PRISON N7 → GOLDERS GREEN STATION NW11

Crime and Punishment — Although Holloway prison is now closed, this run maintains the location – once the largest women's jail in Western Europe – as its start point.

By coincidence, the route passes through several areas associated with infamous crimes and such notoriety can be a useful (albeit grim) aid for jogging the memory. Even the first road, Parkhurst Road, is apt as this is the name of a prison on the Isle of Wight.

The first 'crime scene' is Hilldrop Road. Here we pass the similarly named Hilldrop Crescent which was once home to Dr Crippen who poisoned his wife and buried her in the cellar before fleeing to America with his mistress. After being hauled back to London, tried and found guilty, Dr Crippen took 'the drop' at Pentonville Prison.

Even the relatively genteel Brecknock Road has associations with murder. The building on the corner of Lady Margaret Road was once a post office and in 1886 a young man named George Finch committed a robbery in which an employee named John William Bowes was shot dead.

Finch was clearly no criminal mastermind; living just yards away on Ospringe Road, he pretty much committed the crime on his own doorstep and was quickly apprehended.

On Gordon House Road the run passes the southern tip of Parliament Hill which, according to legend, is said to be where those involved in the 1605 Gunpowder Plot planned to observe the explosive results of their treasonous handiwork.

On South End Road we pass South Hill Park which harbours an extraordinary coincidence. It was here, outside The Magdala pub in 1955, that Ruth Ellis shot dead her abusive lover David Blakely, which resulted in her being the last woman to be executed in Britain.

Many people would struggle to name the second-last woman to go to the gallows. That was Styllou Christofi, who strangled her daughter-in-law to death one night in 1954.

Ellis and Christofi had no knowledge of each other, nor were their crimes related in any way . . . incredibly though, Christofi also committed her murder on South Hill Park, the exact same street as Ellis.

Further up, towards the top of Hampstead on North End Way is Jack Straw's Castle. Now apartments and a gym, this relatively modern building replaced a former inn.

In the 17th century the clump of trees next to this site contained a gibbet in which the rotting body of Francis Jackson, a highwayman who'd terrorised everywhere from Kilburn to Harrow, was displayed as a gruesome warning.

1 HOLLOWAY PRISON

Holloway prison opened in 1852. Its foundation stone bore the ominous legend, 'May God preserve the City of London and make this place a terror to evil doers.' Oscar Wilde was remanded here in 1895 but at the turn of the 20th century the jail switched to incarcerating female inmates only. Consequently, a number of suffragette prisoners were locked up here, including Emily Davison who would later perish beneath the King's horse at the 1913 Derby. The prison was decommissioned in 2016 after it was deemed not fit for purpose.

2 HAMPSTEAD HEATH

Standing at around 800 acres, Hampstead Heath is one of London's best loved open spaces and offers splendid views of the city. Its popularity grew in the 1600s when medicinal springs were discovered, essentially transforming Hampstead into a fashionable spa retreat. Evidence of this medicinal past is referenced in a number of street names such as Well Walk and Flask Walk.

3 NORTH END WAY

Still a pub today, The Old Bull and Bush was a popular day-trip destination for East End cockneys in the late 19th and early 20th century and was celebrated in the popular music hall song, 'Down at The Old Bull and Bush'.

Leave on left: Parkhurst Road
Right: Williamson Street
Right: Camden Road
Right: Hilldrop Road
Right: Brecknock Road
Bear left: Dartmouth Park Hill
Left: Chetwynd Road
Cross: Highgate Road
Forward: Gordon House Road
Forward: Mansfield Road
Forward: Fleet Road
Forward: South End Green
Forward: South End Road
Forward: East Heath Road
Right: Whitestone Pond
Forward: Heath Street
Comply: Roundabout
Leave by: North End Way
Forward: North End Road
Golders Green station on right

1

N

1. Holloway Prison

North End Way
3. The Old Bull and Bush, North End Way
2. Hampstead Heath

BREAKSPEARS ROAD SE4 → LIMEHARBOUR E14

The Docks — The main highlight on this run is Greenwich, a popular destination which has a distinct seaside feel. The Isle of Dogs has quite a unique aura about it too as it's on a peninsula dominated by the soaring, glass skyscrapers of Canary Wharf.

After leaving Brockley we enter Deptford (meaning 'deep ford'), which was once home to a naval dockyard founded by Henry VIII. It was from here that Sir Francis Drake began and ended his circumnavigation of the globe.

The run then takes us through central Greenwich; an old term meaning 'green port'.

College Approach refers to the Old Royal Naval College which once trained officers. It stands on the site of the former Greenwich Palace; birthplace of Henry VIII.

King William Walk is named after a statue of William IV, which can be found at its southern end. This was London's first statue made of granite and it originally stood near London Bridge before being moved to the park in 1935. William himself served in the Royal Navy, earning him the nickname 'Sailor King'.

On Romney Road stands the impressive National Maritime Museum, the largest of its kind in the world, holding over 2.5 million items. One of its most treasured possessions is the uniform worn by Admiral Nelson when he was fatally wounded at the Battle of Trafalgar – so it's apt that Trafalgar Road comes next.

The docks here have mostly been filled in, although it's useful to remember their presence when learning surrounding streets such as Cotton Street, Clove Crescent, Saffron Avenue and Rosemary Drive, which refer to goods once shipped and stored here.

Once we reach Preston's Road we're on the Isle of Dogs, crossing the Blue Bridge which can be raised to let vessels into the former West India Docks. When the docks were still active this function occurred a lot more frequently and would cause traffic to build up – locals referred to such jams as 'Bridgers'.

1 GREENWICH HIGH ROAD

The handsome Greenwich station opened in 1840 and is one of the oldest station buildings in the world to remain in its original form. The line connecting it to London Bridge is entirely elevated, built upon a long, brick viaduct. In the railway's earliest days, some of the viaduct's arches had residences incorporated into them, although today you would be far more likely to find a scrap dealer or mechanic.

2 KING WILLIAM WALK

Taking its name from the Robert Burns poem 'Tam O'Shanter', the *Cutty Sark* was built in Dumbarton, Scotland in 1869 as a 'tea clipper' and was famed for the record-breaking speed at which she could whisk cargoes between China and England. The *Cutty Sark* has been in dry dock at Greenwich since the 1950s and is now surrounded by an innovative, glass visitor centre. During renovation, two fires broke out on board but miraculously no serious damage occurred.

3 ROMNEY ROAD

Beside the National Maritime Museum is Queen's House, designed by Inigo Jones in 1616 as England's first classical building. It is especially famed for its spiralled 'Tulip Stairs' and holds an impressive art collection including works by Hogarth, Reynolds and Turner.

4 COTTON STREET

On the eastern side of Cotton Street you would've once seen blocks of housing flanked by a long concrete structure that resembled the Berlin Wall. This was the Robin Hood Gardens Estate. Designed in the late 1960s by husband and wife team Alison and Peter Smithson, the estate long divided Londoners: some wished to see it preserved while others wanted it reduced to rubble. In the summer of 2017 the latter camp won when bulldozers moved in.

Leave by: Ashby Road
Right: Wickham Road
Forward: Friendly Street
Left: Brookmill Road
Right: Deptford Bridge
Left: Greenwich High Road
Bear left: Greenwich Church Street
Right: College Approach
Right: King William Walk
Left: Romney Road
Forward: Trafalgar Road
Left: Blackwall Lane
Left: Slip Road
Bear right: Blackwall Tunnel Southern Approach

1 Greenwich High Road

2 King William Walk

Romney Road

3

National Maritime Museum

2. The Cutty Sark

Forward: Blackwall Tunnel
Forward: Blackwall Tunnel Northern Approach
Bear left: East India Dock Slip Road
Left: East India Dock Road
Left: Cotton Street
Comply: Roundabout
Leave by: Preston's Road
Forward: Blue Bridge
Forward: Manchester Road
Comply: Roundabout
Leave by: Marsh Wall
Limeharbour on left

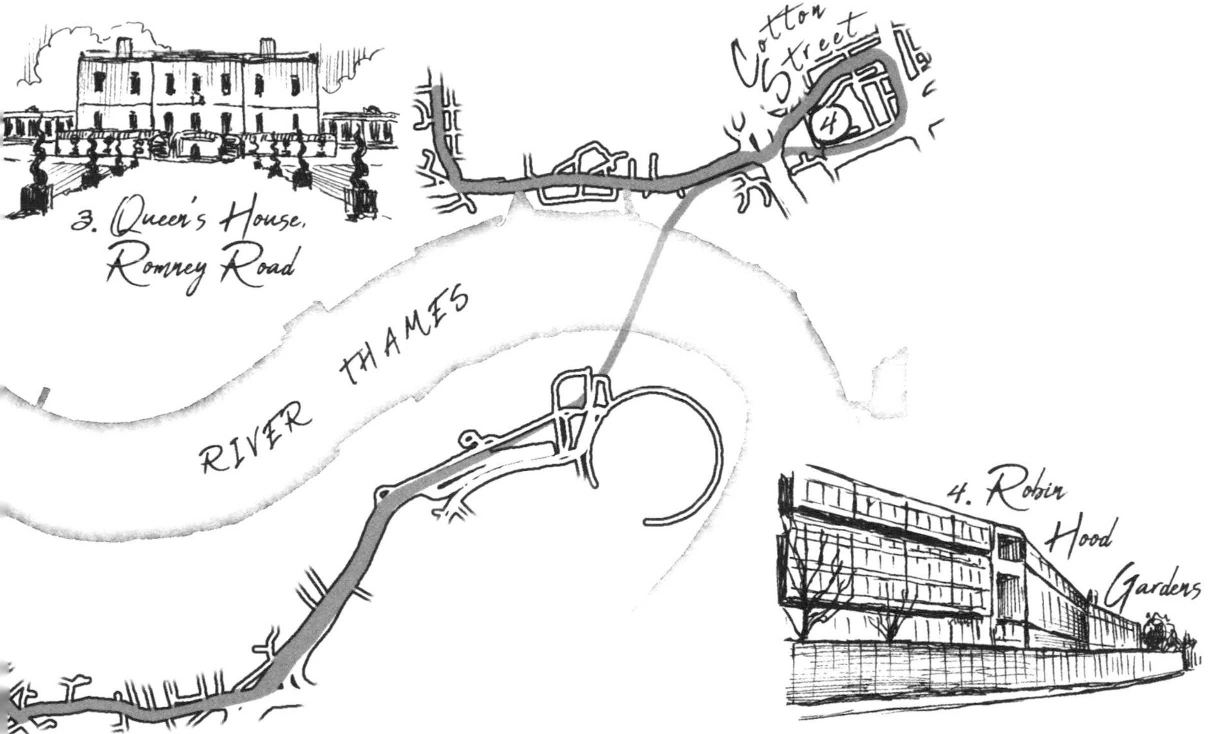

CABOT SQUARE E14 → VALLANCE ROAD E1

Rags to Riches — Surrounded by financial institutions, Cabot Square is a popular place for cabbies to seek a fare. The area around Vallance Road is also a popular cabbie haunt due to the large concentration of taxi depots dotted around the area, mainly beneath the rumbling railway arches.

Although this run begins amidst the glistening towers of Canary Wharf, it passes through areas of the East End which historically have been subject to great poverty, crime and hardship.

Many dockers and their families used to live on the aptly named Commercial Road. The work was dangerous, poorly paid and irregular and in 1889 this resulted in the Great London Dock Strike, led by Ben Tillett. 130,000 came out in support, despite the financial pressures which ensued.

Across Commercial Road, the wives of dockers strung a large banner which read:

Our husbands are on strike; for the wives it is not honey
And we all think it is right not to pay the landlord's money,
Everyone is on strike, so landlords do not be offended;
The rent that's due we'll pay you when the strike is ended.

The dockers were supported by generous donations from colleagues in Australia and after five weeks the strike ended with employers agreeing to demands.

Once on Whitechapel Road one of the first buildings we see is the infamous Blind Beggar pub. It was here in March 1966 that gangster Ronnie Kray shot dead George Cornell, a rival from the Richardson Gang. Ronnie and his twin brother Reggie grew up around the corner on Vallance Road (this run's final destination) and were outraged that Cornell had the audacity to drink on their turf.

259 Whitechapel Road is now an unassuming shop, but it was here in the 1880s that Joseph Merrick, the Elephant Man, was exhibited in a freak show.

After time spent working in Belgium where he was robbed of his life savings, Joseph returned to Whitechapel and spent his final years in the Royal London Hospital, which stands opposite. Today, the hospital contains a small museum, in which items related to Joseph's life, including his iconic hat and mask, can be viewed.

Off Vallance Road is Durward Street. This was once called Buck's Row which, in 1888, was the site of Jack the Ripper's first murder, that of Mary Ann Nichols.

It was also on Vallance Road in March 1945 that the very last V2 rocket to strike London landed. It hit Hughes Mansions where 134 people perished, 120 of whom were Jewish.

1 COMMERCIAL ROAD

The lavish Troxy Cinema first opened in September 1933 with a screening of *King Kong*. One of its earliest managers was Maurice Cheepen, a Jewish immigrant who'd escaped Nazi Germany. He kept the cinema running throughout the war, often rallying audiences to sing as bombs pounded outside. The cinema closed in 1960 with a showing of *The Siege of Sidney Street*, a film based on a real-life event that occurred close by in 1911. Thankfully the cinema has since reopened and is now restored to its former glory. Further up is the George Tavern. An inn has existed on this site for some 700 years and the present building is now an arts and music venue. The pub once had a club attached which boasted a light-up disco floor, and it was here in 1995 that Pulp filmed the video for 'Common People'.

2 VALLANCE ROAD

The triangular building on the corner of Buxton Street is the former Dew Drop Inn which was established by charity worker Mary Hughes in 1926. At the time this area was shockingly poor and Mary did a great deal to help those in poverty; as one visitor wrote in the 1930s, 'Her food is bread, cheese and tea – and if someone else is hungry, she doesn't eat at all.' Mary died in 1941 and is now commemorated at the site by a blue plaque that fittingly describes her as a 'Friend of all in need'.

Leave by: West India Avenue
Comply: Westferry Circus
Leave by: Westferry Road
Left: Limehouse Link
Right: Butcher Row
Left: Commercial Road
Right: Sidney Street
Left: Whitechapel Road
Vallance Road on right

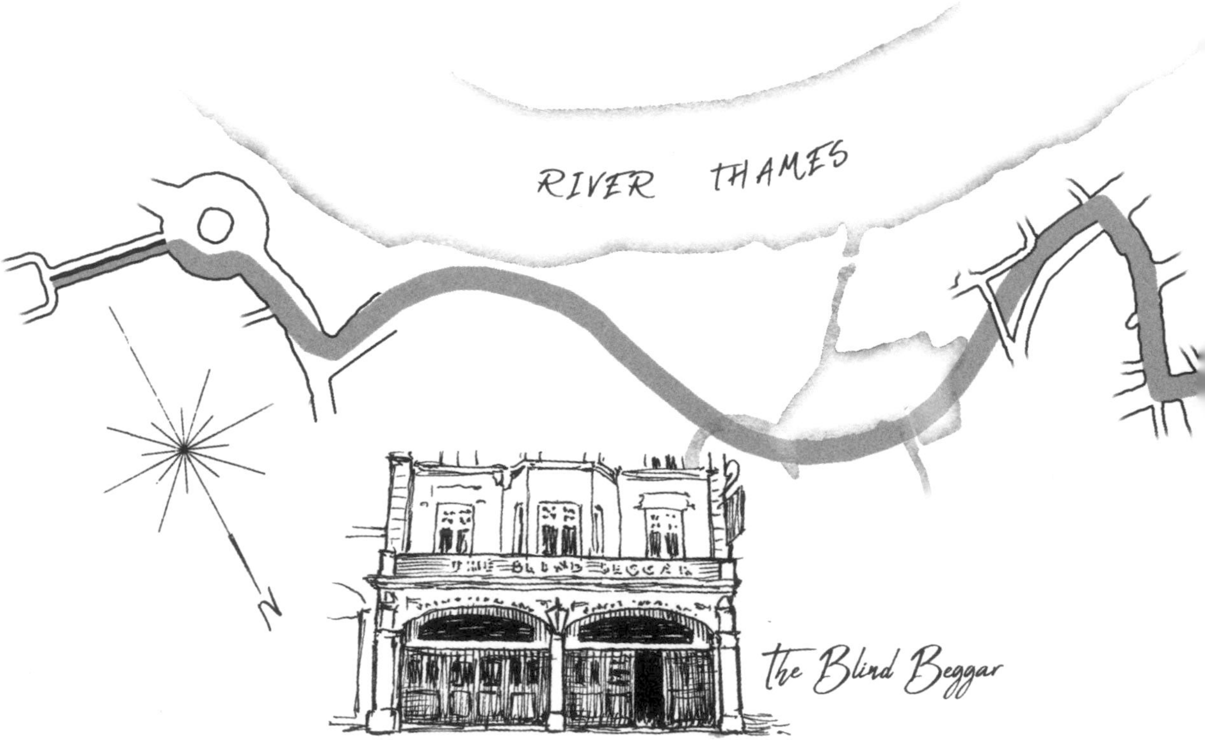

RIVER THAMES

The Blind Beggar

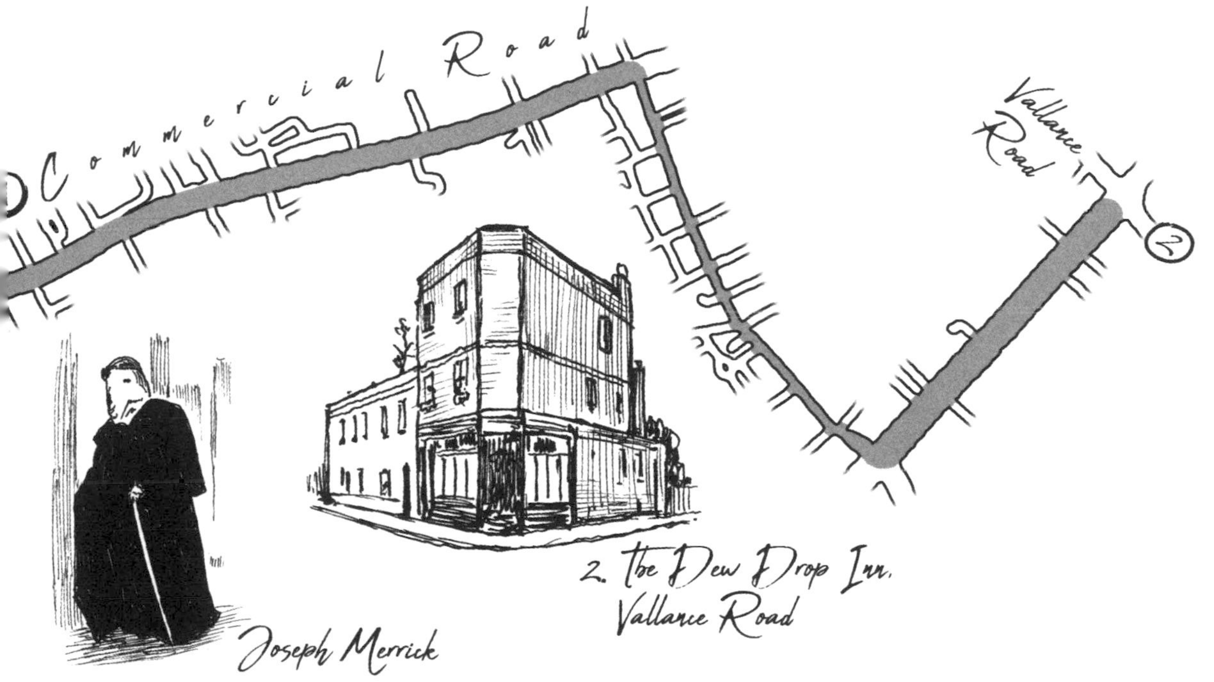
Commercial Road
Vallance Road
2
2. The Dew Drop Inn, Vallance Road
Joseph Merrick

RUNS USING MEMORY CHAMPION TECHNIQUES

Memory champions are mental athletes capable of recalling anything from the order of a deck of shuffled cards to bewildering strings of binary digits: they compete all over the world to outdo each other reciting pi and the like.

The techniques which these masters of recollection use to hone their minds can be traced back many centuries. The earliest recorded example, which occurred in Ancient Greece, makes for an interesting tale.

In the 5th century BC, Simonides of Ceos, a poet and contemporary of Socrates, was invited to give a recitation of his work at a banquet thrown by Scopas of Thessaly. Simonides devoted much of his composition to glorifying his host but, as was customary, also dedicated lines to the gods – in this case, Castor and Pollux, twin sons of Zeus.

Scopas, however, was a notorious cheapskate and after hearing the composition he belittled Simonides in front of his guests, informing him that he would be deducting half the fee, paying only for the lines that had been penned in his honour. If, Simonides was told, he wished to receive the remainder of the money, then it was up to the gods to settle the balance. (I know how Simonides must've felt; I've had a few passengers like that in the cab.)

During the dinner which followed, fate intervened when Simonides was informed there were two young men outside enquiring after him.

But once outside the figures were nowhere to be seen . . . and as the poet looked around, the roof of the building he'd been in only moments before collapsed, killing all inside. According to legend, the two mysterious figures who'd lured Simonides from the building were Castor and Pollux themselves, who saved the poet's life as a means of paying their half of the fee.

When recovered, the corpses were so maimed it was impossible to put names to the victims. This is where Simonides stepped in; by associating specific imagery with each guest, he was able to recall the precise order in which each had been sitting, thus enabling the bodies to be granted proper burials.

When this 'room method' was later popularised by the Roman lawyer Cicero, it gained the name by which memory champions now know it – the 'Method of Loci' (*loci* being Latin for 'locations'). As the process involves envisioning certain objects as they appear along a set line, it is also called the 'Journey Method'.

A popular example of this technique is to apply it to a shopping list. Say we wish to buy:

Apples
Bread
Milk
Soap
Kitchen roll

We now imagine a short journey to the supermarket through a setting you know well or can envision clearly linking your groceries to specific waypoints – ideally with a surreal bent to make each item more memorable.

For instance:

As you open the front door, a bucket of apples perched on top tips, sending the fruit crashing over you.

You walk up the path rubbing your head and notice birds pecking at breadcrumbs on the lawn.

Opening the gate, you see the milkman approach – but he slips on a bar of soap, sending his bottles crashing everywhere. You bend down to help him soak up the mess with some kitchen roll.

A more intricate version of the Method of Loci is the 'Memory Palace', made famous in recent years thanks to the BBC adaptation, *Sherlock*.

This involves devising a building or area within your mind and placing objects representing the aspects you wish to recall throughout, associating each item with a certain feature or piece of furniture. Memory Palaces can grow to contain many rooms.

The examples I've created for the following runs provide something of an insight into my own mind, so please feel free to be creative and adapt them, as these methods work best when they represent places that are personal to you.

FITZJOHN'S AVENUE NW3 → FITZHARDINGE STREET W1

After departing leafy Fitzjohn's Avenue – once described by *Harper's Magazine* as being 'one of the noblest streets in the world' – this run heads through Swiss Cottage towards Avenue Road, a street dominated by grand houses, some of which are diplomatic residences marked by flags flying outside.

Once through Regent's Park it's on to Baker Street, one of London's most famous roads.

Named after Sir Edward Baker who helped develop the area in the 18th century, Baker Street is now of course associated with Sherlock Holmes. A museum dedicated to Sir Arthur Conan Doyle's legendary character occupies the famous 221B and presents the apartment as it would've appeared in the Victorian era.

221B BAKER STREET

Because this run includes Baker Street, an apt memory palace to use is its most famous fictional address, home of a man whose extraordinary powers of memory are legendary: Sherlock Holmes' apartment at 221B.

On the wall of the lobby are several framed certificates (1). Below them is a bookcase where a guide to New York City sticks out, the cover of which is illustrated with an image of Park Avenue (2). A train ticket to Macclesfield is tucked inside as a bookmark (3).

We then enter the next room; Sherlock's office.

In an apparent fit of temper, a compass has been jabbed onto the edge of his desk (4). At the other end of the desk is a framed photo of acclaimed American lawyer Clarence Darrow, who is pictured painting his garden gate (5). Sherlock can't talk yet as he's busy eating a sandwich and his mouth is stuffed full of bread (6).

1. College Crescent
2. Avenue Road
3. Macclesfield Bridge
4. Outer Circle
5. Clarence Gate
6. Baker Street

1 FITZJOHN'S AVENUE

On the corner of Fitzjohn's Avenue and Belsize Lane is the Tavistock Centre, which was established in 1920 to treat soldiers suffering from shell shock. It subsequently went on to pioneer new ways of examining mental illness. Outside the clinic is a statue of Sigmund Freud who lived and died on nearby Maresfield Gardens after fleeing the Nazis in 1938. His former home is now a museum where his famous analysis couch can be seen.

2 OUTER CIRCLE

Set back from the north-western perimeter of Regent's Park is the heavily guarded Winfield House, the official residence of the US ambassador, which has hosted numerous Presidents over the years. The present mansion was built by the American heiress Barbara Hutton in the 1930s after the previous building was gutted by fire. In 1955 Hutton decided to bequeath the grand home to her country, selling it to the US government for the nominal fee of $1. Also on the Outer Circle is the Regent's Park Mosque (also known as the Central London Mosque) with its distinctive gold dome and minaret. The mosque was first suggested by Muslim convert Lord Headley, and in 1940, Sir Winston Churchill authorised a site in Regent's Park to be gifted to Britain's Muslim community. It was not until the late 1970s, however, that the mosque finally opened.

3 BAKER STREET

In 1971 a group of bank robbers rented a leather goods shop called Le Sac at 169 Baker Street. From there they succeeded in digging a tunnel beneath the adjoining shop (now a restaurant) into the basement of Lloyds Bank on the corner of Marylebone Road. Once in, the crooks stole over 200 safety deposit boxes and allegedly left a note on the wall saying, 'Let's see how Sherlock Holmes solves this one.' Although the thieves were eventually apprehended, reports on the case remain sketchy, leading many to theorise that the stolen boxes contained highly sensitive information. Baker Street is also home to London Transport's Lost Property Office which, over the years, has taken in many bizarre items including a stuffed puffer fish, a judge's wig and an urn of cremated ashes.

Leave by forward: College Crescent
Bear left: Avenue Road
Forward: Macclesfield Bridge
Right: Outer Circle
Right: Clarence Gate
Forward: Baker Street
Cross: Marylebone Road
Forward: Baker Street continued
Fitzhardinge Street on left

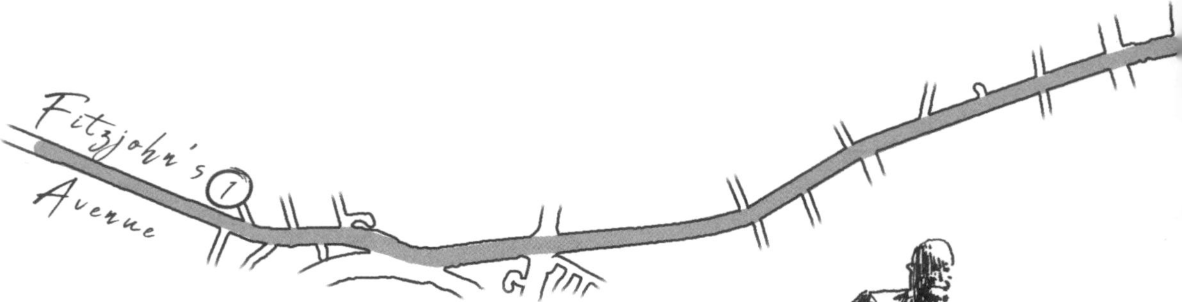

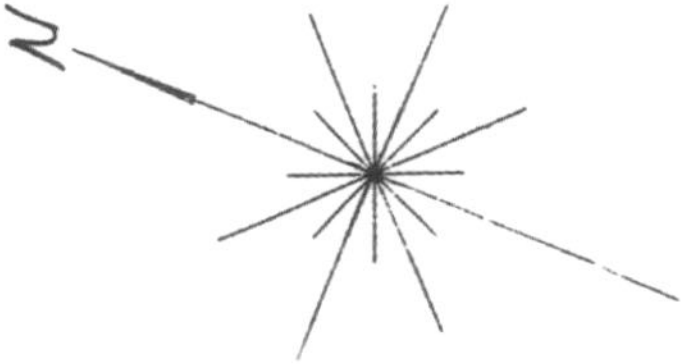

Fitzjohn's Avenue

1. Statue of Sigmund Freud, Fitzjohn's Avenue

2. Regent's Park Mosque, Outer Circle

3. London Transport Lost Property Office, Baker Street

BELGRAVE SQUARE SW1 → BOUVERIE STREET EC4

After swinging around the sweeping curve of Grosvenor Crescent this run plunges into the chaos that is Hyde Park Corner before rewarding us with a trip through what many would consider to be 'classic' London.

This includes iconic sites such as Buckingham Palace and Trafalgar Square with its towering monument to Admiral Lord Nelson – be sure to look out for his 'fleet', a series of model ships topping the lampposts along The Mall.

The run then heads along the Strand, Aldwych, past the gothic Royal Courts of Justice and on to Fleet Street which was the traditional home of Britain's newspaper industry until the 1980s.

A PALACE GARDEN PARTY

This run passes a very real palace – Buckingham Palace – so we can use it as a backdrop for our memorisation and imagine we're attending one of its famous summer garden parties and mingling with some historical figures.

We begin in the conservatory, where the Earl of Grosvenor is being put in his place (1) by the Duke of Wellington (2), bragging about his new home on the edge of Hyde Park (3).

We then enter the garden, walking down a small hill to where Queen Victoria is examining a copy of the American Constitution (4) with King Charles (5).

Further along, behind a hedge, Admiral Lord Nelson (6) is a little worse for wear and is propping himself up against a cannon (7).

We then head for the main stage where Bryan Ferry is singing his hit 'Do the Strand' (8), which some may consider old (9) but is still a great London tune.

In a nook by the stage, sitting alone at a table and toying rather worryingly with his cutlery is Sweeney Todd, the 'Demon Barber of Fleet Street' (10).

1. Grosvenor Place
2. Duke of Wellington Place
3. Hyde Park Corner
4. Constitution Hill and Queen Victoria Memorial
5. King Charles Island
6. Trafalgar Square
7. Duncannon Street
8. The Strand
9. Aldwych
10. Fleet Street

1 HYDE PARK CORNER

On the north side of Hyde Park Corner stands Apsley House, also known rather exclusively as 'Number One London', so called because it stood at the very edge of the city when built in the 1770s. Its most famous resident was the Duke of Wellington who, despite his celebrated victory at the Battle of Waterloo, was forced to install iron shutters after being targeted by disgruntled rioters, thus earning him the nickname 'The Iron Duke'.

2 CONSTITUTION HILL

At the western end of Constitution Hill stand the Commonwealth Memorial Gates dedicated to troops from the Indian subcontinent, Africa and the Caribbean who died fighting in both world wars. Sir Robert Peel – famous for founding Britain's first modern police force – was killed after a riding accident on Constitution Hill, and it was also on this road that several, separate assassination attempts were made on Queen Victoria.

3 QUEEN VICTORIA MEMORIAL

Buckingham Palace was built in the early 18th century for the Duke of Buckingham and passed to the royal family when it was purchased by King George III. But it was not until the reign of Queen Victoria that it became a fully functional royal residence. Today the palace is the royal family's official HQ. It employs 800 people and contains 775 rooms. If you wish to know whether or not the monarch is at home, the flag to look for is the Royal Standard (as opposed to the Union Flag) which is red, blue and gold.

4 ADMIRALTY ARCH

Built as a part of a wider memorial to Queen Victoria following her death in 1901, there are in fact three arches here. The two outer ones are used for squeezing traffic through while the central arch is gated and used only on ceremonial occasions. An apartment within the arch was once the official residence of the First Sea Lord (head of the Royal Navy), although the building is now being transformed into a luxury hotel. Attached to the wall of the northernmost arch you'll find one of the 'London Noses', a humorous, life-sized beak that was installed by artist Rick Buckley in the 1990s.

Leave by: Grosvenor Crescent
Left: Grosvenor Place
Comply: Hyde Park Corner

Leave by: Duke of Wellington Place
Left: Constitution Hill
Comply: Queen Victoria Memorial

Leave by: The Mall
Forward: Admiralty Arch
Comply: King Charles Island
Leave by: Trafalgar Square east side

Right: Duncannon Street
Bear left: The Strand
Forward: Aldwych
Forward: The Strand continued
Forward: Fleet Street
Bouverie Street on right

Hyde Park Corner

1

2

N

Queen Victoria Memorial

3

1. Apsley House, Hyde Park Corner

3. Buckingha

4
Admiralty Arch
Palace
2. Constitution Hill

PARSONS GREEN STATION SW6 → SOUTH LAMBETH ROAD SW8

Parsons Green station to South Lambeth Road is a run that helps understand the quirks of London's geography: even though the route necessitates crossing the Thames, the two points lie roughly parallel, thus demonstrating that the capital's north/south divide can often be ambiguous.

BATTERSEA POWER STATION

Although Battersea Power Station is currently being transformed into a modern development, I think its former, decaying state would make a rather atmospheric mind palace.

In the main hall, a church parson is inspecting a rusty piece of machinery which lies entangled among a green patch of weeds (1) on the floor of the abandoned building. We then find a derelict office where, on a crumbling wall, there's a peeling poster illustrating the Beaufort Scale (2) which Elvis Presley and a medieval monarch (3) are viewing together.

Higher up, on a rickety stairwell, sits the Prince of Wales (4) who is sharing battered fish and chips (5) with the Queen (6 – it is a palace, after all), wrapped in a soggy copy of the *Wandsworth Guardian* (7)

Around the back of the power station lies a rotting Vauxhall Velox (8). The old car's roof has been caved in by a one-ton weight (9) and out of the wrecked engine sprout nine elm trees (10).

1. Parsons Green
2. Beaufort Street
3. New King's and King's Road
4. Prince of Wales Drive
5. Battersea Bridge and Battersea Park Road
6. Queen's Circus
7. Wandsworth Road
8. Vauxhall Cross
9. Kennington Lane
10. Nine Elms Lane

1 BATTERSEA BRIDGE

The first bridge at Battersea opened in the 1770s as a toll crossing established by Earl Spencer, an ancestor of Princess Diana. Constructed from wood and consisting of many narrow arches, this early bridge was considered dangerous and many vessels collided with it during its time. The current bridge was designed in the late 19th century by Sir Joseph Bazalgette, the same engineer who saved countless lives by creating London's first sewer network.

2 PRINCE OF WALES DRIVE

Lined with grand, red brick apartments, Prince of Wales Drive runs along the southern border of Battersea Park. Laid out in the Victorian era, the park is home to a small children's zoo and the beautiful Battersea Peace Pagoda, which was gifted to the UK by the Japanese Buddhist sect Nipponzan Myohoji in the 1980s.

3 BATTERSEA PARK ROAD

Originally founded in Holloway by Mary Tealby, Battersea Dogs and Cats Home has been in the area since 1871. In its time, it's cared for over 3 million homeless animals. Battersea Park Road is dominated by the monolithic Battersea Power Station. When it first opened in the 1930s the plant was half the size – the second section was added in the 1950s, giving the station its famous symmetry. The plant, which famously featured on the cover of Pink Floyd's 1977 album, *Animals*, was decommissioned in 1983 and remained derelict for decades. It is now being redeveloped into offices, restaurants and apartments.

4 NINE ELMS LANE

The huge New Covent Garden Market moved here in 1974 after its former site on the cobbles of Old Covent Garden became impractical. Once again, however, London is changing and a glossy new development means this old stalwart has had to shift yet again. Fortunately not so far this time; it can now be found a little further along towards Battersea Park Road. Another institution to make Nine Elms Lane its second London home is the American Embassy, which for many years was based in Grosvenor Square. The new embassy is an ultra-secure cube-shaped building surrounded by a moat.

Leave on right: Parsons Green Lane
Forward: Parsons Green
Left: New King's Road
Forward: King's Road
Right: Beaufort Street
Forward: Battersea Bridge
Forward: Battersea Bridge Road
Left: Prince of Wales Drive
Comply: Queen's Circus
Leave by: Prince of Wales Drive continued
Left: Battersea Park Road
Forward: Nine Elms Lane
Left: Wandsworth Road
Forward: Vauxhall Cross
Right: Kennington Lane
South Lambeth Road on right

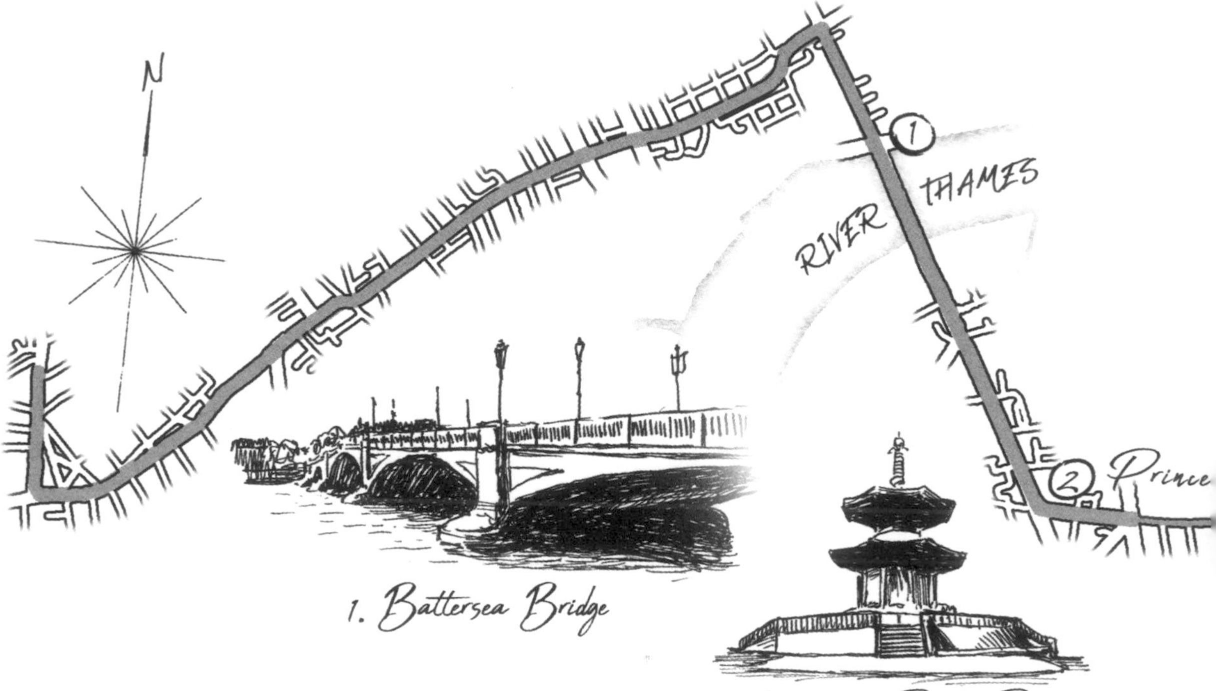

1. Battersea Bridge

2. Battersea Peace Pagoda

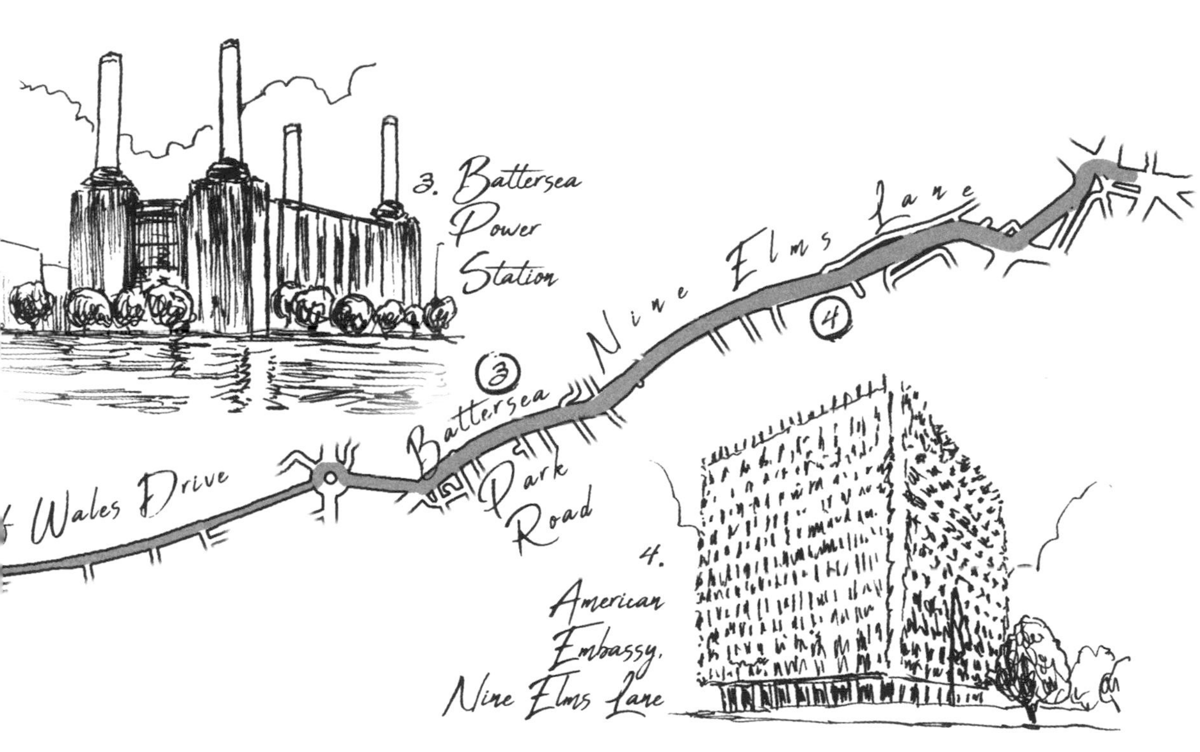
3. Battersea Power Station
Nine Elms Lane
Battersea Park Road
Wales Drive
4. American Embassy, Nine Elms Lane

RAVENSCOURT PARK W6 → GWENDOLEN AVENUE SW15

Hammersmith Broadway has long been a major west London hub. In the 18th century it was an important coach stop and a number of taverns were based here to accommodate travellers, including The Swan, which still exists in rebuilt form.

The Broadway was widened at the turn of the 20th century to accommodate electric trams and is now dominated by the looming Hammersmith Flyover, which opened in 1961.

After crossing Hammersmith Bridge the run heads down through Barnes (an area that on the map resembles a thumb sticking up in the Thames thanks to a long meander in the river) via the Gallic-sounding Castlenau, which owes its name to Major Charles Lestock Boileau, a Huguenot refugee who came to live here – his old family home in southern France was called Castlenau de la Garde.

THE KING'S ORDEAL

This run uses the 'Method of Loci' – imagining a linear journey as opposed to a collection of rooms.

A king (1) puts on a pair of football boots (2), and jogs out of Ravenscourt Park and kicks a thorny bush (3). This disturbs a swarm of bees (4), which chase him towards Hammersmith Broadway.

Once in Hammersmith, the King evades the bees by jumping into a butter churn (5). He is pulled out by Queen Caroline and country singer Garth Brooks (6).

After his ordeal the King crosses Hammersmith Bridge (8) and heads home to his castle (7).

On the way he stubs his toe on a large rock (8) that has dropped off a watermill and rolled downhill (9). The rock must have been lying there for some time because it's bone dry (10).

1. King Street
2. Studland Street
3. Glenthorne Road
4. Beadon Road
5. Butterwick
6. Talgarth Road and Queen Caroline Street
7. Castlenau

8. Rocks Lane
9. Mill Hill Road
10. Dryburgh Road

1 TALGARTH ROAD

The unusual ship-shaped office block on Talgarth Road is called The Ark. It opened in 1992 and has over 4,000 windows. Its curves are a result of its location – architect Ralph Erskine had to find a way of shoehorning the building into a confined space between the Hammersmith Flyover and a set of railway lines.

2 QUEEN CAROLINE STREET

Known by various names over the years, the Hammersmith Apollo opened as a 3,500-seat cinema in 1932 and is now a major venue specialising in music and comedy. In 1958 Buddy Holly performed his last ever UK concert here, and in July 1973 David Bowie shocked fans, and fellow band members, with the sudden announcement that he was retiring his popular Ziggy Stardust character.

3 HAMMERSMITH BRIDGE

This ornate suspension bridge first opened in the 1820s but was rebuilt towards the end of the 19th century over fears it was too weak. In 1939 the IRA attempted to blow the bridge up but luckily a brave passerby spotted the bomb and hurled it into the water. A second attempt in 1996 also failed when two Semtex devices failed to detonate. A third attempt did succeed in 2000. Fortunately nobody was injured although the bridge required extensive repairs and traffic chaos ensued.

4 CASTLENAU

The London Wetland Centre is a nature reserve which opened in 2000 upon land formerly occupied by a set of reservoirs. The centre is now home to an impressive array of wildlife including kingfishers, water voles and all manner of other flora and fauna.

5 UPPER RICHMOND ROAD

The curiously-named Arab Boy pub on Upper Richmond Road is named in honour of a young man called Yussef Sirrie who was the pub's landlord during the Victorian era. Yussef came to Britain as a boy in the 1840s with the pub's developer Henry Scarth who is said to have saved him from being sold into slavery.

Leave on left: King Street
Left: Studland Street
Right: Glenthorne Road
Right: Beadon Road
Forward: Hammersmith Broadway
Right: Butterwick
Right: Talgarth Road
Right: Queen Caroline Street
Left: Hammersmith Bridge Road
Forward: Hammersmith Bridge
Forward: Castlenau
Forward: Rocks Lane
Left: Mill Hill Road
Comply: Roundabout
Leave by: Lower Richmond Road
Right: Erpingham Road
Bear Left: Dryburgh Road
Left: Upper Richmond Road
Gwendolen Avenue on right

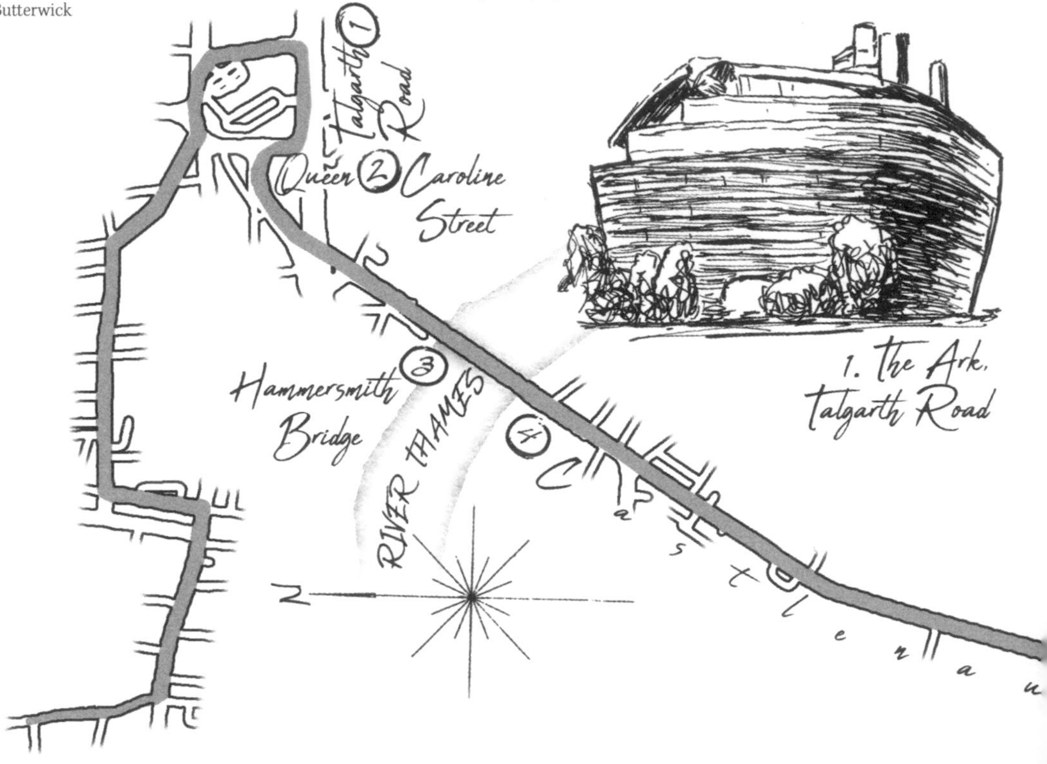

Talgarth Road ①
Queen ② Caroline Street
Hammersmith ③ Bridge
RIVER THAMES
④ Castlenau
N

1. The Ark, Talgarth Road

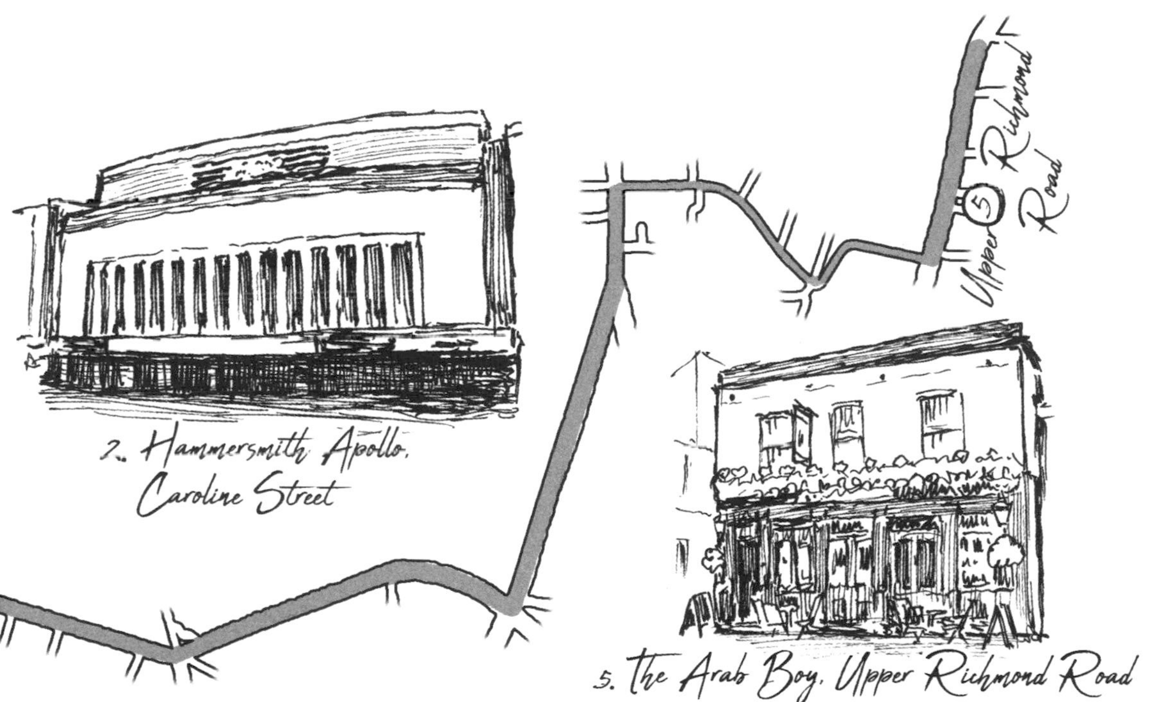
Upper Richmond Road
5
2. Hammersmith Apollo, Caroline Street
5. The Arab Boy, Upper Richmond Road

THE RITZ W1 → BATTERSEA PARK STATION SW8

Although The Ritz famously adorns Piccadilly, the main pick-up and drop-off point for taxis is around the corner on Arlington Street.

Further along on Piccadilly's south side is a curious, tall shelf known as the Porter's Rest. This was originally installed by the Victorians as a spot where servants could temporarily ease their heavy burdens. Sadly though, this one's a replica – Westminster Council controversially removed the original in 2015.

As with many runs this route has to contend with the hair-raising Hyde Park Corner. Grosvenor Place and Buckingham Palace Road are just as fraught, thrumming with long-distance coaches heading to or from Victoria Coach station. It's not until the run reaches Ebury Bridge Road that the pace calms down.

A ROOM WITH THE DUKE

As this run begins at one of the world's most famous and palatial hotels, I think it's only fair we have a peek inside one of its suites for our memory palace.

The Duke of Wellington (1) is staying here and he stands before a gilded mirror adjusting his pointy 'piccadill' collar (2).

He has just arrived in London and has a busy schedule – on the marble dressing table are tickets for functions at the Grosvenor House Hotel (3) and a garden party at Buckingham Palace (4).

An empty vase that he purchased on eBay (5) lies on the four-poster bed. The Duke is planning to fill it with stems from the Chelsea Flower Show (6), which he will then present as a gift to the Queen before he leaves town (7).

1. Duke of Wellington Place
2. Piccadilly
3. Grosvenor Place and Lower Grosvenor Place
4. Buckingham Palace Road
5. Ebury Bridge Road
6. Chelsea Bridge Road
7. Queenstown Road and Queen's Circus

1 ARLINGTON STREET

The five-star Ritz Hotel is named after its founder, Swiss-born César Ritz who opened it in 1906. Over the years the hotel's opulent rooms have hosted all manner of stars and royalty including Anna Pavlova, Dwight Eisenhower, Noël Coward and Tallulah Bankhead, who famously drank a champagne cocktail out of her shoe here in 1951. The Ritz wasn't the first hotel on this site. That accolade goes to the Walsingham House Hotel which, although swanky too, was demolished in 1904 after standing for just 17 years.

2 DUKE OF WELLINGTON PLACE

The Wellington Arch in the middle of the Hyde Park Corner junction dates back to 1828 and was originally topped by a huge statue of the Duke of Wellington mounted upon his horse, Copenhagen. The statue was deemed too cumbersome, however, and was eventually moved to Aldershot where it can still be seen today.

3 CHELSEA BRIDGE ROAD

On the southern side of Chelsea Bridge Road are Ranelagh Gardens, which are part of the Royal Hospital and the location of the annual Chelsea Royal Flower Show. They were originally a popular pleasure garden, the centrepiece of which was the Rotunda, a vast circular hall that hosted numerous entertainments. A view of the Rotunda's interior, painted by Canaletto in 1754, can be seen in the National Gallery.

4 CHELSEA BRIDGE

The first bridge here was originally named Victoria Bridge but as the structure was considered unstable this was changed to Chelsea Bridge to avoid any adverse connection with the Queen in the event of a collapse. During construction, a large hoard of Celtic and Roman artefacts was discovered, leading some historians to summarise that this was the point where Julius Caesar crossed the Thames on his ill-fated invasion of 54 BC. The most notable item uncovered was the stunning Battersea Shield, which is now in The British Museum.

Leave on left: Arlington Street
Left: Piccadilly
Left: Duke of Wellington Place
Left: Grosvenor Place
Left: Lower Grosvenor Place
Right: Buckingham Palace Road
Forward: Ebury Bridge Road
Left: Chelsea Bridge Road
Forward: Chelsea Bridge
Forward: Queenstown Road
Comply: Queen's Circus
Leave by: Queenstown Road continued
Left: Battersea Park Road
Battersea Park station on left

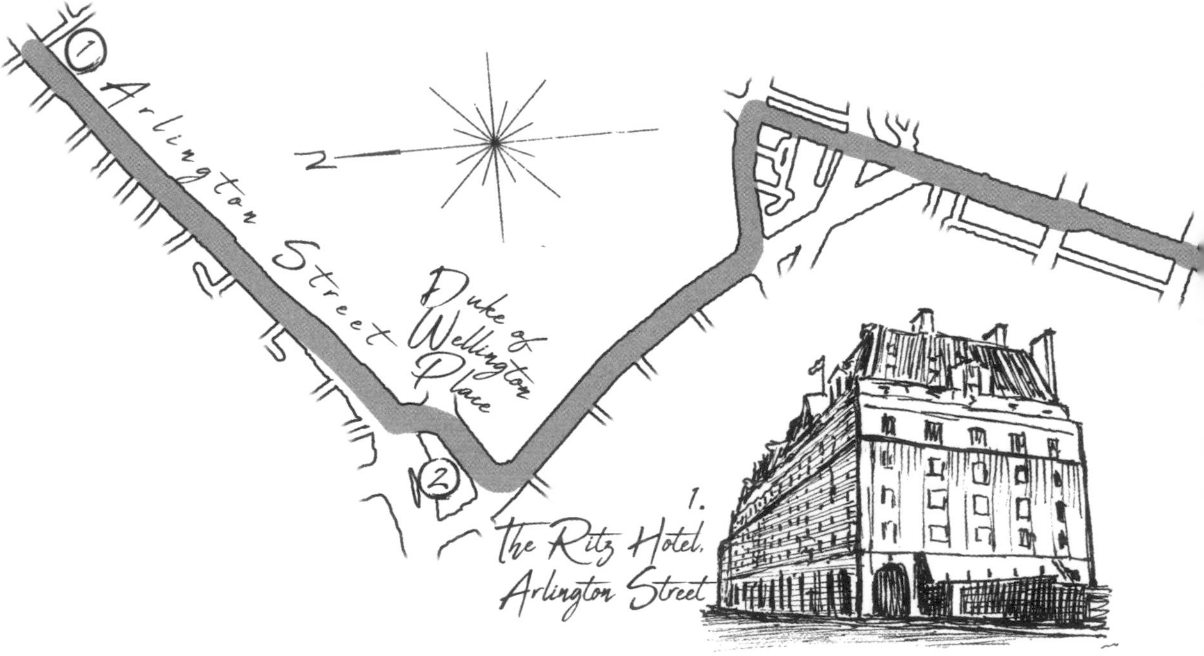

Arlington Street

Duke of Wellington Place

1. The Ritz Hotel, Arlington Street

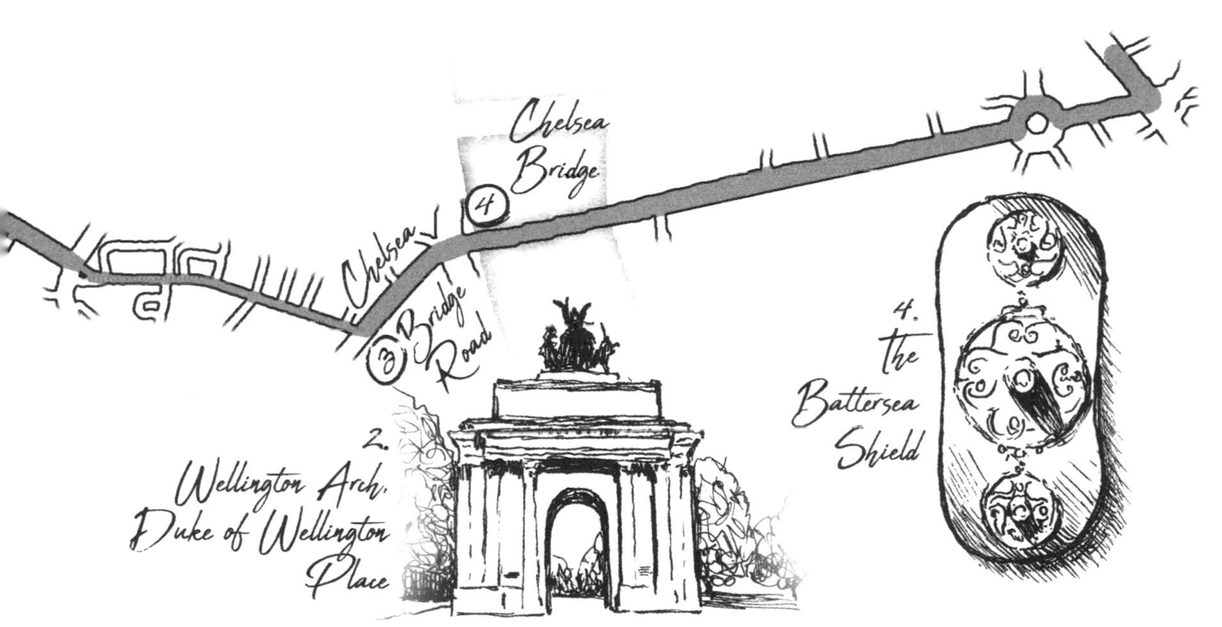
Chelsea Bridge
4
Chelsea
3
Bridge Road
2.
Wellington Arch,
Duke of Wellington Place
4.
The Battersea Shield

SAWLEY ROAD W12 → WARRINGTON CRESCENT W9

This run commences in White City, an area that takes its name from the numerous structures – such as pavilions, art centres and faux palaces – that were clad in white stucco for the 1908 Franco-British Exhibition.

In the same year, the exhibition grounds were hastily improvised as a park for the Olympic Games when the intended hosts, Rome, were forced to cancel. The site is now covered by the 1930s White City Estate whose roads – such as Australia Road, India Way and Commonwealth Avenue – hint at its international past.

The end point, Warrington Crescent, lies in an area many Knowledge students find tricky at first due to the disorientating road layout.

EXPLORING TRELLICK TOWER

This run passes Trellick Tower, a classic building in the brutalist style that can be employed as an interesting example of the Loci Method.

As we enter the ground floor lobby we have to duck to avoid a carpenter (1) who is carrying out repair work on the door frame.

Once inside we meet Nelson Mandela (2), waiting for the lift to arrive. When it does, the doors slide open and someone dressed as Father Christmas (3) steps out.

We take the lift up to the top. On a balcony, Johnny Cash is strumming his guitar (4).

A number of doors line the corridor and we peek through the keyhole of each one. In the first, a priest is pacing around reciting the 'Gospel of St Mark' (5). In the second, a circus performer is lying on the floor, placing heavy weights on his chest (6). In the third, a footballer is practising his goalscoring technique (7), kicking a ball against the wall.

We find the stairwell and decide to explore the roof. Up here someone keeps a pet elk (8), which is roaming among a small allotment of grass and trees (9). Towards the west, there is a great view of Harrow-on-the-Hill (10).

On the way back down, we nearly bump into Donald Sutherland (11). He didn't see us though as he's busy studying an outdated map of Taiwan (12).

1. Wood Lane
2. South Africa Road
3. North Pole Road
4. St Quintin Avenue
5. St Marks Road
6. Chesterton Road
7. Golborne Road
8. Elkstone Road
9. Great Western Road and Harrow Road
10. Woodfield Road and Woodfield Place
11. Sutherland Avenue
12. Formosa Street

1 SOUTH AFRICA ROAD

Named after its south-western entrance, Loftus Road Stadium has been home to Queens Park Rangers on and off since 1917. In 1981 this was the first ground in the English Football League to install an artificial pitch although it wasn't entirely successful, resulting in bouncy balls and painful skin burns. QPR reverted to grass at the end of the decade.

2 WOOD LANE

Between 1960 and 2013 Wood Lane was home to BBC Television Centre; a large, doughnut-shaped complex from which many famous programmes were made and broadcast including *Doctor Who* and *Monty Python's Flying Circus*. As with many London buildings, the former television centre is now being converted into luxury flats, although the new development will include a hotel, restaurants and a cinema as well as maintaining a working TV studio.

3 WARRINGTON CRESCENT

The Colonnade Hotel on the southern end of Warrington Crescent was once a maternity hospital and it was here, on 23 June 1912, that Alan Turing was born. Considered the father of modern computing, Turing was a brilliant mathematician whose work cracking the Enigma code at Bletchley Park in WWII saved countless lives. He died in 1954 aged just 42 after a suspected suicide, and a blue plaque at the hotel now commemorates him.

Leave by right: Bloemfontein Road
Left: South Africa Road
Left: Wood Lane
Right: North Pole Road
Comply: Roundabout
Leave by: St Quintin Avenue
Comply: Roundabout
Leave by: St Marks Road
Left: Chesterton Road
Forward: Golborne Road
Comply: Roundabout
Leave by: Elkstone Road
Left: Great Western Road
Right: Woodfield Road
Left: Woodfield Place
Right: Harrow Road
Left: Sutherland Avenue
Right: Shirland Road
Left: Formosa Street
Warrington Crescent on left and right

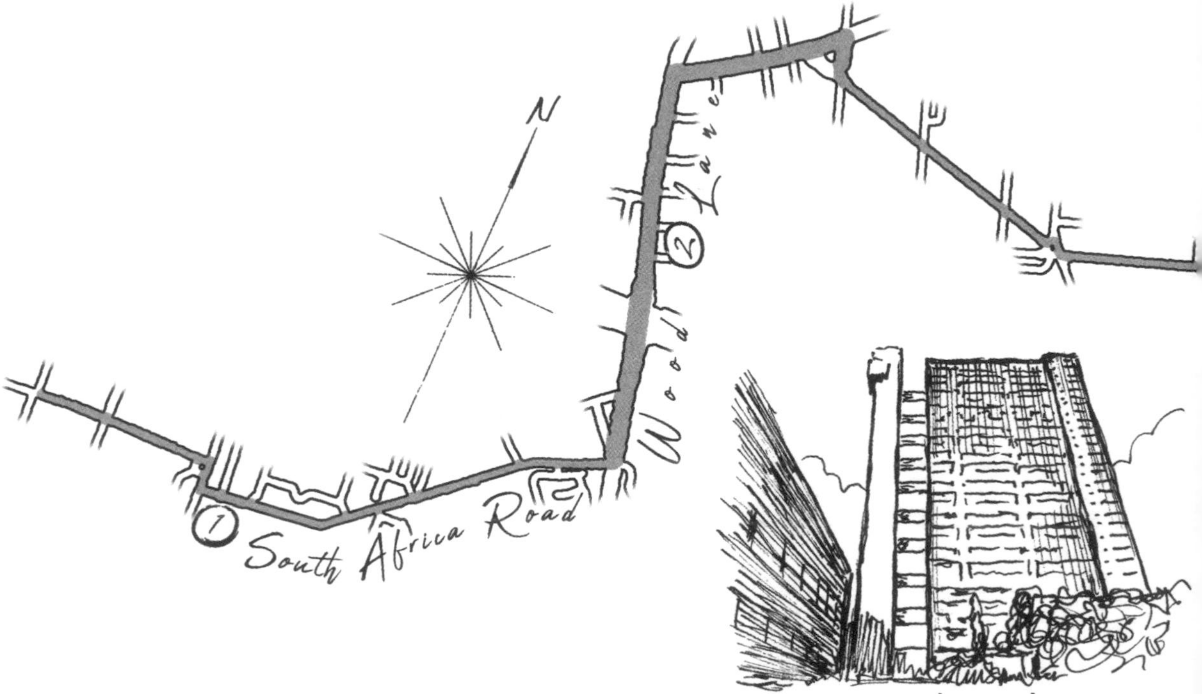

N
1
South Africa Road
2
Wood Lane
Trellick Tower

2. BBC Television Centre, Wood Lane
3 Warrington Crescent

NEW CROSS GATE STATION SE14 → CLAPHAM COMMON WEST SIDE SW4

At first glance this major south London run is relatively straightforward. There are a few twists to master, however.

First, New Cross Gate station (not to be confused with the similar sounding New Cross station on the same road) cannot be left on the right as it's in a dangerous position: there are railings outside and four lanes of traffic.

This means we must leave on the left and use a 'turn around' to point ourselves in the correct direction.

Next is Denmark Hill where you're not allowed to turn right onto Coldharbour Lane – so make sure you don't miss Orpheus Street and Daneville Road, two little streets that will beat this obstacle.

Finally there's Coldharbour Lane to Acre Lane. It may lie directly ahead, but you're not allowed to drive straight forward on to Acre Lane, meaning you must turn left onto Effra Road and then navigate Brixton's St Matthew's triangle in order to access the final leg of the run.

PROMENADE IN THE PARK

For this long run, the Loci Method is best suited.

Imagine taking a stroll through a park (1). There's a cross at its centre, freshly painted (2), and a little further along, sitting on a bench, is the Queen (3) who is laughing at a woodpecker as it's tapping away at a joint of ham that it has mistaken for a tree (4).

Further still, there is a small, green church (5). The vicar is relaxing outside, reading a book of Orpheus poems while eating a danish pastry (6).

We reach the end of the park and here lies a harbour where the breeze gives off a chill (7). A cargo ship called the St Matthew (8) is moored here, waiting to offload its consignment, a ton of bricks (9).

Across the water, it's possible to see acres of land (10) and another park to the south (11), in which a windmill gently turns (12). If we offer to sweep (13) the cargo ship's wooden deck, perhaps the captain will agree to take us across?

1. Parkfield Road
2. New Cross Road
3. Queen's Road
4. Peckham High Street and Peckham Road
5. Camberwell Church Street and Camberwell Green
6. Denmark Hill and Orpheus Street
7. Coldharbour Lane
8. St Matthew's Road
9. Brixton Hill
10. Acre Lane
11. Clapham Park Road and Clapham Common South Side
12. Windmill Drive
13. Broomwood Road

1 NEW CROSS ROAD

On the south side of New Cross Road is the Ben Pimlott Building (part of Goldsmiths College), which is topped by the characteristic Squiggle sculpture.

Opposite is a small supermarket, which used to be a branch of Woolworths. On 25 November 1944, 168 shoppers were killed here in Britain's deadliest V2 rocket attack. A plaque commemorates the tragedy.

2 COLDHARBOUR LANE

Stretched between Moorland Road and Somerleyton Road is Southwyck House, a housing complex dubbed the 'Barrier Block' due to its imposing architecture. The block's thick walls and tiny windows were in fact designed to lessen the impact of a motorway that was scheduled to pass alongside but cancelled by the time the housing was completed in 1980.

3 EFFRA ROAD

Windrush Square was created in 1998 to celebrate the 50th anniversary of the arrival of the ship *Empire Windrush* that carried many passengers from Jamaica who'd go on to settle in Brixton. The square was modernised in 2010 and is now a popular community spot.

The Ritzy cinema, opened as the Electric Pavilion in 1911, can also be found in this area.

4 BRIXTON HILL

Situated in the middle of a busy traffic system, St Matthew's Church has been a Brixton landmark since the 1820s. While still a functioning place of worship, it also incorporates a bar and restaurant within its crypt.

5 WINDMILL DRIVE

There has been a Windmill pub (unsurprisingly named after a windmill that once stood nearby) here since the 1660s. One person who would've been familiar with the tavern is American Founding Father Benjamin Franklin who conducted experiments on Clapham Common's ponds while visiting a friend in the area.

Leave on left: New Cross Road
Right: Amersham Road
Right: Parkfield Road
Right: Lewisham Way
Bear left: New Cross Road
Forward: Queen's Road
Forward: Peckham High Street
Forward: Peckham Road
Forward: Camberwell Church Street
Forward: Camberwell Green
Left: Denmark Hill
Left: Orpheus Street
Right: Daneville Road
Forward: Coldharbour Lane
Left: Effra Road
Right: St Matthew's Road
Right: Brixton Hill
Left: Acre Lane
Forward and right: Clapham Park Road
Left: Clapham Common South Side
Right: Windmill Drive

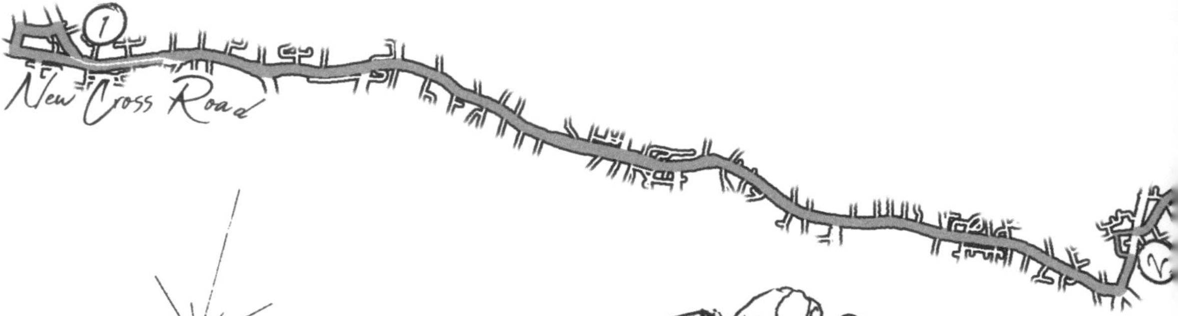

New Cross Road

N

1. Ben Pimlott Building, New Cross Road

Right: The Avenue
Left: Broomwood Road
Clapham Common West Side on left and right

5. The Windmill, Windmill Drive

3. The Ritzy

MYDDELTON SQUARE EC1 → GOLDEN SQUARE W1

The area where this run begins was once the southern end of the New River; a channel created in the early 17th century to bring fresh water into London. A number of roads in the quarter-mile radius are named in conjunction with this; River Street is the most obvious, but there's also Chadwell Street and Amwell Street which are named after Chadwell and Amwell Springs, the river's source.

Myddelton Square is named after Sir Hugh Myddelton, the Welshman who was one of the main people behind the project.

While exploring Myddelton Square, it's worth taking time to look at the adjoining Myddelton Passage where, for reasons unknown, hundreds of Victorian police officers scrawled their initials and identity numbers across a long, brick wall.

INSIDE THE BRITISH MUSEUM

This run passes The British Museum, which makes an ideal memory palace; we can wander around some imaginary exhibits and link them to the roads.

In the Egyptian room there's a relief map of the River Nile (1) along with a model of an Ancient Egyptian well (2). A noisy group of school children are in here too. One of them is having a tantrum as he'd rather be riding the rollercoaster at Thorpe Park (3). His teacher, whose hairstyle resembles Marge Simpson's (4), is telling him off.

The next room is Victorian-themed. Its centrepiece is a cabinet, which contains a stuffed Jack Russell dog (5). Another display features a large pair of bloomers (6), modelled by a waxwork of Lord Shaftesbury (7). He's also wearing a small crown (8) and clutching a Cambridge University degree (9).

In the third room there's a model illustrating the Battle of Lexington (10). Two of the miniature buildings – a windmill and a brewery (11) – appear to have been smashed by cannon fire.

On the opposite side of the room there's a sinister, medieval-plague doctor outfit, complete with characteristic long beak (12).

1. River Street
2. Amwell Street
3. Calthorpe Street
4. Margery Street
5. Russell Square and Great Russell Street
6. Bloomsbury Street
7. Shaftesbury Avenue
8. Prince's Circus
9. Cambridge Circus
10. Lexington Street
11. Great Windmill Street and Brewer Street
12. Beak Street

1 CALTHORPE STREET

Alongside Calthorpe Street is the huge Mount Pleasant Royal Mail depot, which opened in the 1920s. The name is ironic; it refers to a large rubbish dump that once existed here. Mount Pleasant is also home to the Postal Museum where visitors can take a ride on the Mail Rail, a private underground railway that used to whisk letters and parcels deep beneath London's congested streets.

2 GREAT RUSSELL STREET

Opened in 1759, The British Museum was the world's first national, public museum. It owes its existence to Sir Hans Sloane, an avid collector who bequeathed his entire collection of over 71,000 objects to the nation. Today it continues to house treasures from across the globe.

3 GREAT WINDMILL STREET

For much of the 20th century, Soho was considered a sleazy area characterised by adult shops and 'clip joints'. Such businesses have now largely given way to upmarket bars and media offices. An old stalwart can still be found on Great Windmill Street – The Windmill International, which was London's first strip-club when it opened in the 1930s, a time when the law stated women had to remain as still as statues if they were to appear nude.

4 GOLDEN SQUARE

Golden Square was laid out in in the late 17th century and features in Charles Dickens' *Nicholas Nickleby*. Thomas Jefferson also stayed in Golden Square for five weeks on what was to be his only trip to London. The statue in the middle of the square is ambiguous; some believe it represents George II while others say it's Charles II.

Leave by: River Street
Left: Amwell Street
Right: Margery Street
Forward: Calthorpe Street
Forward: Guildford Street
Comply: Russell Square
Leave by: Montague Street
Right: Great Russell Street
Left: Bloomsbury Street
Forward: Shaftesbury Avenue
Right: Prince's Circus
Left: Shaftesbury Avenue continued
Forward: Cambridge Circus
Forward: Shaftesbury Avenue continued

1 Calthorpe Street

2. The British Museum, Great Russell Street

Right: Great Windmill Street
Cross: Brewer Street
Forward: Lexington Street
Left: Beak Street
Left: Upper James Street
Golden Square facing

FINSBURY CIRCUS EC2 → WICK ROAD E9

This run exits the Square Mile – London's oldest area – via the curiously named Norton Folgate, a short section of road that was once its own tiny district, free from the influence of the church.

We then take a complex route through the East End's Bethnal Green, nipping through tight turns and narrow streets – including Columbia Road, which hosts its famous flower market every Sunday, and Broadway Market, a popular destination packed with bars, restaurants and independent shops.

Further along, the tightly terraced Beck Road is one of the East End's best preserved streets.

BUSY FIELDS

This complex route is best suited to the Loci method and requires an array of characters and objects to help us along.

We begin at the circus (1) where a tightrope walker is balancing high along a wall (2). But the pole that helps him balance is riddled with woodworm (3) and not very effective. He tumbles off but is saved by a bishop (4) who holds his cloak out to act as a safety net.

We leave the circus. It's in a field which must be exited by a gate, beside which stands a baby horse (5), trying to steady itself on gangly legs.

On the other side of the gate we have to scramble across a ditch (6) before arriving at a red-painted church (7), outside which King Arthur (8) is playing a game of chance with Arnold Schwarzenegger (9). Whoever wins will get a bottle of hock (10) and the deeds to the state of Virginia (11).

Around the other side of the church, Lieutenant Columbo (12) is examining a body that has been strangled with rope (13); there must've been an awful din (14) when the murder occurred but nobody seems to have heard. The detective has a hackneyed (15) look on his face and is wearing his trademark raincoat (16).

In the next field we meet comedian Peter Kay (17) who is busy counting money (18). He says some of it got burnt and charred (19) and he'll have to go to Broadway (20) to make it up. The role he's been offered is King Duncan (21) in *Macbeth*.

At the other end of the field, a sheep (22) and a horse (23) are watching David Beckham (24) kick a ball. Unfortunately he boots it too far and it plunges into a well (25).

1. Circus Place
2. London Wall
3. Wormwood Street
4. Bishopsgate
5. Norton Folgate
6. Shoreditch High Street
7. Redchurch Street
8. Camlet Street
9. Arnold Circus
10. Hocker Street
11. Virginia Road
12. Colombia Road
13. Ropley Street
14. Dinmont Street
15. Hackney Road
16. Coate Street
17. Kay Street
18. Goldsmiths Row
19. Pritchard's Road
20. Broadway Market
21. Duncan Road
22. Sheep Lane
23. Mare Street
24. Beck Road
25. Well Street

1 BISHOPSGATE

St Botolph is the patron saint of travellers, which is why a number of churches were dedicated to him near London's historic gateways – they offered a place where wayfarers could pray for a safe journey. St Botolph-without-Bishopsgate dates back to Saxon times and it was here in 1795 that the poet John Keats was baptised. The churchyard houses one of London's hidden architectural gems: a Victorian Turkish bathhouse.

2 LIVERPOOL ST STATION

One of the UK's busiest terminals, Liverpool Street opened in 1874. Its platforms are below ground and for many years their Victorian aura remained unchanged – as seen in the 1980 film *The Elephant Man* when Joseph Merrick is hounded through the station by a baying crowd, a terrifying experience that happened to him at the station in real life. In the late 1930s, Liverpool Street was the arrival point for the Kindertransport, the rescue effort established by Sir Nicholas Winton that saved many Jewish children from Nazi-occupied Europe. Two artworks dedicated to the service can be seen at the station.

3 ARNOLD CIRCUS

The Boundary Estate, which surrounds this large circle, was opened in 1900 and was essentially the world's first social housing project. It occupies the site of the 'Old Nichol', which was generally considered London's most ferocious ghetto – it inspired Arthur Morrison's 1896 novel *A Child of the Jago*. The raised bandstand in the middle of Arnold Circus is built upon a mound of soil extracted from the demolished slum.

4 HACKNEY ROAD

Hackney City Farm (entrance in Goldsmiths Row) was established as a little rural oasis in 1984 and is home to pigs, donkeys, goats and other smaller animals.

Leave by: Circus Place
Left: London Wall
Forward: Wormwood Street
Left: Bishopsgate
Forward: Norton Folgate
Forward: Shoreditch High Street
Right: Redchurch Street
Left: Chance Street
Forward: Camlet Street
Comply: Arnold Circus
Leave by: Hocker Street
Right and left: Virginia Road
Right: Columbia Road
Comply: Roundabout
Leave by: Columbia Road continued

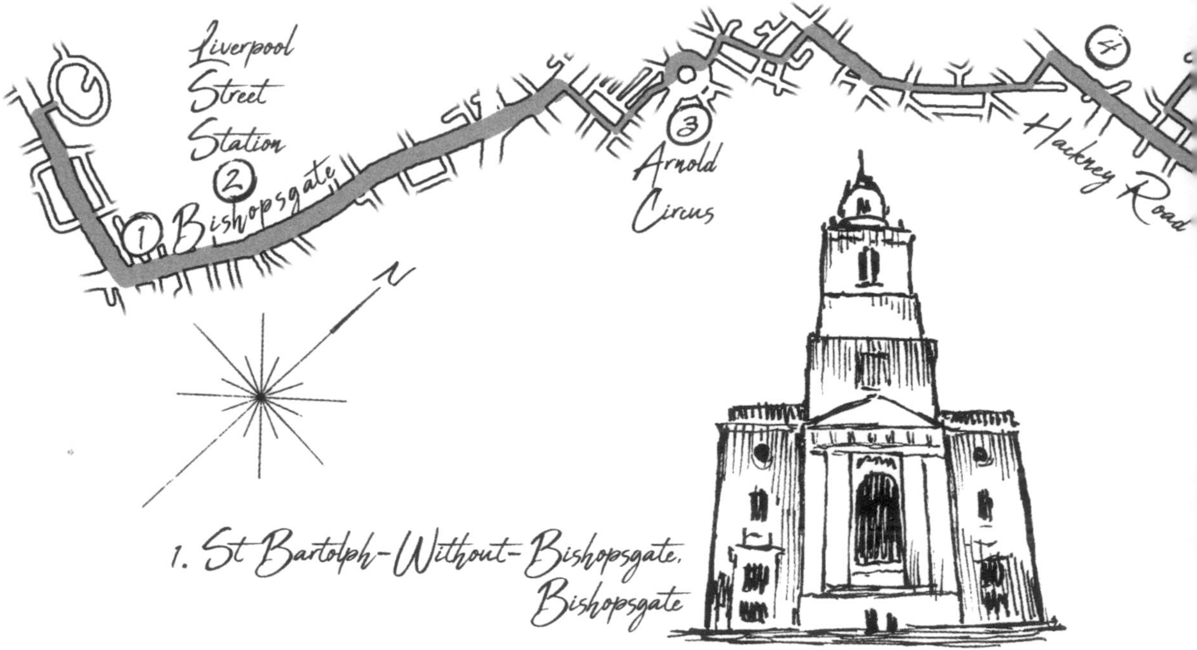

Liverpool Street Station

2

1 Bishopsgate

3

Arnold Circus

4

Hackney Road

N

1. St Bartolph-Without-Bishopsgate, Bishopsgate

Left: Ropley Street
Right: Hackney Road
Left: Dinmont Street
Left: Coate Street
Right: Kay Street
Right: Goldsmiths Row
Forward: Pritchard's Road
Forward: Broadway Market
Right: Duncan Road
Left: Sheep Lane
Right: Beck Road
Left: Mare Street
Right: Well Street
Forward: Cassland Road
Wick Road on left and right

PALLADIUM THEATRE W1 → DEVONSHIRE SQUARE EC2

Starting at one of the capital's best-known theatres, this run has one of the Blue Book's longest calls. Until a few years ago, it involved a group of roads nicknamed 'The Dirty Dozen', a nifty route that zigzagged through Soho's cramped backstreets.

Unfortunately the construction of the deep express railway, Crossrail (officially known as the Elizabeth Line) resulted in these streets being churned up beyond all recognition and this cabbie favourite has now been lost. Due to turning restrictions on Oxford Street, this means the route is subjected to a major detour – either north, via Fitzrovia (as demonstrated here), or south down to traffic-clogged Piccadilly Circus.

Later on, the run passes across Holborn Viaduct, which was essentially the world's first example of a flyover when it opened in 1869.

LIBERTY

Early in the run, this route passes the famous Liberty department store; a charismatic emporium that makes for an ideal memory palace.

We enter via the wool section where argyll (1) tartans are displayed. The odious Prince Regent (2) is arguing with customer services.

Next is the Christmas (3) department, decorated with holly berries and candles (4). Cards depicting the WWI (5) Christmas truce are on sale.

Further along is the toy department where the shelves display Action Man (6), a model castle (7), pots of goo (8), a squeaky toy mallet (9), stuffed Jack Russells (10) and cuddly red lions (11).

We then walk along a corridor where posters advertise travel deals: one with a ship for cruises from Southampton (12), and another for romantic railway travel featuring a steam train puffing high along a viaduct (13).

We wish to go up a floor, so enter an old-fashioned lift guarded by a gate (14). Inside we bump into King Edward (15) and a forlorn Romeo (16).

Now we're higher up, it's possible to peer through a window and see London Wall (17) in the distance. The floor feels a little unstable here though; it's riddled with woodworm (18). A shop assistant approaches us and offers a sample of Camomile (19) tea before showing us the way out through the pet and cutlery departments (20).

1. Argyll Street & Little Argyll Street
2. Regent Street
3. Noel Street
4. Berwick Street
5. Wardour Street
6. Newman Street
7. Eastcastle Street
8. Goodge Street
9. Malet Street
10. Russell Square
11. Red Lion Square
12. Southampton Row
13. High Holborn & Holborn Viaduct
14. Newgate Street
15. King Edward Street
16. Montague Street
17. London Wall
18. Wormwood Street
19. Camomile Street
20. Outwich Street, Houndsditch & Cutler Street

1 GREAT MARLBOROUGH STREET

Now a five-star establishment, the Courthouse Hotel was once indeed a court – Great Marlborough Street Magistrates.

Many famous people are associated with the former court – a young Charles Dickens worked as a reporter here and trials involving Oscar Wilde, Christine Keeler, John Lennon, Mick Jagger and Johnny Rotten all occurred at the court.

2 NEWGATE STREET

The Central Criminal Court – a.k.a. the Old Bailey – looms here. There has been a court associated with this site since the 1500s although the current building dates from 1907.

3 ROTUNDA

Cabbies nickname the large, brick structure in the middle of this roundabout the 'Wall of Death', most likely because it resembles the drum-like structures in which daredevil bikers defy gravity.

Above the rotunda is the Museum of London, which opened in 1976 and offers a fascinating insight into the capital's history from Roman times all the way to the present day.

Leave on right: Argyll Street
Left: Little Argyll Street
Left: Regent Street
Left: Great Marlborough Street
Forward: Noel Street
Right: Berwick Street
Left: D'Arblay Street
Left: Wardour Street
Cross: Oxford Street
Forward: Berners Street
Right: Eastcastle Street
Left: Newman Street
Right: Goodge Street
Left: Tottenham Court Road
Right: Chenies Street
Right: Gower Street
Left: Keppel Street
Right: Malet Street
Left: Montague Place
Comply: Russell Square

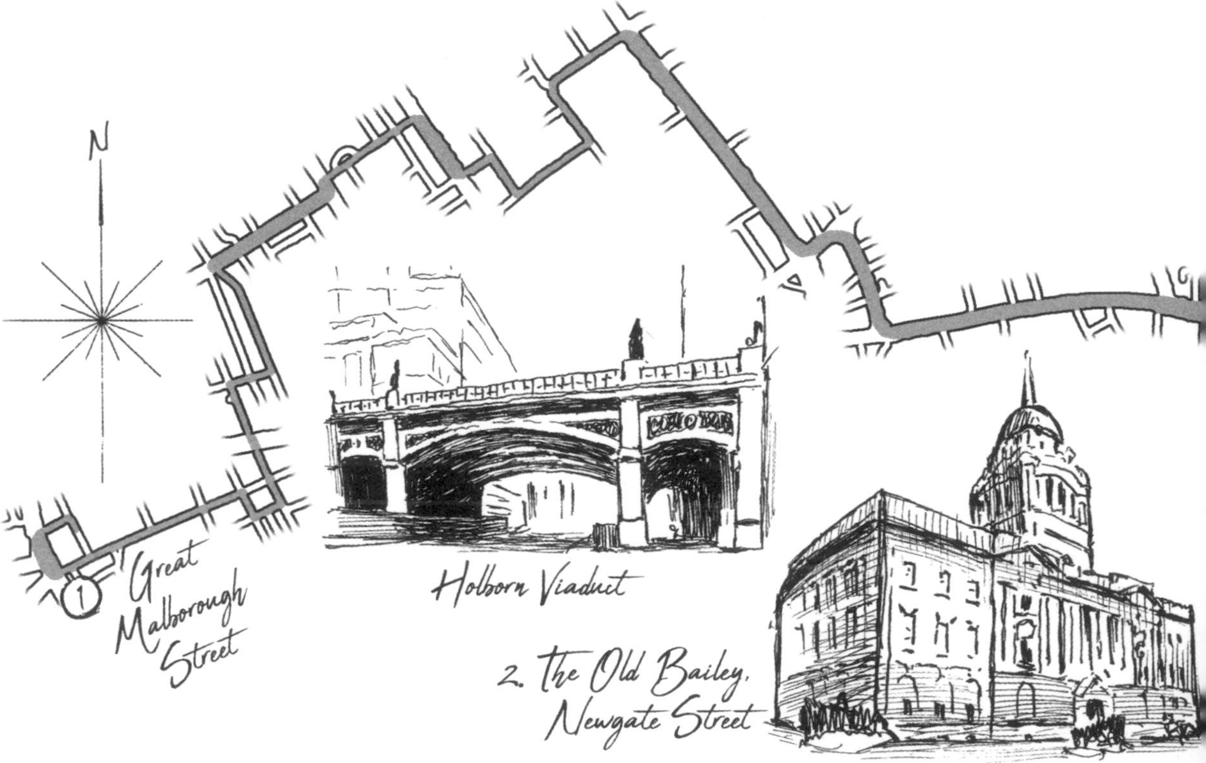

N

1 Great Malborough Street

Holborn Viaduct

2. The Old Bailey, Newgate Street

Leave by: Southampton Row
Left: Theobalds Road
Right: Drake Street
Forward: Red Lion Square
Forward: Procter Street
Left: High Holborn
Forward: Holborn
Forward: Holborn Viaduct
Forward: Newgate Street
Left: King Edward Street
Forward: Montague Street
Comply: Rotunda
Leave by: London Wall
Forward: Wormwood Street
Forward: Camomile Street
Left: Outwich Street
Bear right: Houndsditch
Left: Cutler Street
Devonshire Square on left

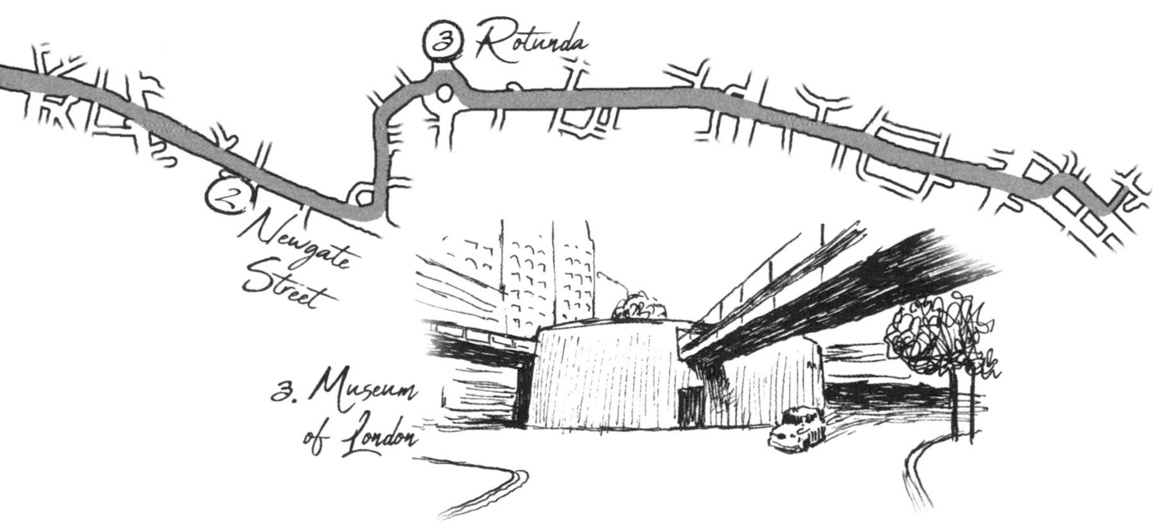

RUNS WITH A PERSONAL CONNECTION

Training our memories to recall reams of information is one thing, but there are times in our lives when certain moments are so sharply defined that the brain automatically logs the experience forever.

Such instances tend to be *episodic memories*; recollections of a time and place which are deeply personal and, in many respects, shape the people we are.

Sense and emotion play a major role in forming these types of memories. Think back to your earliest recollection – it's sure to include a stimulation of at least one of the senses and perhaps a strong impression of location too.

In my own case this involves standing (in a rather unsteady, toddler kind of way) in my grandmother's kitchen one autumn evening. I'm on the step of the back door, which leads to the garden. The kitchen is warm and brightly lit, enhanced by the colourful wallpaper – a kitsch collage of flowers in oranges, yellows, browns. And then it happens. I trip, tumbling backwards into the dark night, cracking my head on the chilly concrete. An abstract blur of sensations follows; cries, the feeling of being whisked up and sodium streetlights bobbing past as I'm hurried to some place unknown.

With its kaleidoscope of sights, sounds and smells, London is a fertile place for generating special-long-lasting memories. As a cabbie, I've been privileged to meet many people who've been happy to share their own personal ones with me.

Some have been funny – such as the woman who recalled driving her Mini through the arches outside the Ritz hotel on a Sunday morning many years ago.

Others have been an education – learning about places in London that no longer exist, such as the commuter who'd regularly pass through the now vanished Broad Street railway terminal, or tales of wild nights in night clubs long gone.

In some cases, these memories have been heartbreaking, apparently shared as a way of achieving some catharsis. I will never forget the elderly gentleman – a Lord, no less, picked up from the Houses of Parliament – who gazed longingly at certain buildings we passed as he told me about the role they'd played in his long relationship with his recently deceased wife.

Traditionally, the majority of students who embark upon The Knowledge are from the London area and as such will have numerous memories reignited as they revisit certain parts of the capital.

Once their goal is achieved and they finally become a working taxi driver, many new memories of remarkable passengers and interesting encounters will be acquired, thus ensuring that, while all cabbies may share the same map etched upon their brain, the mind of each individual also harbours a special and unique patchwork of the city.

MANOR HOUSE STATION N4 → GIBSON SQUARE N1

This fairly straightforward route takes us through a good swathe of north London, including the major junction at Highbury Corner.

It's when learning the quarter-mile radius around Gibson Square that things get tricky due to the number of restrictions and blocked-off roads within the area.

STARTING OUT

As the first run on The Knowledge, *Manor House station to Gibson Square* holds a special place in every cabbie's heart.

I remember arriving at Manor House very early one Sunday morning; it was cold and misty and, as I expect many fellow students did, had a brief moment of crisis when I asked myself what on earth I was getting myself into.

But this thought was quickly expelled when I stood up to stretch my legs – and promptly trod in some dog mess, which in hindsight was probably a symbol of good luck although it certainly didn't feel like that at the time.

1 MANOR HOUSE

The area is named after the former Manor House pub which opened in the 1830s and provided the original starting line for The Knowledge when it was introduced a few decades later.

In the 1960s the pub gained prominence as a popular music venue, providing a platform for fledgling acts such as The Rolling Stones and The Jimi Hendrix Experience.

London's cabbies aren't the only titans of memory associated with Manor House. In 1893 an elephant named Jim was being paraded outside the pub alongside two llamas when he broke free, blasting a 'Fantasia on the trumpet' before charging into nearby Finsbury Park where he trampled the bandstand and smashed several walls.

2 GREEN LANES

Travelling along Green Lanes you'll spot one of London's most curious structures; a looming fortress which wouldn't look out of place in the Scottish Highlands. This is the Castle Climbing Centre, an ornate pump house built in the 1850s to supply Londoners with pollution-free drinking water. The works remained in service for over 100 years and, after narrowly avoiding demolition, were converted in 1995 into an indoor centre for budding rock climbers.

3 HIGHBURY NEW PARK

Tucked away behind St Augustine's Church is a quaint gothic hall which was transformed into an unlikely recording studio after being acquired by The Beatles' producer, Sir George Martin, in 1965.

The Sex Pistols' blistering *Never Mind the Boll*cks* album was cut here, as was *London Calling* by The Clash and the iconic drumbeat to Queen's 'We Will Rock You'.

4 UPPER STREET

Like St Augustine's, Union Chapel is another north London church with close musical ties. As well as offering weekly prayer and Bible study it is a celebrated concert venue that has hosted many big names over the years including Amy Winehouse, Patti Smith and Sir Elton John.

Another type of rock associated with Union Chapel is Plymouth Rock, the boulder upon which the Pilgrim Fathers famously set foot in 1620. In 1886 a visiting group of Americans gifted the church with a small chunk of the fabled relic, which can still be seen on display today.

5 GIBSON SQUARE

Like the Manor House pub, Gibson Square dates back to the 1830s. It was laid out by Francis Edwards, an architect who'd studied under the Bank of England's designer, Sir John Soane.

Gibson Square's most unusual feature is its little 'temple', a Greek inspired building which popped up in the early 1970s as a cunning disguise for a ventilation shaft linked to the Victoria Line which runs deep below.

Leave on left: Green Lanes
Right: Highbury Quadrant
Left: Highbury New Park
Comply: Roundabout
Leave by: Highbury New Park continued
Left: Highbury Grove
Right: St Paul's Road
Comply: Highbury Corner
Leave by: Upper Street
Right: Islington Park Street
Left: College Cross
Right: Barnsbury Street
Left: Milner Square
Forward: Milner Place
Gibson Square facing

Manor House

Green Lanes

Highbury Ne

2. Castle Climbing House, Green Lanes

3. St Augustine's, Highbury New Park

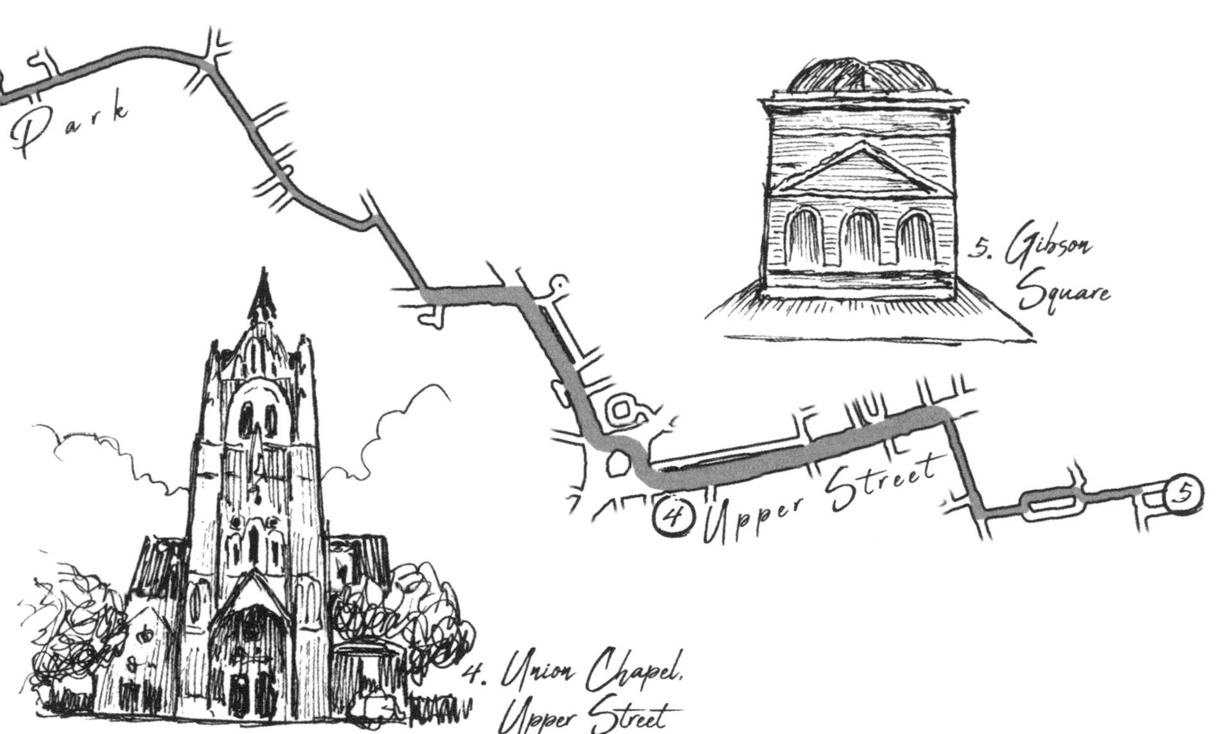
Park
5. Gibson Square
Upper Street
4
5
4. Union Chapel, Upper Street

SAVILE ROW W1 → SPA ROAD SE1

I've always enjoyed reading and one of my favourite books as a child was Jules Verne's *Around the World in Eighty Days*, which encouraged me to nurture a desire to explore new places; a useful hobby when studying The Knowledge.

That's why this run's start point is special to me; number 7 Savile Row was Phileas Fogg's fictional home and it's from here that he begins his epic journey, the very first leg being a cab ride to Charing Cross station.

This run has echoes of another favourite author of mine, Charles Dickens, whose descriptions of London are legendary.

One such link can be found on the junction of Blackfriars Road and The Cut – a curious sculpture known as the *Dog and Pot*. This is a replica of an old shop sign that once stood on the same spot, which Dickens wrote about when recalling his own childhood.

Dickens himself was a keen explorer of London, eager to learn the city's most intricate details – rather like an early Knowledge student in that respect.

Further along is Marshalsea Road, named after the former prison in which Dickens' father was incarcerated for debt. Part of the prison wall remains today and can be seen behind St George the Martyr church (on the junction of Borough High Street and Great Dover Street), which itself appears in *Little Dorrit*.

Literature aside, this run also includes Waterloo Bridge – my favourite Thames crossing, which I never tire of driving over – and Transport for London's Palestra Building, which is where I passed my final Knowledge exam and finally received my green badge; one of the proudest moments of my life.

1 PICCADILLY CIRCUS

Gleaming bright day and night with its spread of illuminated advertising screens, Piccadilly Circus is one of London's most iconic spots. At its centre is the statue of *Eros* (also known as the Shaftesbury Memorial Fountain), which dates from the 1890s. The figure is in fact the *Angel of Christian Charity* but, most likely due to his bow and arrow, has come to be associated with the Greek god of love instead.

2 TRAFALGAR SQUARE

Like Piccadilly Circus, Trafalgar Square is world-famous. It wasn't always so glamorous though; before the square was laid out in the 1840s, the site was occupied by grubby stables.

Nelson's Column was created soon after as a tribute to the great naval hero. The four lions around the base were sculpted by Sir Edwin Landseer, a Victorian artist famed for his depiction of animals, his most notable painting being *Monarch of the Glen*. When sculpting the lions Landseer had to work quickly as the beast he was provided with as a muse was dead and rotting.

3 WATERLOO BRIDGE

This bridge provides one of the best views of London with a panoramic sweep taking in Westminster, the South Bank and the City.

The first bridge opened in the 19th century but began to deteriorate as motor vehicle usage increased. Today's Waterloo Bridge was built during WWII, with much of the workforce comprised of women. The remains of two columns from the previous structure can be seen below on Victoria Embankment.

4 UNION STREET

On the corner of Union Street and Blackfriars Road is Palestra House, a modern glass building which is now home to Transport for London.

The term *palestra* is ancient Greek for 'wrestling arena' and is named so because a boxing venue called The Ring once occupied the spot. It was managed by Bella Burge – affectionately nicknamed 'Belle of Blackfriars' – who is believed to have been the world's first female boxing promoter.

The Ring was destroyed in WWII – bomb damage from that night can still be seen in the tiles beneath the adjoining railway bridge. The Ring pub, however, remains open across the road.

5 SPA ROAD

Located inside a former Victorian school is the Kagyu Samye Dzong London Buddhist Centre, which holds workshops and free meditation sessions. The centre also has a shop and Tibetan Tea Room.

Leave by: Vigo Street
Right: Regent Street
Comply: Piccadilly Circus
Leave by: Coventry Street
Right: Haymarket
Left: Pall Mall East
Comply: Trafalgar Square
Leave by: Duncannon Street
Bear left: The Strand
Bear left: Aldwych
Right: The Strand
Left: Lancaster Place
Forward: Waterloo Bridge
Forward: Waterloo Road
Comply: Tenison Way
Leave by: Waterloo Road continued
Left: The Cut
Cross: Blackfriars Road
Forward: Union Street

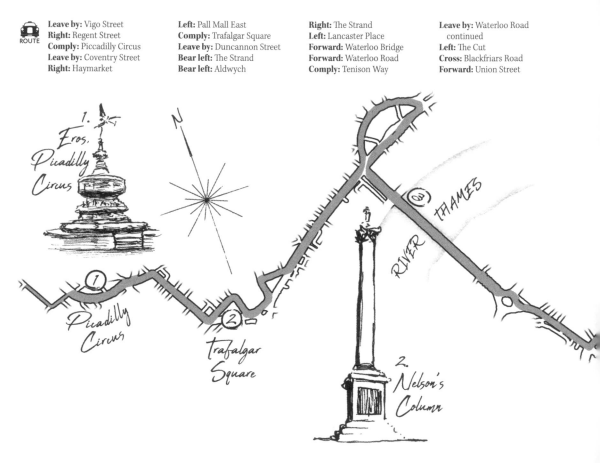

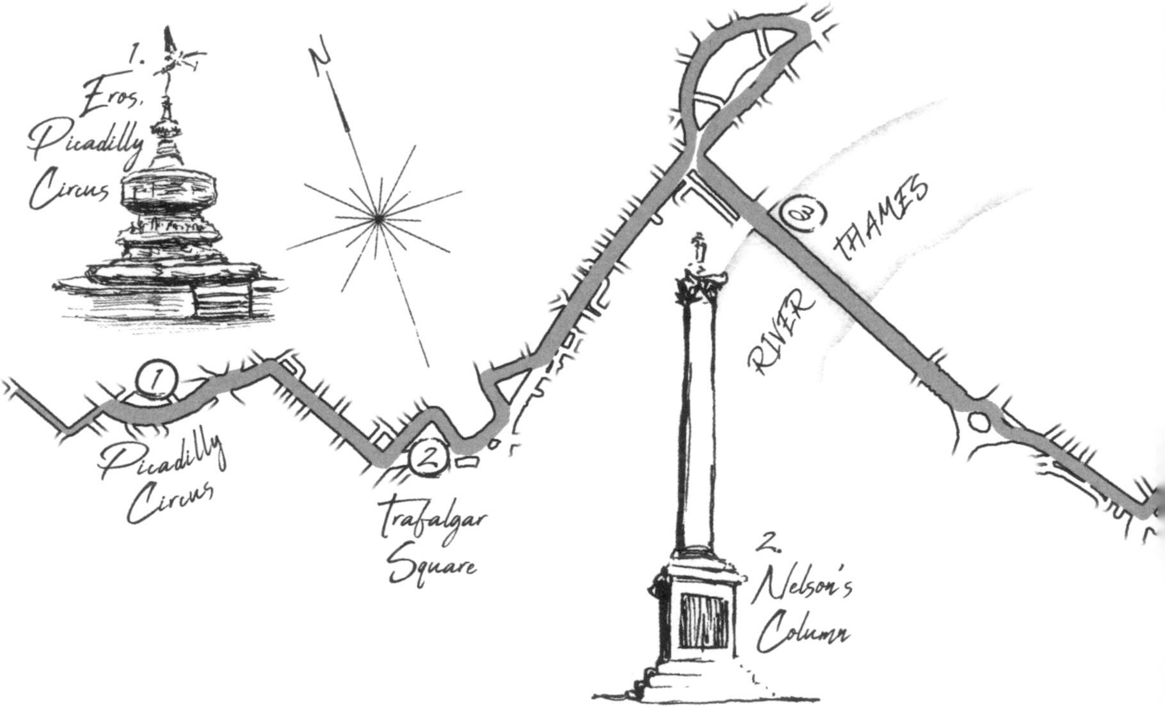

Right: Great Suffolk Street
Left: Copperfield Street
Right: Great Guildford Street
Left: Southwark Bridge Road
Right: Marshalsea Road
Forward: Great Dover Street
Left: Long Lane
Right and left: Bermondsey Street
Cross: Tower Bridge Road
Forward: Grange Road
Spa Road on left

CROWN DALE SE19 → CROFTON PARK STATION SE4

Beginning six miles south of Charing Cross, this lengthy run hugs the south-eastern perimeter of The Knowledge area.

This is a pleasant drive, taking in a good number of steep, leafy roads and passing through areas with distinctly rural sounding names such as Forest Hill and Gipsy Hill (which is named after a large traveller community who were based in the area during centuries past).

London is vast; you can live in the city your entire life and never see many parts of it.

As someone who grew up in north London this run was the deepest south I'd ever ventured and it gave me a real sense of the enormity of the task at hand (and I'm sure this experience is mirrored by many south London Knowledge students when heading northward).

Discovering this new area was a real treat for me; south London feels a lot leafier than the north and Crystal Palace Park has become one of my all time favourite places in the capital.

And don't worry . . . as a cabbie I'll happily take you south of the river!

1 HAWKE ROAD

Although unassuming at first glance, Pear Tree House is one of London's most extraordinary blocks of flats.

Peer over the low concrete wall on Hawke Road and you'll see why: the apartments are built on top of a nuclear bunker, complete with a thick, reinforced blast door. The shelter was built in tandem with the flats in the 1960s and was designed to act as a local control centre in the event of a nuclear attack (although it's safe to say the residents above would not have been allocated a space).

2 CRYSTAL PALACE PARADE

Crystal Palace Park was created in the 1850s when the celebrated Hyde Park venue for the Great Exhibition – the glass and iron Crystal Palace – was dismantled and rebuilt on Sydenham Hill.

The building remained a popular attraction for many years until it was consumed by an almighty blaze in 1936 – it's said light from the flames could be seen as far away as the south coast. Today, a number of eerie statues (some headless) and windswept staircases and terraces are all that remain.

Despite the palace's destruction, however, the park is host to a number of attractions, most famously its collection of over 30 model dinosaurs that provide a fascinating insight into how the Victorians imagined prehistoric creatures to look.

Also in the park you'll find a maze, a small museum and an outdoor concert venue where, in 1980, Bob Marley gave his last ever UK performance.

Towering over the park is the elegant Crystal Palace Transmitter, which was erected in 1956 and continues to broadcast television across the London region. The tower can be spotted in the 1969 film *The Italian Job*.

3 LONDON ROAD

Named after its founder, Frederick John Horniman, the Horniman Museum opened on Christmas Eve 1890.

As a tea trader, Horniman had travelled the world, acquiring a huge array of artefacts that provided the basis for the museum's collection. Today, the Horniman holds over 350,000 objects related to anthropology and natural history, and recently opened a butterfly house within its grounds.

4 BROCKLEY ROAD

The Rivoli Ballroom is the last such building of its kind in London. Maintaining a distinct 1950s feel, it is a popular location for film crews. Oasis, Tina Turner and Elton John have all recorded music videos here.

Leave by forward: Central Hill
Left: Gibbs Avenue
Right: Bloomhall Road
Forward: Hawke Road
Left: Lunham Road
Forward: Highland Road
Left: Gipsy Hill
Right: Colby Road
Right: Dulwich Wood Avenue
Left: Farquhar Road
Right: Dulwich Wood Park
Bear right: College Road
Left: Crystal Palace Parade
Comply: Roundabout
Leave by: Westwood Hill
Comply: Roundabout

2. The Crystal Palace

① Hawke Road

② Crystal Palace Parade

Leave by: Sydenham Hill
Comply: Roundabout
Leave by: Sydenham Rise
Right: London Road
Left: Honor Oak Road
Right: Honor Oak Park
Left: Stondon Park
Forward: Brockley Road
Comply: Roundabout
Leave by: Brockley Road
Crofton Park station on right

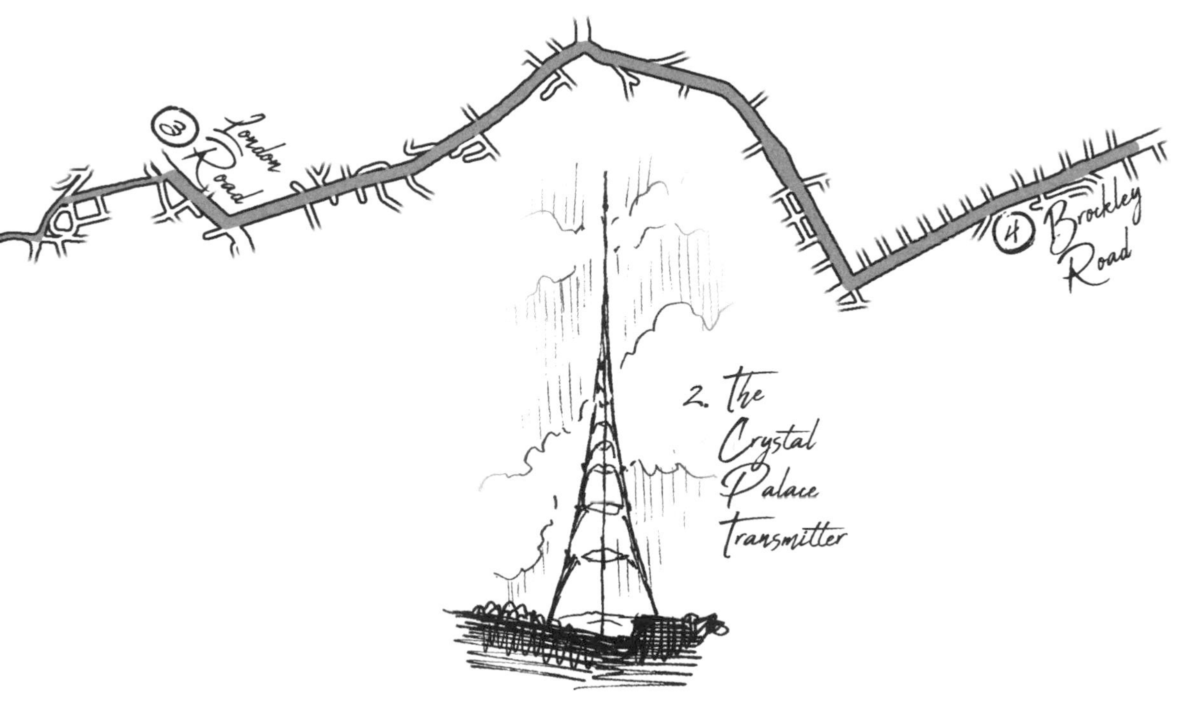

CALEDONIAN ROAD STATION N7 → ALEXANDRA PALACE N22

For many years Caledonian Road was home to Knowledge Point School, which I attended (it has since moved to the London Taxi Company showroom on nearby Brewery Road).

When I first started The Knowledge I needed guidance and this school (one of several across the city) was invaluable. I made some wonderful friends there – 'callover partners' – with whom I'd revise and we still keep in touch today.

The school was an atmospheric place, full of row upon row of large laminated maps, over which anxious students would sit, frowning, chewing pens and squinting at the ceiling in a desperate attempt to salvage a memory.

Every so often, someone would walk in, smartly-suited, meaning they'd had an appearance and others would be eager to find out what points and runs they'd been asked.

On rare occasions someone would announce that they'd received their 'req' (meaning they'd finally reached the required standard) and sweets would be handed out to celebrate.

Lessons were held at the school too, which could be potentially nerve-racking if you were asked to recite a run in front of the rest of the class.

This run's end point, Alexandra Palace, was a favourite with the teachers; they'd often ask you to go from there to Crystal Palace, the furthest north-to-south route possible on The Knowledge. This was a good way of demonstrating how runs should not be taken in isolation; they simply provide the framework that eventually knits an entire mental map together.

1 CALEDONIAN ROAD

Caledonian Road ('The Cally' to locals) is named after the former Royal Caledonian School, a home originally established for Scottish children who'd been orphaned by the Napoleonic Wars. It stood next to Pentonville Prison. The site is now occupied by the Caledonian Estate, where metal thistles can still be seen along the railings outside.

2 CROUCH END BROADWAY

There has been a convergence of routes here since ancient times, *Crouch* being derived from the Latin for 'cross'.

A building of note here is Hornsey Town Hall, which was Britain's first modernist building when it opened in the 1930s. It's now used as an arts centre.

It was also on The Broadway that the opening credits for the long-running comedy series *Peep Show* were filmed (even though the show was set much further south in Croydon).

3 ALEXANDRA PALACE

Built to mirror Crystal Palace in the south, Alexandra Palace first opened in 1873, and promptly burnt down just sixteen days later. It reopened in 1875 and staged an eclectic range of events including early airship displays and horse racing. During WWI the building was used to house Belgian refugees and, later in the war, German and Austrian prisoners.

In 1936 the BBC began broadcasting the world's first high-definition television service from the palace. Sets were extremely expensive at the time, however, meaning audiences were small. The service abruptly went off air just hours before the outbreak of WWII and would not return until 1946.

The palace was once again gutted by fire in 1980. Now thankfully restored, it includes an ice rink, ten-hole golf course, restaurants, cafes and a boating lake.

Leave on left: Caledonian Road
Left: Hillmarton Road
Cross: Camden Road
Right: Parkhurst Road
Left: Holloway Road
Right: Tollington Way
Left: Hornsey Road
Forward: Hornsey Rise
Forward: Crouch End Hill
Forward: The Broadway
Bear left: Park Road
Bear right: Alexandra Palace Way
Alexandra Palace on right

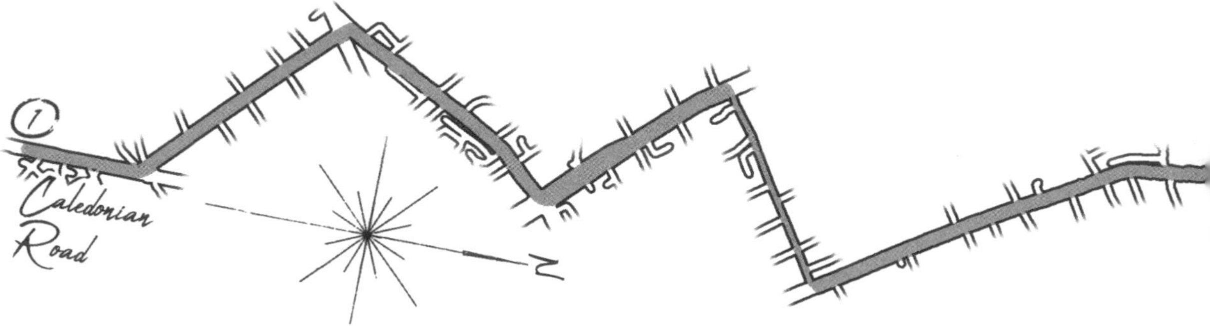

1 Caledonian Road

2. Hornsey Town Hall, Crouch End Broadway

Crouch End Broadway
2
3
3. Alexandra Palace

GOLBORNE ROAD W10 → PENNINE DRIVE NW2

As mentioned on the Crown Dale to Crofton Park station run, London is so huge that there are many places its inhabitants will never encounter.

The other side to that of course is that there are plenty of other places with which a born and bred Londoner will be very familiar, and I certainly found studying The Knowledge to be quite a nostalgic process at times.

My great-great grandmother, Bo, lived on Kilburn Lane. I was very young when she died and had not returned to her road for many years. As soon as I drove along Kilburn Lane, however, I recognised her old home – a terraced house with red bricks arched around the windows and front door. It immediately evoked memories of Bo sitting in her armchair, frail but inwardly strong, the smell of the gas stove distinct in the air.

When we visited my great-great gran we'd take the train to Queen's Park and driving past this station also invoked memories. I could see myself sitting on the springy seats of an old British Rail train, the type that had a corridor and doors that slammed, as it clattered and groaned through north London.

On one trip I found a forlorn teddy bear abandoned at the junction with Salsbury Road. For some reason my parents allowed me to keep it (he was given a good scrub of course) and I still have him to this day as a kind of mascot, safely tucked away in a cupboard.

Kilburn High Road holds special memories too.

When I was growing up, my father would sometimes treat us to a drive into central London, usually to see the Christmas lights along Oxford Street and Regent Street. I adored those evening excursions, driving down the long stretch of Kilburn High Road, which always seemed to be alive, twinkling with light from the buses, taxis, shops and pubs. It's a memory that always puts a smile on my face when working late.

My father grew up in Kilburn but sadly the block of flats where he lived, Marshall House on Albert Road (near Salsbury Corner), has been demolished and replaced with the inevitable luxury apartments.

1 GOLBORNE ROAD

Completed in 1972, Trellick Tower is one of London's most iconic late-20th-century buildings. It was designed by the Hungarian-born architect Ernö Goldfinger who was said to be notoriously grouchy (although it must be said, I did once have the fortune of picking up a passenger who'd met Goldfinger many years previously and he attested that he was most charming).

James Bond author Ian Fleming was no fan of the architect, due to a project he didn't agree with on Willow Road, Hampstead. As a result, he decided to name his most famous villain Goldfinger after him.

In the early 1980s, Trellick Tower was used as a secret transmission site for the popular pirate radio station DBC: Dread Broadcasting Corporation.

2 KILBURN HIGH ROAD

Established in 1980, the Tricycle Theatre is a popular venue for drama, and also contains a gallery and cinema. New writers are encouraged, especially those covering contemporary issues.

3 PENNINE DRIVE

It's difficult to imagine now, but the neat suburban houses that cover this area stand upon what was once the site of an early London airport, Cricklewood Aerodrome. The aerodrome began life as a factory for Handley Page who built heavy bombers for use in WWI.

Shortly after the war, the company began offering civilian flights to Paris and, on 14 December 1920, one such flight took off from here. Unfortunately the aircraft struggled to climb and crashed into a back garden a short distance away on Basing Hill. A number of crew and passengers died, making this the first fatal crash of a civilian airliner.

Today, the only remnant of this area's aviation past is a small factory building that can be seen on the The Vale, parallel to Pennine Drive.

Leave by: Elkstone Road
Left: Great Western Road
Cross: Harrow Road
Forward: Elgin Avenue
Left: Chippenham Road
Left: Warlock Road
Right: Fernhead Road
Left: Carlton Vale
Forward: Kilburn Lane
Right: Premier Corner
Left: Salusbury Road
Right: Victoria Road
Left: Kilburn High Road
Forward: Shoot Up Hill
Right: Mill Lane
Left: Fordwych Road

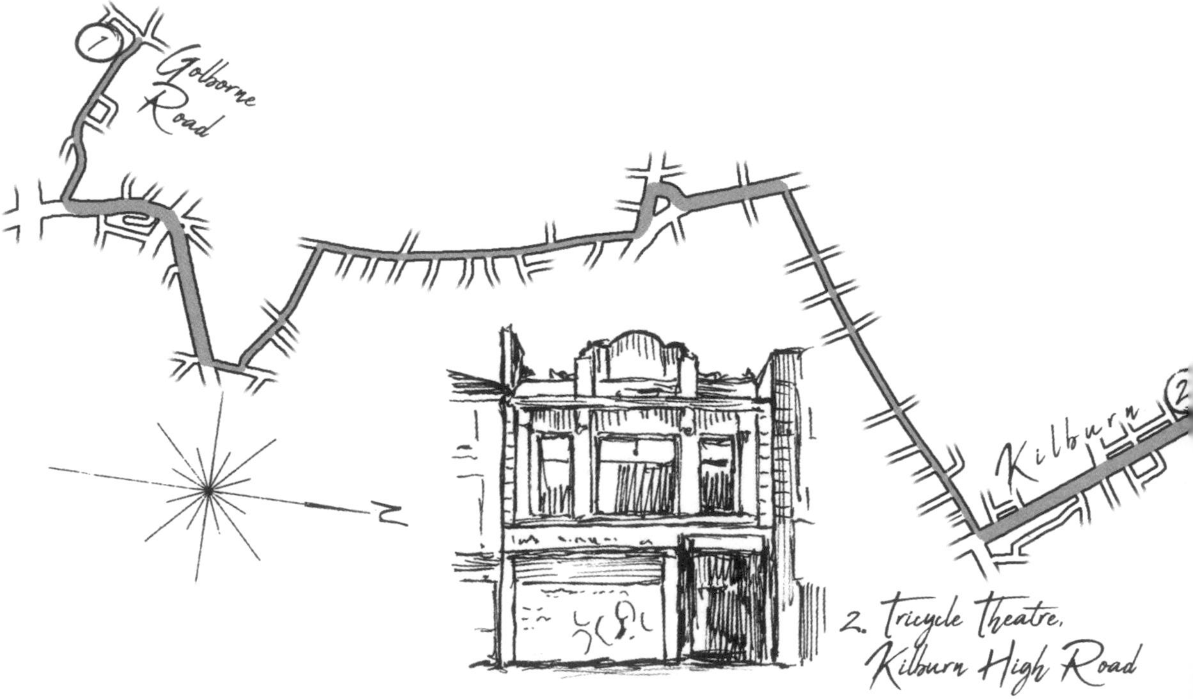

Golborne Road

Kilburn

2. Tricycle Theatre, Kilburn High Road

Right: Minster Road
Left: Westbere Road
Forward: Lichfield Road
Cross: Cricklewood Lane
Forward: Claremont Road
Pennine Drive on right

BLACKFRIARS STATION EC4 → BRYANSTON STREET W1

This central London run twists and turns through some well known areas, including Covent Garden, one of the city's most popular tourist spots.

It also reminds me of two special passengers I picked up on separate occasions.

The first was an elderly gentleman who – it transpired – was one of 'The Few', a former RAF pilot who fought in the Battle of Britain.

I took him to St Clement Danes RAF church on the Strand, close to the junction with Arundel Street. The former pilot had made the same journey many times over the decades to pay his respects to his mates who didn't make it.

The second was a famous actress; the delightful Samantha Bond (famous for her appearances in the James Bond series and *Downton Abbey*) who was in a hurry during a Friday evening rush hour. When we arrived at our destination, she announced that the route we'd taken was 'genius', a kind compliment that made me feel rather proud – and a little tongue-tied too!

Black taxis offer a rare private space, so it's no surprise that cabbies pick up celebrities on a regular basis. Other friendly famous faces I've encountered include satirist and *Private Eye* editor Ian Hislop, illusionist Derren Brown, American actor and singer David Soul and the late comedian and actress Victoria Wood.

1 QUEEN VICTORIA STREET

The wedge-shaped Blackfriar pub stands on the site of a former friary and is an excellent example of art nouveau architecture. At one point it was threatened with demolition but, like St Pancras station, was thankfully saved by Sir John Betjeman.

2 TEMPLE PLACE

The distinctive green hut on Temple Place is a tiny cafe for licensed cabbies. In Victorian times, cabs were of course horse-drawn – meaning drivers were open to the elements. As such, cabbies often found refuge in the pub – with inevitably detrimental results (hot chocolate laced with rum is said to have been a popular cabbie tipple). To combat this, the Cabmen's Shelter Fund was established to provide cabbies with a place where they could remain sober and enjoy a warm meal.

Today, as well as the hut on Temple Place, there are 12 other examples across the city. Only cabbies are allowed to dine inside, but the public are welcome to use the take-away hatch where you'll find the cheapest cuppa in town. In 2017 these little cafes were granted Grade II listed status in honour of their historical importance.

3 BOW STREET

The point where Wellington Street meets Bow Street provides a good view of Covent Garden's piazza, which dates back to the 17th century. Although designed to be a grandiose square, it didn't take long for market traders to muscle in on the patch, resulting in the place becoming pretty grubby as the years passed.

The food and flower market remained right up until 1974 when it moved south to Nine Elms. It was then reborn in the early 1980s as a major tourist destination as cafes, pubs, arts and crafts and the London Transport Museum moved in.

4 WARDOUR STREET

Bordering the south-eastern section of Wardour Street is St Anne's Church and garden. The church (which is accessed via a modern, neon-lit entrance on Dean Street) has a spire topped with an unusual cylinder and sphere. The gardens hold the former burial ground that contains an estimated 80,000 bodies – rather eerily, this is why the ground is raised considerably above street level.

5 OXFORD STREET

One of the world's most famous department stores, Selfridges, holds pride of place here. The store was opened in 1906 by Harry Gordon Selfridge, a successful businessman from Chicago who is said to have coined the phrase, 'The customer is always right.'

Harry Selfridge was a born promoter and would often organise special events to draw in crowds. One such display occurred in 1925 when the Scottish inventor John Logie Baird was invited to give the world's earliest public demonstration of a device called television.

Sadly, Harry Selfridge's fortunes would not last. His wife died in the 1918 influenza pandemic and he became a heavy gambler. He died poor in a small flat in Putney in 1947.

Leave on left: Queen Victoria Street
Bear right: Embankment Slip Road
Bear right: Victoria Embankment
Right: Temple Place
Left: Arundel Street
Left: The Strand
Right: Aldwych
Left: Catherine Street
Left: Exeter Street
Right: Wellington Street
Forward: Bow Street
Forward: Endell Street
Left: Shorts Gardens
Comply: Seven Dials

Victoria Road

Bow Street

N

St Clement Danes

1. The Black Friar, Victoria Road

Leave by: Mercer Street
Left: Shaftesbury Avenue
Forward: Cambridge Circus
Forward: Shaftesbury Avenue
Right: Wardour Street
Left: Broadwick Street
Right: Poland Street
Left: Oxford Street
Forward: Oxford Circus
Forward: Oxford Street continued
Right: Portman Street
Bryanston Street on left

5. Selfridge's, Oxford Street

2. Temple Place

4. St Anne's Church, Wardour Street

ORMONDE GATE SW3 → LEMAN STREET E1

When on The Knowledge – especially when attending an appearance – the golden rule is that any run you call must be as straight as possible.

Because of the way in which the Thames twists and turns this can mean that on some journeys the most efficient way – as shown on this run – is to cross the river twice.

This run's end point presents another common anomaly – it is forbidden to turn right onto the northern end of Leman Street from Whitechapel High Street, meaning a diversion must be taken via several back streets.

I've always strived to explain such obstacles to passengers and practically everyone I've met has been completely understanding. However, there have been a number of occasions when I've been verbally abused for 'taking the wrong way', accused of attempting to rip people off and I've even had the partition between me and the passenger bashed.

Such accusations are a rare aspect of the job, but they can be upsetting because like the majority of my fellow drivers, I do my best to uphold the level of service expected of us.

I was reminded of this standard one evening while sitting in my cab at a red light on the junction with Mansell Street. My window was slightly down when I heard a polite voice enquire, 'Mr Lordan?'

It was one of The Knowledge examiners who was out 'pointing' – looking for any new places or changes that had materialised in the area. He enquired how I was, how business was and so on. This was some three years after I'd passed, yet the examiner could still put a name to my face. An epic memory.

1 PIMLICO ROAD

The patch between Pimlico Road and Ebury Street is called Orange Square. In the middle stands a statue of Wolfgang Amadeus Mozart depicted as a boy. This is in honour of the time he spent living on Ebury Street where, aged just eight, the little Austrian composed his first symphony.

2 BROAD SANCTUARY

Westminster Abbey – officially named the Collegiate Church of St Peter at Westminster – is one of London's most historic sites. Its origins essentially come from a broken promise: Edward the Confessor had vowed to make a pilgrimage to Rome, but once he became king this proved impractical. To make amends, the Pope instructed Edward to establish or renovate a monastery dedicated to St Peter.

Luckily, a monastery existed on what was then a remote, marshy area. It had been founded in 960 AD and it was this building that Edward set out to expand. He established himself at a palace opposite (now the Palace of Westminster) in order to oversee the work.

Edward died on 28th December 1065, just days after his project was consecrated. But he'd made history. The following year, Norman William the Conqueror battled his way to the English throne and was crowned inside the Abbey on Christmas Day 1066. Ever since then, every monarch's coronation has taken place here.

3 TOWER BRIDGE

London's most eye-catching crossing, Tower Bridge was built between 1886 and 1894. Its deck was designed to rise in order to allow tall ships to pass through, a mechanism that was steam powered until 1976.

In its early days, busy river traffic necessitated frequent raising of the bridge deck, so two walkways were built high above to accommodate pedestrians wishing to cross. These were soon closed to the public, however, after becoming a popular haunt for criminals. They now accommodate the Tower Bridge Exhibition, complete with a glass floor for a unique perspective.

In December 1952, a bus driver named Albert Gunter was driving towards Shoreditch when, terrifyingly, the deck began to rise. Taking the initiative, Albert hit the accelerator and leapt over the widening gap, landing safely. For this stunt he was awarded the grand sum of £10.

4 TOWER BRIDGE APPROACH

To the left is an excellent view of the Tower of London. It is intrinsically linked to Westminster Abbey, which we pass earlier on this run, the Tower having being established by William the Conqueror.

The first section was the formidable White Tower, which stands at the centre and is constructed from both Kentish rag and French Caen stone. Over the years the tower has grown to include other famous icons such as the Bloody Tower (where the most important political prisoners were locked up) and Traitors' Gate.

Leave by: Royal Hospital Road
Forward: Pimlico Road
Forward: Ebury Bridge
Comply: Roundabout
Leave by: Warwick Way
Cross: Vauxhall Bridge Road
Forward: Rochester Row
Comply: Roundabout
Leave by: Greycoat Place
Comply: Roundabout
Leave by: Great Peter Street
Left: Great Smith Street
Right: Victoria Street
Forward: Broad Sanctuary
Comply: Parliament Square
Leave by: Bridge Street
Forward: Westminster Bridge
Forward and bear left: Westminster Bridge Road
Right: Station Approach Road
Comply: Roundabout
Leave by: Spur Road
Left: Baylis Road
Forward: The Cut
Cross: Blackfriars Road
Forward: Union Street
Left: Southwark Bridge Road
Right: Union Street continued

1 Pimlico Road
2 Broad Sanctuary
River Thames
N

2. Westminster Abbey

Right: Borough High Street
Left: Mermaid Court
Right: Tennis Street
Left: Long Lane
Forward: Abbey Street
Left: Tower Bridge Road
Forward: Tower Bridge
Forward: Tower Bridge Approach
Left: Tower Hill
Bear right: Minories
Right: Goodman's Yard
Left: Mansell Street
Right: Whitechapel High Street
Left: Old Castle Street
Right: Pomell Way
Right: Commercial Street
Leman Street facing

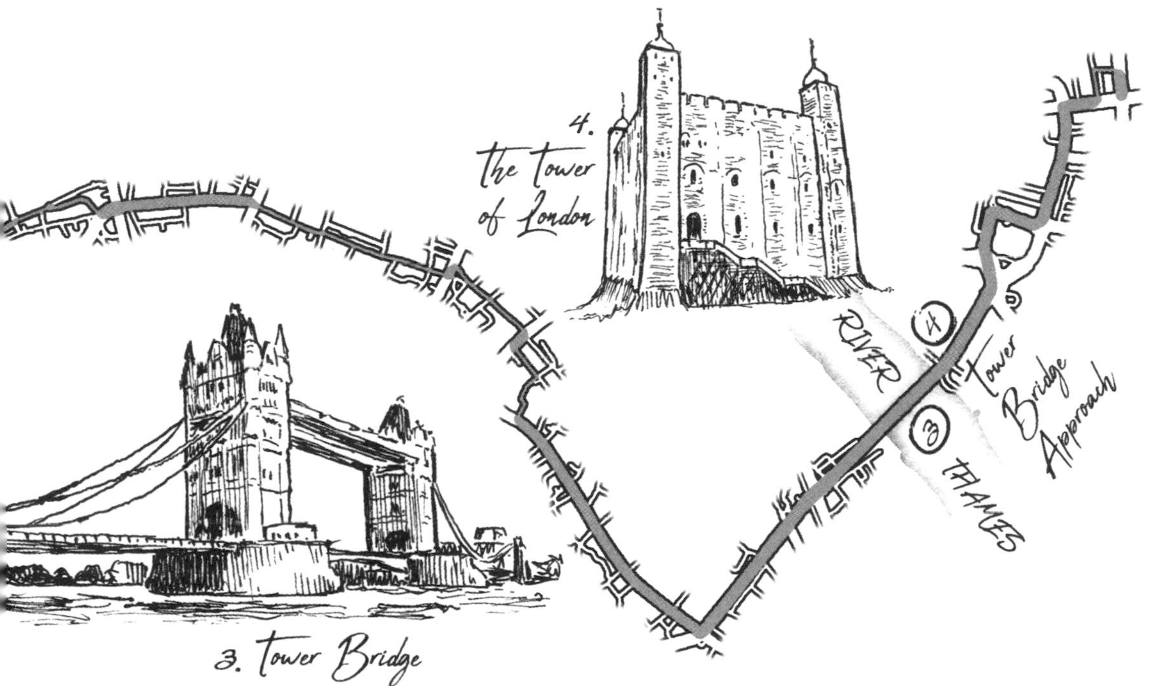

COPENHAGEN STREET N1 → CHARING CROSS STATION WC2

Copenhagen Street is fairly long and there are several points from which you can leave it. In this case I've opted for Barnsbury Road, which takes us through the back streets of Islington and Clerkenwell – including Percy Circus where, rather surprisingly, Vladimir Lenin lived for a period in 1905.

Charing Cross is named after a memorial to Queen Eleanor of Castille who died in 1290; the grief-stricken King Edward I had twelve crosses installed between Lincoln and London to mark the route of her funeral procession.

The Charing Cross originally stood just south of what is now Trafalgar Square and marked the official centre of London (that job is now carried out by the mounted statue of Charles I).

Today's Charing Cross, which stands in the station's forecourt, is an enhanced replica created in 1863. Despite the slight shift, it is still symbolically used as the end point for the last run on The Knowledge.

Copenhagen Street to Charing Cross station is the Blue Book's final run so to reach this point is an achievement in itself.

Although all of the runs have now been studied this is by no means the end . . . the Blue Book is essentially the basic framework of The Knowledge and it's now up to a student to develop their understanding of the city, to examine the smaller details and keep on top of any new or changing points.

Every time I had to pass the old, quietly menacing Public Carriage Office on Penton Street where I had my initial talk, and would go on to sit the majority of my appearances, was a stark reminder of this.

Having said that, I still felt a celebration was in order once I'd completed this run. I used to study The Knowledge late at night, so I headed to a 24-hour diner near Smithfield and ordered a decadent milkshake.

1 HUNTER STREET

The distinctive Brunswick Centre was built in the 1960s and was originally intended to stretch as far as Euston Road. This plan was scuppered, however, by the Territorial Army Centre on Handel Street who refused to budge.

2 BOW STREET

Bow Street is dominated by the facade of the Royal Opera House, which dates back to 1858. There is some interesting architecture on either side; to the north is the twisting Sky Bridge, which passes high over Floral Street as a connection to the Royal Ballet School. To the south is the former Floral Hall, which bears a passing resemblance to the old Crystal Palace and now forms part of the theatre.

Directly opposite the Royal Opera House is the imposing Bow Street Magistrates building which closed in 2006 after a 260-year history. There are currently plans to turn it into a luxury hotel that will incorporate a police museum in the old cells.

3 THE STRAND

Directly opposite Exeter Street is The Savoy hotel, the entrance to which is the only road in the UK where drivers are required to drive on the right side of the road (although there are private examples too, such as Hammersmith bus depot). Countless big names have stayed here over the years, including Monet – who painted the Thames from his balcony – George Gershwin, Charlie Chaplin, Harry Truman, Audrey Hepburn and Marilyn Monroe.

Another famous face who stayed at The Savoy was Bob Dylan who, in 1965, filmed the famous promo to 'Subterranean Homesick Blues' behind the hotel on Savoy Hill.

4 CHARING CROSS STATION

Opened in 1864, the station backs right onto the Thames (the name Charing itself comes from the Anglo-Saxon word *cerring* which means 'turning', a reference to the bend in the river). The site was originally home to Hungerford Market – hence Hungerford Footbridge, which links the station to the south bank.

Leave by: Barnsbury Road
Forward: Penton Street
Forward: Claremont Square
Forward: Amwell Street
Right: Great Percy Street
Comply: Percy Circus
Leave by: Great Percy Street continued
Left: King's Cross Road
Right: Frederick Street
Left: Gray's Inn Road
Right: Sidmouth Street
Forward: Regent Square
Forward: Tavistock Place
Left: Hunter Street
Forward and comply: Brunswick Square
Leave by: Grenville Street
Right: Colonnade
Left: Herbrand Street

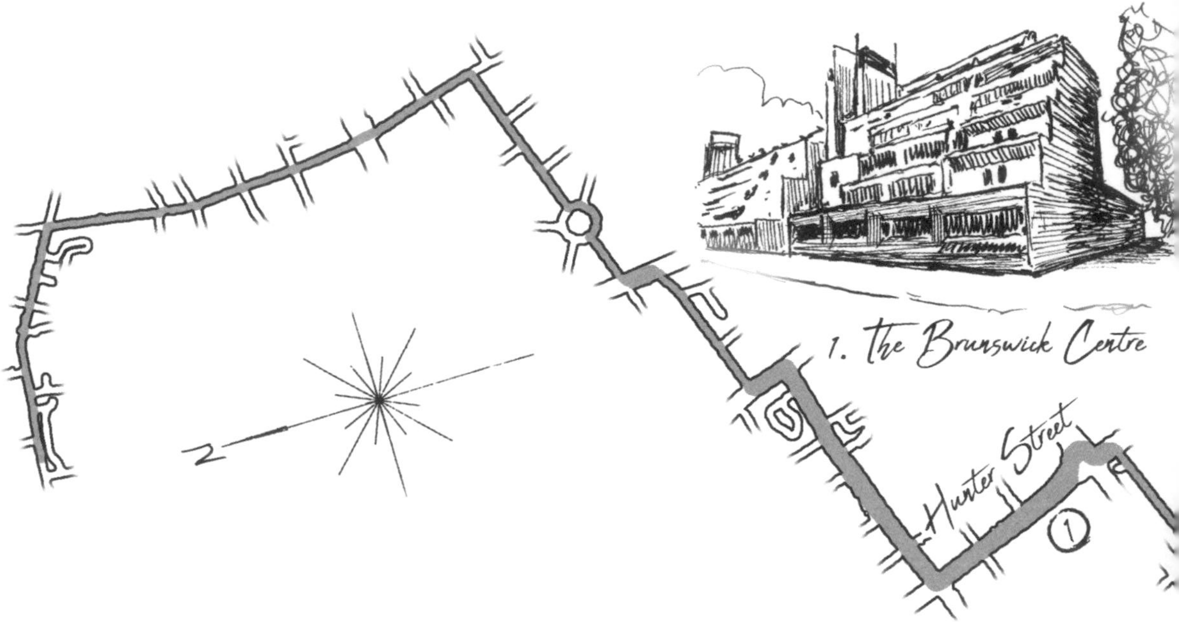

1. The Brunswick Centre

Hunter Street

(1)

Right: Guildford Street
Left and right: Russell Square
Left: Montague Street
Right: Great Russell Street
Left: Bloomsbury Street
Forward: Shaftesbury Avenue
Right: High Holborn
Left: Endell Street
Forward: Bow Street
Forward: Wellington Street
Right and left: Exeter Street
Right: The Strand
Left: Station forecourt
Charing Cross station on left

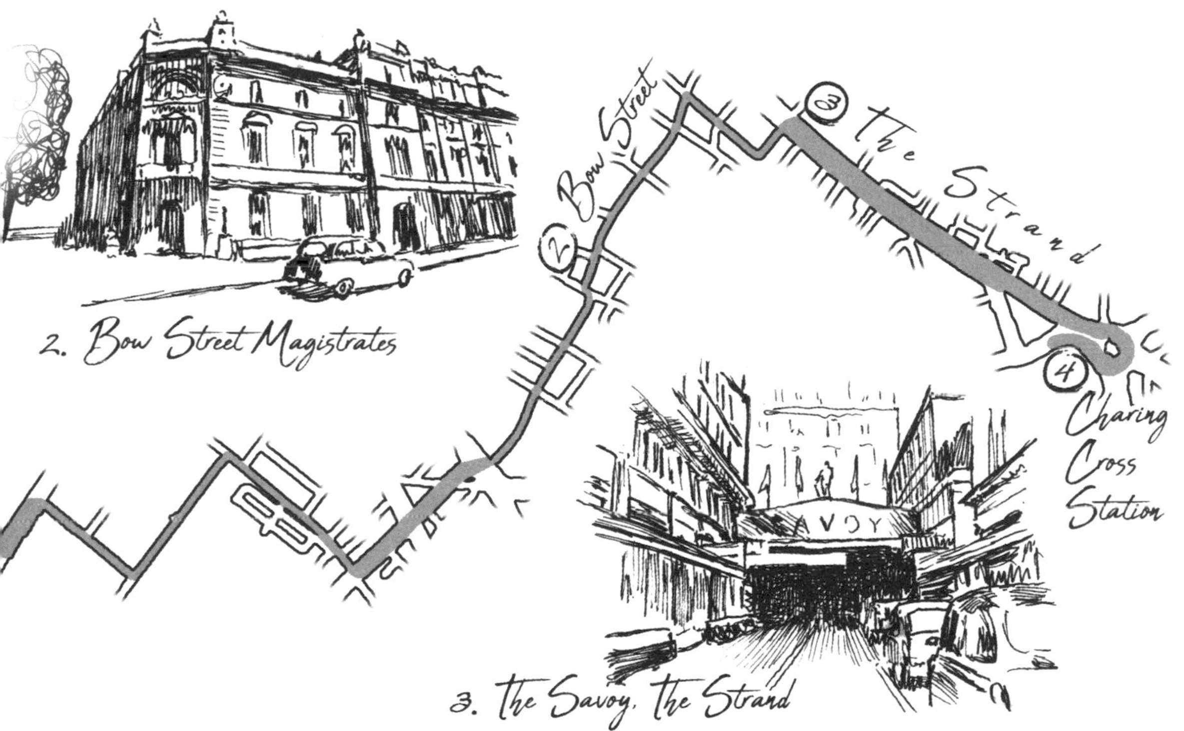

2. Bow Street Magistrates

3. The Savoy, The Strand

MARSHALSEA ROAD SE1 → TOLLINGTON ROAD N7

On an appearance, it's rare that an examiner will ask a straightforward Blue Book run. Almost all questions are random routes that a candidate is expected to calculate using their acquired Knowledge.

On my final appearance, the very last run I was asked was Cannon Street station to Archway station.

This run, Marshalsea Road to Tollington Road, was useful for calling it as it closely matches the route once north of the river. I called it in a daze . . . and then the examiner asked me to do it in reverse. Once done, he scribbled down some notes and then came the immortal words.

'Ok, I'll pass you today.'

1 MARSHALSEA ROAD

When learning the quarter-mile radius around Marshalsea Road there are some particularly interesting streets to discover. The first is Redcross Way, at the northern end of which is Crossbones Garden.

This community project is built upon the site of Cross Bones Graveyard, a mass pit for unconsecrated burials. It originated in the medieval era and at first was used for local prostitutes. They were nicknamed 'Winchester Geese', a reference to the Bishops of Winchester who owned much of the property in lawless Southwark – including the numerous brothels.

The second is Disney Place (which leads into the tiny dead-end, Disney Street). Although not a reference to the famous film company (the name is of Norman origin), a cabbie couldn't help telling Walt Disney about these two little streets when he happened to pick up the filmmaker and his wife Lillian in 1965. Naturally, Walt wanted to see for himself and had his photograph clicked beneath the sign.

2 SOUTHWARK BRIDGE

Cheerfully coloured in green and yellow, Southwark Bridge was opened in 1921 as a replacement for a previous toll crossing.

Due to the limited access at its northern end, it's one of London's quieter bridges. It can be seen in the climactic scene to Guy Ritchie's film *Lock Stock and Two Smoking Barrels*.

3 NEW CHANGE

New Change takes us around the eastern side of Sir Christopher Wren's masterpiece: St Paul's Cathedral. There has been a place of worship on this site dedicated to St Paul since the year 604 AD.

Today's cathedral, which was completed in 1711, is the fifth such building to stand on the site. Prior to that, St Paul's was a huge, wooden structure built by the Normans – the spire was even taller than today's cathedral. It was destroyed in the Great Fire of London.

On the night of 29 December 1940 St Paul's was almost destroyed again by flames, this time during the heaviest raid of the Blitz.

During the raid, Churchill gave the order that the cathedral 'Must be saved at all costs'. Fire watchers based around the dome dealt with incendiaries while firefighters battled the surrounding inferno. St Paul's became a symbol of defiance that night when a famous photograph, showing the cathedral seemingly immune to the smoke and flames, was snapped from the top of a nearby building, the location of which now happens to be the office for Quercus, the publisher of this very book.

4 LITTLE BRITAIN

Inside Postman's Park is the Memorial to Heroic Self-Sacrifice, a covered wooden walkway featuring a collection of plaques in honour of individuals who've died while saving the lives of others. Most of them date from around the turn of the 20th century and detail people killed in gruesome incidents such as drowning, fires and vehicular mishaps.

Leave by right: Southwark Bridge Road
Forward: Southwark Bridge
Forward: Queen Street Place
Left: Upper Thames Street
Right: Puddle Dock
Right: Queen Victoria Street
Left: Friday Street
Left: Cannon Street
Right: New Change
Left: Newgate Street
Right: King Edward Street
Forward: Little Britain
Forward: Montague Street
Comply: Rotunda
Leave by: Aldersgate Street

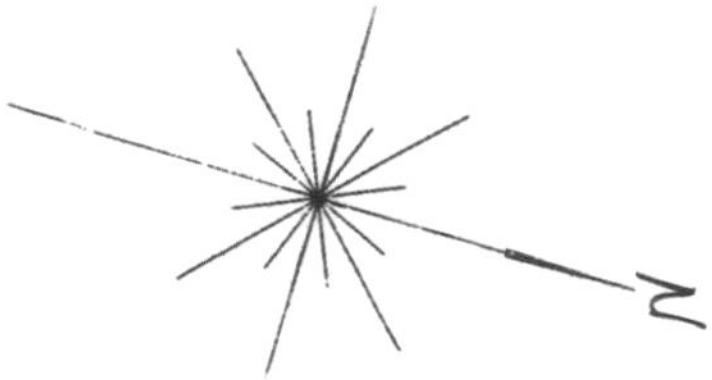

Marshalsea Road
1
2
3
New Change
4 Little Britain

N

1. Cross Bones Graveyard

Forward: Goswell Road
Right: Angel Junction
Forward: Islington High Street
Left: Liverpool Road
Left: Holloway Road
Tollington Way on right

KENTISH TOWN STATION NW5 → WEST SMITHFIELD EC1

Most cabbies have a favourite route they like to begin their shift on. For those who live towards the east, it could be Canary Wharf, those in the south perhaps Clapham High Street.

Living as I do towards the north-west, this run has become quite a habit of mine as I head into town, especially as it provides the opportunity of ranking at St Pancras International. If work looks light there, no problem; I'll keep going and try my luck in the City.

I've picked up some wonderful people on my travels; fares that have blessed me with many cherished memories. The violinist with the Stradivarius, the choreographer from *The Lion King*, the family from Cambodia, the couple taking their newborn baby home for the first time . . .

The people I'm fortunate enough to meet in this job are as varied, intriguing and indeed as complex as the streets of London themselves.

1 KENTISH TOWN ROAD

Opposite the junction with Royal College Street is a pawnbrokers shop housed in a distinctive ox-blood-red tiled building. This was originally South Kentish Town, one of the tube's many abandoned stations. It had a short life, closing in 1924 after just 17 years' use.

In 1951, Sir John Betjeman wrote a darkly humorous short story about a Mr Basil Green who became stranded in the station after accidentally alighting . . .

2 PANCRAS ROAD

Saint Pancras, after whom the station and area are named, was a Roman martyr, beheaded for being a Christian when he was just 14 years old.

St Pancras Old Church is one of the oldest places of worship in England, dating back around 1,700 years. The churchyard contains some particularly interesting sites – for example, the Tomb of John Soane (designed by the architect himself) was the inspiration for the distinctive red telephone box.

Also here is The Hardy Tree, which is encircled by a curious cluster of gravestones. The tree is named after the author Thomas Hardy who, while working as a young apprentice architect, was forced to exhume some 7,000 bodies to facilitate the expansion of the railway into St Pancras.

This is believed to have inspired Hardy's later poem, 'The Levelled Churchyard', which contains the lines:

We late lamented, resting here
Are mixed to human jam
And each to each exclaims in fear
I know not which I am

3 FARRINGDON ROAD

The Betsy Trotwood pub first opened in 1865 and was one of the first buildings to be built above London's newly opened underground railway (the tracks into Farringdon can be seen if you peer over the wall into the cutting alongside Farringdon Lane).

The pub's present name dates from the 1970s and is a reference to a character in *David Copperfield* by Charles Dickens. The area around Clerkenwell and Farringdon also has numerous.links to *Oliver Twist* – Fagin's den and the Three Cripples pub were described as being located in this area.

4 WEST SMITHFIELD

Smithfield is a corruption of 'smooth field'. Combined with the Fleet, which once flowed nearby, this made the ideal location for the cattle market that originated here during the Middle Ages.

Today's covered market buildings date from the 1860s and originally incorporated a subterranean freight link with the Metropolitan Railway.

Alongside the meat market, Smithfield was for many centuries London's most brutal execution spot; burning and being boiled alive in oil were common methods. The most notable person put to death here was the Scots rebel knight Sir William Wallace who was hanged, drawn and quartered in the early 14th century. A memorial to him can be seen on West Smithfield's southern branch.

Leave on left: Kentish Town Road
Left: Royal College Street
Bear Left: St Pancras Way
Left: Pancras Road
Forward: Midland Road
Left: Euston Road
Forward: Pentonville Road
Right: King's Cross Road
Forward: Farringdon Road
Left: Farringdon Lane
Cross: Clerkenwell Road
Forward: Turnmill Street
Bear left: Cowcross Street
Right: St John Street
Left: Charterhouse Street
Right: Lindsey Street
Right: Long Lane
West Smithfield facing

Kentish Town

Pancras Road

1. South Kentish Town Station

2. St Pancras Old Church, Pancras Road

3. The Betsy Trotwood

GLOSSARY OF KNOWLEDGE TERMS AND CABBIE SLANG

Acceptance interview
A group talk in which new Knowledge candidates are issued with their copy of the Blue Book and given a general overview of what The Knowledge entails.

All Nations, The
The green cab shelter on Kensington Road. So called because it is close to the location of the former Crystal Palace, home of the Great Exhibition in 1851.

Appearance
A one-to-one oral exam in which a student is tested on their knowledge of London. Appearances are ongoing and are divided into three stages: 56s, 28s and 21s. These numbers denote the number of days between each test and indicate a student's progress. Numerous exams must be successfully completed before advancing to the next stage. *See Score.*

Bat-cave, The
A shortcut between York Buildings and Savoy Place that is officially known as Lower Robert Street and runs through an unusual subterranean service road.

Banker
A favourite run commonly asked by a Knowledge examiner.

Baze, The
Bayswater Road.

Be lucky
A popular term that cabbies use when bidding farewell to one another.

Bell and Horns, The
The green cab shelter on Thurloe Place. Named after a pub that once stood nearby.

Bilker
A passenger who runs off without paying the fare.

Blue Book, The
A Knowledge student's Bible: the pamphlet listing the 320 basic routes that aspiring cabbies must drive, explore and commit to memory.

Bone, The
Marylebone station. If the terminus is busy, it's said that there's 'meat on the bone'.

Burst, The
The collective moment in the West End when shows end and audiences pour from theatre exits.

Butter boy/girl
A newly-qualified cabbie. The term's origin is uncertain – some believe it's a corruption of the phrase 'but a boy' (i.e., suggesting naivety) while others say it stems from a time when older drivers used to accuse newcomers of pinching their 'bread and butter'.

Cabbed out
An area experiencing a sudden influx of available taxis.

Calling over
The process of revising The Knowledge indoors with a map. Ideally this is done with a fellow student known as a callover partner.

Canary
A cabbie licensed to work within one of London's suburban sectors (each of which has its own, smaller Knowledge area). So called because their badges are yellow as opposed to the green 'all London' licence.

Chucker
A passenger who vomits inside your taxi.

Churchill, A
A meal. Derived from the fact that it was Sir Winston Churchill who granted cabbies the right to refuse a fare if they were in the middle of eating.

Comply
A term used for acknowledging a roundabout or major junction when reciting a run – e.g., 'Comply Highbury Corner, leave by Upper Street.'

Corridor of Fear
The long walk between the waiting room and examiner's office that was a feature of the Public Carriage Office when it was based at Penton Street. Still recalled with dread by many cabbies.

Cross, The
King's Cross station.

Dead Zoo
The Natural History Museum.

Den of thieves
The Stock Exchange.

Do your porridge
To spend a long time waiting on a slow rank. Also known as Stewing.

Drop, I got my
A successful appearance in which a student progresses to the next stage. *See Score.*

Drive, The
A difficult driving test that each student must pass (regardless of any previous driving experience) in a black taxi before being licensed.

Duck and dive
To take a route using many back streets.

Dungeon, The
Old nickname for the grim Victorian building which was home to the Public Carriage Office prior to 1966.

Flyer
A fare to the airport.

Gas Works, The
Slang term for the Houses of Parliament (no doubt coined due to the volume of hot air that emanates from there).

Handshake, The
The moment when an examiner offers their hand to signify you have achieved your req. Any attempt to shake an examiner's hand before this point is considered taboo.

Hummingbird
A nickname for the Bersey, London's first electric taxicab, which was unveiled back in 1897. The name is a reference

to the gentle buzzing noise it made.

Iron Lung, The
A handy public convenience on the junction of Regency Street and Horseferry Road that resembles a traditional French *pissoir*.

Journeyman
A cabbie who rents their taxi from one of London's many dedicated garages. *See also Musher.*

Kipper season
The time of year – traditionally January and February – when work levels fall flat, primarily due to the public saving the pennies after the excesses of Christmas.

Knowledge boy/girl
Any student studying The Knowledge – usually identifiable by the fact they're riding a moped with maps attached to the handlebars.

KWAK
Acronym for 'Kojak with a Kodak'; a police officer armed with a speed-check device. Also known as a Blue Tree.

Leather arse
A driver who works exceptionally long hours. Also known as a Copper Bottom.

Leave on left/right
When describing a run, this informs the examiner that you know which side of the road the start point is located on.

Legal
A passenger who pays the exact fare without granting a tip.

Magic Roundabout, The
The busy gyratory at Shepherd's Bush.

Map Test
A written examination that must be completed before beginning the Appearance stage. This includes identifying points and roads on a map where all wording has been removed.

Mr Ormes' Parrot
In the late 20th century, Mr Ormes (who can be seen in the 1996 BBC documentary, *Modern Times: Streetwise*) was one of the most formidable Knowledge examiners. He was famous for keeping a small model of a Guinness toucan in his office that would face towards or away from

the window depending on his mood; this quirk has since become part of Knowledge folklore.

Musher
A cabbie who owns their cab as opposed to renting. *See also Journeyman.*

On the bounce
To have numerous jobs in quick succession.

On the cotton
When revising, Knowledge students call a run and pen it on to a laminated map. Once drawn, a length of cotton is stretched between the start and end points to ascertain accuracy – the aim being to ensure the line is as straight as possible.

Oranges and lemons
Main roads – so called because they are coloured orange and yellow on an A–Z map.

Padders
Affectionate term for Paddington station.

Pipe, The
The Blackwall Tunnel. Appropriate as it's frequently blocked.

Point
Any place of interest which a student must note and commit to memory. There are tens of thousands of points across the city. On an appearance, an examiner will ask a start and end point and the student must correctly identify the location of each before being permitted to recite the run.

Point Sheets
Lists of current trends asked by examiners – are published every weekday by various Knowledge schools in order to help students revise.

Putting on the foul
To squeeze on to the back of a taxi rank that is already full.

Ramble
Extra routes drawn up by the Knowledge schools that enhance the Blue Book runs.

Redlined
The demoralising process of being sent back to the beginning of a stage. This occurs when a student is unable to

attain a score of 12 within the space of seven appearances. If redlined twice, then a student must regress even further to the previous stage.

Req
Short for Required Standard; the name given to a student's final appearance in which they finally pass The Knowledge of London. It is a moment of great elation. *See also The Handshake.*

Roader
An especially long journey.

Run
A route between any two given points, whether it be from the basic framework of 320 as provided by the Blue Book, or any two points selected at random by a callover partner or Knowledge examiner.

Score
If successful on an appearance, a student may score, depending on their performance, an A (6 points), B (4 points) or C (3 points). To progress to the next stage, a total of 12 points must be accumulated. If a student does not demonstrate sufficient Knowledge on an appearance, they receive a D meaning 0 points.

Seeing it
The moment when a run – or indeed entire sections of the map – achieves clarity within a student's mind.

Set down on left/right
When describing the conclusion of a run, this term is used to denote which side of the road the end point is based on.

Sherbet
A taxi. Shortened from Sherbet Dab; Cockney rhyming slang for cab.

Six-Mile Radius
The area covered by The Knowledge – a six-mile radius centred around Charing Cross, which extends to Alexandra Palace in the north, Crystal Palace in the south, Acton in the west, and City Airport to the east.

Sticky run
A particular run that a Knowledge student consistently struggles to recall.

The Burbs
Short for the suburbs. After acquiring their req, a student must spend several weeks studying a set of basic runs that cover residential zones outside the Six-Mile Radius.

Heathrow Airport is also included.

An understanding of these areas must be successfully demonstrated in one final appearance.

Turnaround

For points where it would be considered dangerous to set down a passenger on the opposite side of the road (for example due to railings, multiple lanes of traffic or other obstacles), a turnaround must be employed. This means utilising a number of roads to direct your taxi towards the correct side of the road.

Up the Stairs

A term meaning there is lots of work at Euston station – so called because queues of passengers form on the stairwell leading down to the taxi rank.

Woosher

A student capable of calling runs with great speed and fluidity.

ACKNOWLEDGMENTS

In writing this book – and during the years preceding it – I've been blessed with immeasurable support from some truly amazing people.

To my grandmother Jo; I'd be lost without you.

To my partner, Elaine; you are my rock.

Sincere thanks also to Irene, Stewart and Neil, and to my folks in Canada for your consistent positivity and for encouraging my creative side.

To my friends: in London, Alex, Mike, Ainslie and Doug, fellow-cabbie Phil and all from the Demby family. In Glasgow; Melanie and Stuart, Mark and Caroline... your support, kindness and encouragement means more than you'll ever know.

To Roff Smith; your friendship and wisdom is an absolute gift and I'm honoured to know you. Thank you also to Elizabeth Dalziel and Francis Hardinge for your advice and inspiration, and to Matilda Egere-Cooper for granting me a voice.

To Tony Curran, Anthony Johnson and Harpaul Singh: your patience, guidance and friendship has helped me through some bumpy times. I can't thank you enough.

Special appreciation too to my former English teacher, Melanie Branton who inspired me at A-level and continues to encourage my writing 20 years on, and to all others who've read and supported my blog.

I would also like to extend my gratitude to Ben Brock and the team at Quercus for believing in me, and also to Jamie Whyte whose beautiful illustrations have perfectly encapsulated the spirit of the city I love.

To my late grandfather, Michael and other absent souls. You'll never be forgotten.

And finally to the passenger who urged me to write... your short hop to Knightsbridge that Autumn evening set me on a journey which has finally arrived at this page. Whoever you were, thank you.

First published in Great Britain in 2018 by Quercus.

Quercus Editions Ltd
Carmelite House
50 Victoria Embankment
London EC4Y 0DZ

An Hachette UK company

A CIP catalogue record for this book is available from the British Library.

HB ISBN 978 1 78648 969 2
Ebook ISBN 978 1 78648 970 8

10 9 8 7 6 5 4 3 2 1

Printed and bound in Italy by L.E.G.O. S.p.A.